TWIN FLAME
CODE BREAKER

11:11 KEY CODES

THE *Secret* TO UNLOCKING UNCONDITIONAL LOVE & FINDING YOUR WAY *Home*

DR. HARMONY

Published by Ask DrH Healthy Solutions, LLC
Twin Flame Code Breaker is a trademark of Ask DrH Healthy Solutions, LLC
http://www.twinflameexpert.com

The author of this book makes no claims or recommendations for medically prescribed treatments of any kind. The intent of the content is for educational purposes only and help assist you to progress along your spiritual journey. This book contains information that is intended to help the reader be better informed about a twin-flame relationship. It is presented as general advice on relationships. Always consult your doctor for your individual needs. It is not intended to be a substitute for the medical advice of a licensed physician. The reader should consult with their doctor in any matters relating to his/her health.

Editorial Services: Aileen Cho
Logo and Graphic Designs: Jonathan Gundry
Cover & Interior design: CreateSpace Independent Publishing Platform

Library of Congress Cataloging-in-Publication Data
Harmony, Dr.
Twin Flame Code Breaker: 11:11 key codes; the secret to unlocking unconditional love and finding your way home. / Dr. Harmony – 1st edition.
pages cm
ISBN-13: 9780692794920
ISBN-10: 0692794921
1. Relationships — Twin flame aspects. 2. Love — Religious aspects.
3. Self-realization — Spirituality. I. Title.

Library of Congress Control Number: 2016917247
Ask DrH Healthy Solutions, LLC, St Peters, MO

ISBN-13: 9780692794920
ISBN-10: 0692794921
First Edition November 2016
11 10 09 0807 6 5 4 3 2 1

May 10, 1940 – August 29, 2015

In Memory of My Spiritual Teacher, the Late Dr. Wayne Dyer.

"We are not our bodies, our possessions, or our careers. Who we are is Divine Love and that is infinite."

— *Dr. Wayne Dyer*

If you are familiar with the teachings of Dr. Wayne Dyer, you might find that my *"words of wisdom"* sound similar. He has been my spiritual inspiration for nearly two decades. The first time I met him in 2003, the following words unconsciously slipped out of my mouth: *"As long as I am living, your work will never die."* He in his Zen-like presence, bowed and nodded his head while placing his hands in Namaste prayer position – expressing his gratitude in silence. Finally, he responded with his famous line: *"I am glad to hear you won't be dying with your music still in you."*

In the couple of months before his passing, I got to learn straight from the heart and mouth of his infinite wisdom what *"writing from the soul"* really means. Now my words have come to pass! *As long as I'm living, Wayne, your work will never die!*

To My Twin Flame,
Thank you for sharing "The Gift" of Unconditional Love by choosing the heavier karmic load – so that I could align with my Divine mission and find personal freedom during this lifetime!
May You Find Personal Freedom – Inner Peace & Happiness
– Always & Forever!
Follow Your Heart – Live Your Brightest Dreams!

Contents

To My Reader:

I BEGIN THIS PERSONAL QUEST to fulfill my own twin-flame mission by sharing my message and spreading a new world order – heaven on earth. I hope to enlighten the globe by giving back *"The Gift"* of unconditional love that I received from my own twin flame, which has fueled my beacon for other twin flames to follow. *"Twin-Flame Code Breaker"* and the *11:11 Key Codes* contain The Secrets I discovered to unlock personal freedom and find my way home to a place of inner peace and happiness. These *11:11 Key Codes* have been Divinely orchestrated and *"Twin-Flame Code Breaker"* has been infused with spiritual energy in order to share with you the twin-flame prophecy in the same way that it has been shown to me. For nearly 20 years, I have been a spiritual advisor with a background in holistic chiropractic, vibrational medicine and remote-energy healing, helping people remove energetic blocks that had been keeping them stuck in life. Combined with my expertise, personal experiences, extensive research and my Divinely-guided messages, I help other twin flames around the world to find their way home.

I must say, I am honored to be *"The Chosen One"* to have the opportunity to deliver such a powerful message to the world and express my truths, so my soul can finally rest. Throughout *"Twin-Flame Code Breaker,"* I share the deepest secrets of my soul, while at the same time shifting into full radiance and not caring what others think of me – or who I am. I am no longer running from myself. *Learning to view life with my heart and not my head has taught me how to be emotionally receptive while giving to others with no expectations – only appreciation.* I have become an expression of the Creator, sharing *"The Gift"* of unconditional love – the new earth heart language.

Reflecting back on my journey, several questions come mind – *"How do I begin such a book as Twin-Flame Code Breaker?" "What words of wisdom will lie between the pages as this book unfolds?"* and *"How will this message affect you, the reader?"* Even more importantly, *"How will my own twin-flame mission impact the world?"* As these questions race through my mind, I stumbled across my personal journal. Upon opening it, I immediately found this entry dated *11-11, 2004* (I will share the meaning of *"The 11:11 phenomenon"* in *Key Code* 7:7). This was just after I had divorced. I am pleased to share this powerful message with you:

> *The storm is over and as the darkness rolls across the sky – behind it, "I can see clearly now," with a new perspective on life. I can feel the warmth from the rays of light forming on the horizon shining down on me. I know that this dark season was necessary for the nitrogen to mist amongst the foliage, offering a green canvas for the spring flowers to sit amongst. As I reflect on this rocky journey we call life, "I can see clearly" now what I could not see before. Suddenly, light rays begin to beam through the clouds and this offers me assurance that I have made the right decision by choosing to shift my life in a new direction. I feel relief—my soul has been led towards inner peace and happiness. I understand that every dark season of my life has been a necessary part of my journey and that my challenges have molded me into the person that God intended for me to become.*
>
> *Far too many people live with emotional scars that are embedded deep within the DNA of their Being and in their hearts. It is my mission to help others who have experienced a similar journey to heal their past pain and negative experiences. I have listened to my heart and now I am experiencing inner peace, happiness, harmony, serenity and unconditional love. As I transcend through the wings of*

God towards heaven, there is light at the end of the tunnel. Moving forward, I will be eternally grateful for my past and that which it has taught me. My life lessons have strengthened my inner Being and I have demonstrated great dignity which has helped me to build inner strength, creating personal empowerment. God has prepared me to become a great leader! These lessons have taught me to open my heart and to listen to the song deep inside my soul. When I am ready, I will share my music with the world.

Ever since I was a child, I have felt that there has been a book within me – ready to express the symphony of my heart and soul. However, my spirit has never been able to fully express the deepest secrets that are hidden inside me. I understand that my gut instincts must develop and become strong enough to override the knowledge that my mind holds.

Not understanding what my purpose is, I begin to ask, "Why?" "Why me?" "What is my message?" "What is my mission?" I start to hear the inner voice getting stronger – saying to me that I would know when my Divine message is ready to share with the world. That still inner voice begins speaking louder, telling me – the time will be right when you get out of head space and move into the place of heart. I know that God uses people and their experiences to help bless the lives of others. I know that I have been chosen as a prophet to share all that I have come here to experience and understand, when the time is right. Then I will share my wisdom with the world: a new way of life – a new way to love unconditionally – experiencing heaven on earth!

WOW – reading those words that I wrote to myself, so very long ago on *11-11-2004*, gives me confirmation that I have finally arrived and that I am in full alignment. That same inner voice is not only still present inside me, but it has evolved. "*I can see clearly now*" that unlocking "*heaven's gate*" and discovering the "*11:11 Key Codes*" in "*Twin-Flame Code Breaker*" was "*Key*" to unleashing personal freedom, so that I could find my way home. *"I can see clearly now"* the portrait that I have been painting my whole life. My past, present and future have collided like the *"big bang theory."* This book has become an expression of my truth and my heart, and I'm about to catapult my soul into the stratosphere.

I would like to encourage you to also reread that message from *11-11-2004* after you have finished reading this book. In doing so, I think you will gain the same revelation I did. You will see a real demonstration of how the power of Divine order handles everything in our lives, and that when we get out of our own way and allow ourselves to shift into full alignment, the spirit infuses our Being with everything that we need for our journey. We begin to realize that what we need is already there. You can then look back as I did and say, *"I can see clearly now!"*

Finally, I can say that I have learned to speak words of wisdom and view life with my heart and not my head. Without doubt, I know that the Divine time has come for me to become a vessel and to share with others the highest form of unconditional love known to mankind. I will help the world open up to a new way to practice the unconditional love imprint that is expressed through hearts of twin flames. *"Twin-Flame Code Breaker"* is a blueprint that has been part of the Divine plan since the beginning of time. *The intent of this twin-flame prophecy is to spread this new world order so that we can raise the unconditional love vibration of the planet.* I am quite confident that if you put these same *11:11 Key Codes* into action, it will also help you unlock The Secret to finding personal freedom. It will raise your unconditional love vibration and help you find your way home to heaven on earth – a place of inner peace and happiness.

Much Love and Many Blessings!
Dr. Harmony

Introduction

What Does It Mean To "Find Your Way Home?"

THERES IS A LOT OF CONTROVERSY AND MISUNDERSTANDING about the twin-flame concept. Some people confuse it with love at first sight, searching for a fairy-tale relationship with hopes of living happily ever after. It's no wonder they seek someone else to fill a void that can only be filled from within! Therefore, it's important to develop a better understanding of a true twin-flame relationship and what it means to find your way home. You can stop searching outside yourself by learning to practice unconditional self-love, which will *"free your soul."*

Perhaps you too have been searching for something your whole life, but are not sure what you were looking for. *Have you had a longing to go home, but can't seem to find your way? Do you feel incomplete? Maybe you are feeling stuck in every area of your life and have experienced the pitfalls of hell and are not sure how to climb your way out.* Most likely, you are one of the majority of individuals out there who are sleepwalking through life, *"spiritually unconscious"* and searching for something to complete you! I, too, was one of society's statistically *"unhappy"* people until I became aware of the fact that only I could change it. *As you "awaken" you will start to shift from the darkest night of your soul and soon become the brightest beacon for others to follow.* Looking back, you know that it has taken every obstacle and every struggle to facilitate your transformation and nothing represented failure – only accomplishment. Once you finally surrender to the idea of seeking change in your life, acknowledgment forces you to redirect your path; it will continue until you completely let go and get out of your own way. This process opens the space for your soul to expand, so that you realize that if you just get in alignment and show up, everything that you need for the journey will appear. You no longer have to force things to happen. You enter the vortex of all possibilities and your soul can finally rest. Until you fully understand this and learn to go with the flow, you only prolong the process. How long it takes you to find your way home is ultimately up to you.

Personally, I have searched my whole life for my inner calling. I never dreamt that becoming a twin-flame expert would be my life's purpose. To be completely honest, I spent a lifetime beating my head against a brick wall. Mainly due to logical thinking, I processed my feelings and emotions from my head rather than listening to my heart. Being a strong-willed individual has caused many hardships. However, the obstacles that I experienced were exactly what I needed to learn before I could get out of my own way. The art of letting go and surrendering to a power greater than oneself might sound simple enough, but it literally took being shoved off a cliff by the Universe before I got it. But once I started to free fall, I aligned with my destiny and everything I needed to fulfill my soul's agreement appeared.

Many of you will be able to identify with this intense battle of head versus heart. A few people may already identify with what it means to move through life with ease and grace, but for most it requires an intense shift; whether you are starting an "*awakening*" or moving beyond the illusion of your "*dark night of the soul.*" Twin flame or not, "*Twin-Flame Code Breaker*" is a blueprint designed to assist you along your journey as you transcend by letting go of your karmic patterns and shift towards your radiant self.

To some readers the term "*twin flame*," may be something that you have never heard of. To others the definition offered in "*Twin-Flame Code Breaker*" may provide a new perspective on this sacred relationship. *Regardless, understanding what it means to be a true twin flame will help you gain a much better understanding of the "real reason" for a twin-flame journey.*

Expanding your twin-flame wisdom, will help break energetic barriers that are blocking you from moving forward in life and in your twin-flame union. Your karmic past no longer has to keep you stuck in life or in any of your relationships. By identifying why you are being called to connect with your twin flame, you will come into alignment with your own personal peace and gain the desire to honor your twin flame agreement – rather than running from it.

The term "*twin flame*" refers to an "*individual*" twin soul seeking "*self-transformation*" along one's "*personal path*" in attempt to learn one's "*own*" life lessons so that one can master one's "*own*" portion of a joint mission – a contract that you make with your other half at the time of inception, creating the power of two that is greater than one. Upon incarnation of souls, an energetic spark splits into two complete, whole and individual souls. Throughout each twin soul's evolutionary journey, they parallel, creating a mirrored reflection for each other – forcing the other to see what it is they each need to work on within themselves. After mastering their agreed-upon lessons they join together, sharing their lessons, and then reunite for eternity.

Whether you have a twin flame incarnated during this lifetime or not, this message will provide an understanding that will enhance your personal relationship with yourself, thus creating more self-love. This will not only feed your soul with the vital ingredients needed to produce self-worth, self-acceptance and personal fulfillment, it will also enhance all your relationships.

Think of this message as the *Universe's attempt to speak to your heart* and for good reason. Spirit has a mission of speeding up your twin-flame agreement. *Why? Because as a unified twin-flame group – the mission of all twin flames must be fulfilled – it is necessary in order to balance unconditional love throughout the world.* These *11:11 Key Codes* are *"The Gift"* to you so that you don't have to walk your journey alone, as I did. *"Twin-Flame Code Breaker"* will provide you with the *"Keys"* to unlock *"heaven's gate,"* putting you on a fast track towards harmonizing unconditional love, connecting to your "ultimate calling" and finding your way home, as you embrace *"The Gift"* within your twin-flame mission and reunite with your twin flame.

While reading *"Twin-Flame Code Breaker," I ask that you show up with love and be present with an open mind, process with a ready heart and integrate with a willing spirit.* You may not agree with everything that this message has to offer, but the more you stay in "non-judgment" the more you will experience and personally receive. Take away from this message that which resonates with your soul and leave the rest.

You may find that the first couple of *"Key Codes"* contain in-depth information that my guides have assured me are important for you to understand why you are going through such intense experiences. Practicing patience while reading them will be your first lesson to accomplish; they set the premises for what is guaranteed to be worth the wait. I will also share many of my own personal experiences throughout these *11:11 Key Codes* with the intent to confirm the validity of the power of these principles. You will find a few repetitions throughout *"Twin-Flame Code Breaker,"* I have been instructed by my guides to leave those repetitions — they are there in order to help the readers fully grasp the knowledge and wisdom. Studies have proven that hearing something again and in a different context facilitates processing and integration of information before comprehension.

I would like to mention that I wrote *"Twin-Flame Code Breaker"* in its entirety in a six-week time frame and it has had minimal standard edits. The content flowed through in the context that it is presented. There are a few things that have been left intentionally; given the window of time that I was given to have this message ready to present, there may be a few editorial errors. But I am being told that is intentional — proving the point to release perfectionism (head) and focus on the beauty of the message (heart). The information provided in the *11:11 Key Codes*, will not only give you a better understanding of the background of twin flames, but you will also gain clarity as to why you should continue your twin-flame journey. The goal is for you to say, "*I can see clearly now!*"

The intention of this "unconditional blueprint" is to become the catalyst so that you may find the personal freedom that your soul longs for. The second purpose of this message is to raise the unconditional love vibration by expanding into multidimensional planes of the Universe – by *raising the unconditional love vibration throughout all humanity not only during this life span but throughout the remainder of eternity*. This revolutionary "*conscious expansion*" will help society as a whole move away from our old belief paradigms and shift into higher vibrational emotions, creating a *new earth heart language*.

The mission of all twin flames around the globe is to reunite during this era, to tear down the *old conventional belief systems and collectively restore heaven on earth, so that all mankind can find their way home to a state of harmony, peace, happiness and unconditional love*. So, whether you have a twin flame incarnated during this lifetime or not, if this revolutionary message has crossed your path, this is a Divine appointment. There are no accidents – everything happens for a reason, and when the student is ready, the teacher appears. So here I AM – the vessel. Are you ready to find your way home?

KEY CODE 1:1

Understand the Twin Flame Prophecy

PART ONE

Once Upon a Time in a Land Far, Far Away

SINCE THE BEGINNING OF TIME, humans have held the concept of a soul splitting upon inception — the idea of creating two individual twin souls; generating the power of two that is greater than one. Upon incarnation, the twin souls create an agreement, and each soul selects their portions of the lessons that they agree to learn during their joint evolutionary journey. They lead parallel lives; throughout each life, typically only one twin incarnates at a time. They share the goal of gathering knowledge and wisdom from each of their individual experiences and then share with each other the awareness they learned through the process. *This joint venture helps both to evolve further and faster as they transcend to their higher selves.* The mission is that, by the end of their journeys, they both have mastered all the lessons that they agreed to learn along the way. The culmination of their final lessons requires them to come together in order to create a mirrored reflection that is necessary to clear out all karmic debris.

Ultimately, they are able to fulfill a greater mission than either one of them could have done alone. At the end of their evolutionary journey, they reunite and become one again. *Then the ultimate goal is to pay forward and give back to the Universe —to help others using all the lessons, knowledge and wisdom they gained during their transformational journey.* The lessons they learn then become part of the Universal intelligence that is collectively used to create a new blueprint and a legacy for others to follow.

One of the most important lessons each individual twin soul must master during their joint venture is the art of self-love, and then to share *"The Gift"* of unconditional love with each other and then together share it with the world. *The plan of the Universe is to use this collective higher vibrational energy and magnify the power of unconditional love, then to bring it into the physical plane by infusing this energetic force within the physical bodies of all human beings.* Human beings are an expression of the Divine love of God, the Creator of all things, generating oneness amongst all humanity. Therefore, it is important to experience oneness with self before being able to share unconditional love with another.

Once the twin souls are close to mastering their agreed-upon lessons near the end of their journey, they subconsciously begin to remember their Divine origin. Then they begin to energetically seek each other out and incarnate at the same time with the intention of reuniting. Due to their agreement on the higher planes, their soul acts accordingly to accomplish their mission. Through the process, they continually communicate energetically by connecting to their higher selves. When the timing is right and it is time for them to connect on the physical plane, a *"soul awakening"* transpires, creating *"conscious awareness"* that helps them identify each other again. They begin to remember who they are. The entire process from incarnation to transcending to their higher selves is Divinely guided. Once they physically join they begin releasing all the karmic debris of their past. This happens during the final stages of their evolutionary journey before completing their soul agreement and returning to the Source for all eternity.

The twin-flame or twin-soul relationship plays a very important role in the evolutionary process of every human. Everyone has a twin soul, but not all twin souls are incarnated at the same time. Once the twin souls join in physical form, they become twin flames. *This means that the individual sparks energetically connect and create a flame – this demonstrates the difference between the terms "twin soul" verses "twin flame."*

Once twin flames complete the final stages of their mission, they are granted what is known to be the most satisfying relationship — and one that every soul seeks. This is usually the relationship most people are seeking when they express their desire to connect with a soulmate. Online, you can read many romantic love stories, with each source giving a different version of the twin-flame phenomenon. Many of the sites will give you the impression that a twin-flame relationship is love at first sight, and that you will unite and live happily ever after. Others make mention of the intensity of this relationship, which can give the impression of doomsday. However, if properly viewed, these ideas are far from the truth. *A true twin-flame relationship doesn't include self-desire. It is deeper than love at first sight. This sacred couple is a representation of unconditional love and should be just that – no conditions on another person to fill a void within one's self.* It is important for a person to be whole and complete. That raises one's own love vibration and eliminates the need for codependency and addictive behaviors. These are just symptoms of the self in search of something to fill its inner void. One should learn to release the expectations of others, including their twin flame.

While working with twin flames from all over the world, I repeatedly hear a few common comments such as: *"He or she is not doing for me what I think they should,"* or *"They are doing to me what I think they shouldn't be doing." "I would let it go and practice patience in this situation; after they show me respect." "I want my twin flame to do what I think they should before I am willing to surrender and let go and trust that they are going to give me what I need and what I want from them."* I am always reminding these twin flames that this is an unconditional relationship. Therefore, there should be no expectations or conditions placed on their twin flame. Placing these type of conditions on their other half is not unconditional love! A twin-flame relationship is a self-journey – all about your own self. Your twin flame is only present to mirror the reflection of what it is you need to work on within yourself. Until you understand this concept and make a connection with yourself, generating self-love, you cannot experience true love with anyone or in any relationship. *It is imperative that you are a whole, complete and unified person who is one within yourself first.* You must first love yourself enough to balance and unify your oneness before you can share this unconditional love with another person, whether you are a twin flame or not.

I also hear the repeated questions: "*When is he or she coming back?*" "*When will we be together?*" My answer to either of these questions is this: When one twin flame tends to focus on the other and view their twin as the "*runner*," it is actually you focusing on who you believe to be the "*runner*." You are not focusing on what your twin flame is teaching you. *When doing this, that makes you the "runner" – running from yourself! Let me repeat this: YOU are the one not focusing on your own self and your own journey.* Like it or not – it's true! And it takes this kind of self-awareness to raise your own energetic vibration, which is required before you can ever have a chance to come into complete harmonization with your twin soul and manifest the full twin-flame union.

Being that I work with twin flames every day, some of the best advice I can give you is: *If you are truly seeking a reunion with this Divinely-orchestrated relationship, it's time to get back to the meaning of what a true flame relationship is all about.* Start sacrificing your own self-desires for the purpose of reconnecting and uniting with complete wholeness within yourself. It is this selfless act that has to occur in order to connect to the true meaning of a true twin-flame union.

"In the Beginning, God Created the Heavens and the Earth." – Genesis 1:1

Whether you believe in the ancient story of the sunken utopia – Atlantis — or not, its metaphor can be demonstrated in the Book of Genesis. Since the beginning of time, there have been documented stories of the sacred union of twin flames. Of course, one is the story of Adam and Eve. *Theologies often state that the Book of Genesis depicts the story of Atlantis, which preceded the same self-destruction that occurred in the Garden of Eden — also a place called heaven on earth.* Atlantis, similar to Eden, was a place intended for all mankind to experience eternal inner peace and happiness (i.e., heaven on earth). This is said to have changed when Eve partook of the forbidden fruit from the tree of knowledge, which represents the duality of good versus evil. *Eve was tempted by a serpent, a snake that was thought to be evil; but could it have really just been a representation of the activation of her kundalini energy* (I will discuss more about this in *Key Code 10:10*)*?* When we activate this energy from within our sacral chakras (I will present a full understanding of chakras in *Key Code 5:5*), it becomes the catalyst to activating the art of sacred sexuality. *The purpose is to help a person tap into the Divine creativity, which can only be accomplished once a human Being connects to their higher consciousness.* As energetic Beings, we are granted expanded wisdom and Divine knowledge by connecting to our highest cosmic self. Tapping into this wisdom at the highest vibration can only take place once both souls have fully awakened and have learned how to fully surrender and let go.

It is in the cosmic energetic planes that the Universal intelligence exists. It must be brought down to the earthly plane and channeled into physical form through our connection to our higher selves or higher consciousness. This concept is similar to the tree of knowledge where Eve shared the wisdom of truth with Adam. *Did her decision to connect to the higher realms really cause them damnation? Or was it that they opted to make a self-sacrifice by choosing to create the dualities of good versus evil, heaven versus hell, happiness verses sorrow, personal freedom verses bondage?* The truth is – we must experience the bad in order to feel the good. *Could it be that this sacred couple knew that it would be necessary to clear karmic patterns of all past negative soul trauma in order to restore heaven on earth as it was before the fall of Atlantis?* We could view this as a sacred sacrifice: these twin flames gave up their eternal joy so that they could help clear the karma for the world.

This exemplifies the mission of a twin-flame union to sacrifice self-satisfaction, so that together all twin flames can help save the world from self-destruction. It also teaches us that the end of times are really just the end of the old ways, letting go of old karma. When we release the past and begin demonstrating acts of unconditional love by taking on and then releasing the karma of the world, this generates a new blueprint for the new world order.

Historians continue to make the connection between Atlantis and Eden. Both became egotistically tainted and turned the heart of heavenly bliss into a strife, hardships, struggles, pain and suffering. *Both worlds allowed inner ego battles to win — head over heart – evil over good – hell over heaven.* It was this imbalance of negative verses positive energies that caused a shift in the physical plane of Atlantis that ended in complete devastation, and the empire was cast into the Atlantic ocean. The *Fall of Atlantis* occurred in the area we know today as Egypt. *It was this self-destruction that has been thought to have created tremendous soul trauma, leaving souls in a state of complete despair.* This has also produced feelings of abandonment for massive amounts of souls. Twin souls were ripped apart, creating a void with a feeling of missing their other half and a feeling of wanting to return home.

I continually hear these exact words when working with twin flames. I clearly see that this soul trauma is very real. *I help twin flames release these past energetic imprints and create freedom of their soul so they can find inner peace and happiness once more.* I am also working with the leaders of twin flames to remove these negative energetic blocks so that together we can all restore heaven on earth. It is my duty to fulfill my twin-flame mission by helping to prevent self-destruction once more. If you were to research all of the ancient and biblical concepts, they all talk about this same type of self-destruction; it dates back all the way to Abraham's teachings of Babylon. Damnation of Atlantis and Eden also parallels the same destructive patterns found in the ancient Greek, Celtic, Hellenic, and Roman mythologies.

The story of Adam and Eve is also a perfect example of how the energetic forces of the trinity and pyramid energies began with God as head of the throne: the alpha and the omega – the yin and the yang – creating both the perfect harmonic balance of the Divine masculine and the Divine feminine energies. These two energetic forces are also represented by the infinity symbol, which has no beginning or ending. Comparing the trinity to the sacred geometry of the Star of David, the merkaba and the Sephirah Tripheret, which stands for harmony and the Sri Yantra (also called the unified field); all are produced by a sequence of triangular shapes that produces pyramidal energies. Each symbol forms a perfect combination and balance of the masculine and feminine energies. The particular shape of the symbol determines its energetic frequency creating the term sacred geometry. Adam the masculine and Eve the feminine also represent the perfect image of unconditional love embodied in the human flesh; they were considered the first pair of twin flames in physical form. Adam was created by God and Eve from the rib of Adam; they came from the same source, never to be separated, connected in their Divinity for all eternity. This is the first documented inner sacred marriage of twin souls becoming twin flames.

As we investigate further into the sacred geometrical energy produced within these pyramidal structures, we can get a better understanding of God's energetic connection to the trinity and the head of the pyramid, called Kether in Hebrew. Adam is the son of God, Chokmah in Hebrew, sitting at the right side of the pyramid and representing the masculine image of God, known for his wisdom. Eve is symbolized by the Binah in Hebrew, sitting to the left of God at the base of the pyramid. She is the feminine energy and represents the Holy Spirit that energetically connects to the physical body of Adam. This also demonstrates how the energy from man is an extension from the Source, in addition to emanating Source energy on an earthly plane. When the masculine and feminine energies are merged, it produces the infinity symbol. Together they create an ebb and flow of God's energy. *When the masculine and feminine counterparts intersect at the exact zero point, this is where the two sparks ignite, creating the flame that represents the sacred union of the energy produced by all twin flames.*

The masculine destruction of the *Fall of Atlantis* can also be compared to the feminine expression of the Great Flood of Lemuria which took place off the Pacific coast – where Hawaii is now. It is believed that highly vibrational crystal beings once lived in this land of paradise, also a heaven on earth. We can also see the same self-destruction as Atlantis when researching the story of Lemuria. The highly vibrational beings of Lemuria were aware of the flood predictions. They heard stories of the end of times, but only a few listened and built underground housing. The ones that listened returned to a new earth and found a new way of living. Like Atlantis, both Lemuria and the Mayans also built pyramids with the energy that they created through the access to their Divine intelligence; which gave them access to the Divine creativity. That granted them such great knowledge and wisdom.

Personally, I find it very interesting that they all accessed the same higher intelligence and created a similar concept of time and space despite being thousands of miles apart without any direct form of communication. I have visited Egypt, Hawaii and Mexico. Recently, I discovered I have energetic grid points in each of these areas, which energetically anchors me in physical form to these places. By processing my own experiences while visiting all three of these places, it has helped me to connect my past to my present so that I can release it; allowing me to move forward during this lifetime.

The Holy Grail - Jesus and Mary Magdalena

There are a variety of theories on the subject of Jesus and his twin flame Mary Magdalena. If you research this – the most famous unconditional love story of all time – you will find a host of evidence that proves that the union of Jesus and Mary Magdalena to be true. All controversy stems from the conflicting belief systems of society as a whole — beliefs that have been taught from generation to generation, and in the process, passing down truths that have been watered down (not to mention many cover-ups that have taken place within the church doctrines). It is very important to remember that the only thing that is truly the truth is that which resonates within your own heart and your understanding of your own twin-flame journey. Regardless, when you get to the heart of the matter, the essence of their story cannot be denied. This couple is a perfect example of what a true twin-flame journey is all about. Together, they offer a beautiful representation of the highest form of unconditional love that has ever exist between two human beings.

In Da Vinci's painting of the Last Supper, we can see the Holy Grail, an open vessel formed between the physical bodies of Jesus, the masculine, on the right and Mary Magdalene, the feminine, on the left. It is thought to represent Mary's uterus and depicts a feminine expression of what it means to open up and receive unconditional love. The masculine or giving of unconditional love is represented by the cup that Jesus drank out of during the Last Supper. This idea of giving and receiving follows the energetic laws of the Universe – the harmony of both energies are necessary to balance oneself first and then all relationships. If you examine this portrait in further detail, however, you will not find a single cup on the table.

Looking at the deeper meaning of this idea it teaches us that it is that same vessel that holds the Christ consciousness of the planet. It took the masculine and feminine energetic connection between Jesus and Mary Magdalena to produce a higher unconditional love vibration. For the purposes of this concept, periodically throughout "*Twin-Flame Code Breaker*" I will use the term "*Christ consciousness*" in reference to the phrase "*raising your unconditional love vibration.*" Christ consciousness exudes once the merger of two twin souls has occurred, and is the energetic exchange between the harmonic balances of these souls to produce an unconditionally high force that is so strong, it must be housed in an etheric or third energy body. Both the hearts of Jesus and Mary Magdalena had to be present in order to create the Christ consciousness vibration needed to generate unconditional love. Just like the same masculine and feminine duality of the Divinity, it is necessary to experience much pain and sorrow to feel such great joy and unconditional love.

Together, this twin flame couple took on the karmic vows of pain, suffering, struggles and hardships for the world. All twin flames have agreed to participate in this same assignment. Jesus, the masculine, took on the heavier karmic load so that his feminine counterpart, Mary Magdalena, could carry out their agreed earthly mission. We know this to be true because after Jesus's crucifixion, Mary Magdalena fled to France to continue to spread Christ's teachings. Note that several churches throughout France were built with stained-glass images placing hers and Jesus together. True twin flames are not only encoded with the same innate healing abilities that Jesus had, but they also are "*The Chosen Ones*" taking on the same self-sacrifice and carry the karmic patterns of the world. *Therefore, twin flames can be viewed as wearing the same crown of thorns as Christ did during his crucifixion on the cross. It represents the deaths of all of our karmic pasts, transcending and then resurrecting to heaven where we become enlightened.* This is exactly what twin flames do when they shift from their lower self and experience a rebirth that occurs during the Ascension process (I provide a complete explanation of this process in *Key Code 4:4*).

All twin flames must experience this personal resurrection before coming into full reunion with their other half. A twin-flame relationship is the treasure that every soul seeks and it becomes the sum of all rewards that you are granted for making such deep sacrifices and bearing the burdens of the world. Most twin flames don't realize that they have volunteered for this assignment. The purpose is so that all humans might find the same unconditional Christ love for themselves first and then share that love with each other and then the planet. In order to do so, you must first "*unlock*" the personal freedom required to find inner peace and happiness – heaven on earth. It is the *11:11 Key Code*s found in "*Twin-Flame Code Breaker*" that will help you learn how to release your own karmic past and heal yourself. It is not until you find unification within yourself that you can find the harmonic balance within your twin flame relationship. Once you do, you are to share this harmony with others. Jesus and Mary Magdalena represent the purest form of this harmonic balance. They are examples for all twin flames to follow. Being able to find the same harmonic balance that this holy couple found becomes the Divine mission of all twin-flame reunions. The goal is to shift into the same Holy Grail vessel of unconditional love.

Everyone has the same Holy Grail imprint that Jesus and Mary Magdalena had; their imprint has been energetically encoded within every cell in every body. Expressing this same Christ consciousness creates the healing power that all twin flames have and will share with the world. By following this unconditional act together, all twin flames can continue to keep the truth about Jesus and Magdalena alive. Their teachings create the healing miracles that lie within the hearts and hands of all twin flames. Once you awaken and activate these healing powers found within the DNA of your soul, you will receive these same Holy Grail codes within your twin-flame heart. This will open you up to all possibilities and help you align with the mission of your twin-flame Divine plan.

The Incarnation of Twin Souls and How They Become Twin Flames

Humans are energetic light beings. God said, "Let there be light," and there was light. Light is energy, and energy creates a magnetic force that constitutes the connection of all matter and on every plane. This energy produces an aura or energetic field around every living creature. As I mentioned, we have an etheric body – a third body that is created to house the energy of two souls. This third body is produced between the interaction of any two people no matter what type of relationship, and it houses the collective energy produced between every physical and energetic interaction that occurs. Once twin souls fully awaken and fully merge into twin flames, the energetic forces produced between them can become so powerful that it cannot be housed in either one of their physical bodies. Twin flames always merge energetically in the etheric body before merging on the spiritual, mental, emotional and physical planes. It is this third body that also keeps them continuously connected during all lifetimes, even while only one twin soul is incarnated and the other twin soul parallels in an energetic formation. This is how your twin is able to assist you from the other side at all times.

Energy is ever-changing and cannot be created nor destroyed. Albert Einstein scientifically proved with his famous physics formula: E = MC (2). Here, these energetic forces can only be measured when there is a harmonic balance between the masculine and feminine energies – the positive and negative polarities. This formula also links the concept of light versus darkness. It scientifically proves that when these two energies merge, creating balance, the process generates space that creates room for expansion. It is this same energy that is in everything and everyone. It is infused with God's innate intelligence that magnetically produces the power within us that keeps us breathing, our hearts beating and every other system in our bodies functioning at optimal level — without any conscious effort or actions needed on our part.

I, having a scientific and analytical mindset for the majority of my life, have found this energetic concept a way that I can make a direct connection with God. This has allowed me to consciously create my own personal relationship with this Universal intelligence. I developed this connection through my own experiences, studies and Divine understanding, which started when I gained firsthand experience in receiving healing energy therapies that removed interference in the proper energetic flow within my body. Since then, I have acquired a wealth of wisdom and understanding of these Universal laws associated with quantum physics. I experienced firsthand the healing powers of these energy forces after a major car accident. The benefits that I received is what later prompted me to become a chiropractor. As my practice evolved, I also became an energy-healing practitioner. Today, I remotely use my energetic healing knowledge to help twin flames break the barriers that are holding them back, both personally and in their twin-flame union. My experiences paved my energetic path with the necessary stepping stones to direct me towards my own twin-flame mission. To date, I have accumulated 30-plus years of energetic wisdom. With everything in this universe being made up of the same energetic force as the Creator, these principles gave me a better understanding of how God is in and with everyone at all times.

As previously mentioned, when we spark from this innate energetic power Source — God if you will — we split into two perfect energetic souls. Both carry a balance of the masculine and feminine energies. *When the twin souls divide and before incarnating in attempts to become twin flames, each soul carries a 60/40 percent ratio of the masculine compared to the feminine energies.* One twin will carry 60% masculine energy, making them the masculine-dominant twin. The other twin soul carries 60% feminine energy, making them feminine-dominant. Once the two individual souls finally clear enough of their individual karmic debris and are ready to start making a connection to their higher self, which is what happens through the Ascension process, it is during this time that they come together in physical form to begin to help each other to balance these masculine and feminine energies at 50/50. Keep in mind the balance of these ratios can vary, here I'm referencing the ratios that occur when twin souls have matured enough and are ready to reincarnate with attempts to reunite becoming twin flames.

After the two twin souls spark from the light of God and assist each other throughout their individual journeys, and once they are ready to unite into physical form, their individual sparks will merge back together. It is their physical union that creates the flame. This flame generates a higher frequency of energy than either one's individual energy. This becomes the conductor of a great mission that can only be fulfilled once the twin souls have reunited. This concept offers a better understanding of the difference in the terms "twin soul" and "twin flame"; the flame only ignites after the souls have recognized each other and have physically merged. However, this does not necessarily mean that they have yet or will merge into a full romantic union. The ultimate goal of this relationship is to fulfill the mission that each twin-flame couple agrees to at the beginning of their evolution.

Once the twin souls have energetically merged, one twin flame becomes the generator of this energy, while the other is the electric (I will provide a deeper understanding of the concept in *Key Code 8:8*). It takes the combination of these joint forces to generate a great electrical powerhouse in the etheric body that is needed in order to complete their Divine mission. This explains the concept of two being greater than one.

Rainbow – The Color of God's Love

Psalms 104:1-4 (NIV): 1 Praise the LORD, my soul. LORD my God, you are very great; you are clothed with splendor and majesty. 2 The LORD wraps himself in light as with a garment; he stretches out the heavens like a tent. 3 and lays the beams of his upper chambers on their waters. He makes the clouds his chariot and rides on the wings of the wind. 4 He makes winds his messengers, flames of fire his servants.

These bible verses deliver very powerful messages. First, verse 2 indicates that God is made of light and that his beams spread amongst all things. Verse 3 indicates that God shares light with others. In verse 4, God sends messengers or flames who are extensions from light beams; these twin flames are appointed as servants. When we incarnate, we spark from the same white light of God.

"If you are filled with light, with no dark corners, then your whole life will be radiant, as though a floodlight were filling you with light." –Luke 11:36 (New Living Translation)

It was physicist Isaac Newton who discovered how to refract the spectrum of white light and proved that the seven colors of the rainbow exist when white light is split through a prism. *Each life that we incarnate, we spark from one of the seven rays of God's white light.* Therefore, we originate from one of the seven colors of the rainbow – the color of God. Also, each time that we incarnate, we can come from a different color ray. Since twin flames split upon incarnation, they are of the same color ray. At the end of each lifetime, everyone returns to the same ray of light that they incarnate from. I think it is important here to point out that not everyone believes in the concept of reincarnation. Personally, I feel that this is due to a lack of personal research and understanding of this concept, and because most belief systems are not fully researched; opinions rarely rely on facts. Most people's belief systems are passed down to them. Let me also say – I will be the first to admit, I am not a Bible scholar. Therefore, I encourage you to investigate this concept in further detail for yourself. However, what I will say is this: the Bible was compiled of a series of man-made prophecies;

not everyone realizes that it was man and the church that decided to eliminate a few books from the Bible – some of which contained the teachings on the subject of reincarnation. Please know that I am not presenting this information for a debate – this is not about being right or wrong, but only to encourage you to do more study for yourself and to create your own understanding of God and to connect with your own truth. If you would like to research more about this subject, I would highly recommend you look up information using this phrase: "The missing books of the bible."

God appointed a Chohan or Lord over each color ray. Each having Ascended Masters and an Archangel to assist us during out journey. These entities transcend religion and so they are non-denominational; they have to report to God to get permission to act and help you on God's behalf. They are also not able to assist you without your request for assistance. Each color ray and entity also carries virtues that are to be learned each time that we are incarnated. Each virtue is associated with a particular color ray (I will share more details on the virtues and their connection to the twin-flame mission in *Key Code 2:2*). This is why I perform incarnation color ray readings for twin flames. Once you determine which ray you and your twin soul have incarnated from, and which leaders govern that ray, it will help you to connect with your mission and have a better understanding of what lessons you and your twin flame came here to learn during this life. That in turn helps you implement the joint mission of the twin-flame union.

Each of these seven rays of light are associated with a specific energetic frequency that produces the associated color. Twin flames can carry multiple light rays, being that they incarnate from different rays during each lifetime. However, a person is always more dominant in one specific light ray during each lifetime. We can also carry different color rays within each plane of our being, e.g., our energetic or light body, and spiritual, mental, emotional and physical bodies; these planes become the genetic makeup of our Being. The energetic or light body becomes the glue that connects the physical body to the spiritual, mental and emotional bodies. *At the end of each life cycle, the energetic light returns to the color ray from which it came from – this becomes the passing of the soul from the physical body.* We have all heard stories of this; when people experience near-death experiences they report seeing a bright light.

ENERGY IS OUR DIRECT CONNECTION TO THE SOURCE

These color rays come to us directly from the Creator. They have always been and always will be a part of our existence. These seven rays emanate from God and extend to each of us, becoming the Source of our energetic genetic makeup. Each ray represents a different aspect of who we are in each of our planes: etheric, energetic, spiritual, emotional, mental and physical. *The color of the rays that we each carry and the colors of the chakras do not have any direct correlation, but the rays do help shape our personality characteristics.* Just like the color rays, each chakra color also operates at a very specific frequency of energy. The chakras are our direct connection to the Source at all times. The aura or energy field that is produced becomes the filter of our energetic operating system – filtering the internal and external energetic exchange of energy.

Now that you have an in-depth understanding of the twin flame prophecies, let's shift gears in part two of *Key Code 1:1*, and gain a better understanding of what it means to be a true twin flame during this era.

PART TWO

What is a True Twin Flame?

I HAVE ALREADY GIVEN AN in-depth description of twin-flames origination, history, incarnation and what it means to be a twin flame. One of the most important ways to identify a true twin-flame union is that it is always connected to a Divine calling and worldly mission. Later in *Key Code 2:2*, I will go into greater detail regarding the connection of twin flames and their mission. In this section, I want to review what it means to be true twin flames with hopes of creating clarity on the idea and clearing up some of the confusion that exists. So, here we will also explore their general traits, characteristics and synchronicities.

As you may have realized, there is so much controversy about the description of a true twin flame. If you were to do a google search on twin flames, you might find some of the information in this revelation. However, you are more likely to read articles about how twin flames are romantically attracted, raving about how you will experience an intense physical attraction. A true twin flame connection is if anything the opposite. It is part of the Divine plan to remove this physical appeal in order to break down ego and also to connect on the energetic and spiritual planes before it can be converted into a physical attraction.

For this reason, it is the purpose of "*Twin-Flame Code Breaker*" to clarify and redefine the true nature of real twin-flame relationships and their prophecies, creating a deeper understanding of who they are and why they are on the planet during this timeframe of our world's existence, and to reveal the reason for their return. Twin flames are mirror images of each other. *Their number one purpose for coming together in physical union is to become a reflection for each other, so that each individual twin can work on their own individual journey while being available for each other as they travel their individual paths to enlightenment.* They must evolve as two individual souls, reaching full maturation before they can complete their joint evolutionary agreements. Then and only then is it possible for a full reunion to occur; this is why generally full union only happens less than 1% of the time. However, now more than ever in the history of time, more twin souls are coming together into a full twin-flame union. I will give a full understanding of why in *Key Code 2:2.*

Twin souls typically incarnate at a time when their souls' journeys are coming to a close because together they have evolved enough and are nearing the mastery of their life lessons; each twin soul has had to extensively break their chosen karmic vows. At the beginning of their journey, they not only choose which lessons they will master, but also which virtues they will learn, and they also decided who will take which karmic vows. When one twin masters their own lessons, the other twin soul benefits as well. *A true twin-flame relationship is all about a spiritual awakening, letting go of the old self and transcending to the higher self.* That is the Ascension pathway that leads them back home as they find their way out of the darkness and into the light. A twin-flame relationship does not always have to be romantic in nature. The twin flames can be siblings, parent-child or even friends. One twin soul is usually more awakened than the other, and they usually do not come into full physical contact until their other half has begun or ready to achieve this awakening. Occasionally, this does happen, but when coming together too soon, it creates more separation because there are many obstacles that must be cleared before they can completely unite on all levels.

It is not until both twin flames are ready for this fully awakened state and both have or are ready to break their karmic vows that they can fully accelerate through their Ascension process. After reaching full Ascension, twin flames are then granted the opportunity to receive their ultimate reward by experiencing the ultimate relationship that a twin-flame union offers. If you have reached this state of being, but your twin flame is not available or ready to commit to a physical relationship, then you will be granted a soulmate or a twin-flame facilitator (I will explain more about this towards the end of this chapter). That way, you will closely mimic a full-union twin-flame experience. This is necessary for a person to continue their own personal mastery to complete their joint mission.

Most of the time, true twins don't even find out about the term "*twin flame*" until after they have met their twin soul on a spiritual level. This is because this arrangement is so Divinely guided; it is revealed to you at the exact time you are ready. That way, you will be able to recognize your twin flame when you meet them on the physical plane. As I mentioned, usually there is no initial physical chemistry or instantaneous love. That is a sign of a false twin and is karmic nature. It could even be a very deep soulmate that gets a twin soul ready for their twin flame. *Most of the time, a true twin flame is not someone you would have chosen for yourself – I hear this phrase from twin flames all the time.* That is because it is ego that is still involved, and this becomes part of the lesson that has to be mastered. Because of ego or circumstances, it can take years before a twin-flame relationship develops into a physical connection.

Once the twin souls incarnate together, they usually have a lot of life lessons in parallel or similar life events happening at the same time. They usually have opposite characteristics in some of their personal traits but complement each other in all the ways that they are different. Their lives can parallel and merge in and out of each other's lives before there is a spiritual connection.

True Twin-Flame Characteristics

- Twins feel the need to be honest. The ultimate truth comes up and they feel the need for confession.

- Twins can communicate about anything and everything and can spend hours talking.
- Twins feel that they are born to carry out a great mission or have a greater purpose.
- Twins emit creative energy used to create something productive individually and together.
- Twins know the other person as well or better than they know themselves.
- Twins enter 5D – 5th dimensional time, where time goes by fast – the point is to accelerate the process, getting them on the same page faster.
- Twins get on a fast track of esoteric cosmic wisdom.
- Twins start seeing 11:11 around the time of physical connection.
- There is usually not a chemical attraction; they are typically "not your type."
- Twins prepare for advanced Ascension work and do this work together after each have awakened spiritually, or at least are in the process.
- Twins can see issues that need resolving in other people and they know how to help them.
- Twins are always teaching each other.
- Twins are very intuitive; one or both have a strong connection and is guided by spirit.
- Twins feel each other's pain – even when separated.
- Twins come together to help complete the balance of their masculine/feminine energies.
- Twins feel an emotional and spiritual connection.
- Twins have suffered much pain in previous soulmate relationships.
- Twins usually have some form of telepathic communication.
- Twins have the ability to heal others.
- Twins look, feel and act younger.
- Twins are capable but have trouble asking for help.

- Twins activate past life awareness's in order to clear the past.
- Twins connect through the chakras and are encoded with *"The 12 Chakra Template"* (This will be fully explained in *Key Code 5:5).*

Twin-Flame Synchronicities

In this section, I will share examples of my own twin-flame synchronicities. I think this demonstration will give you a better idea of how the lives of twin flames are in parallel and how their individual paths align during their journey together:

- We both started college to become medical doctors.
- We both were in a car accident that redirected our paths to become chiropractors.
- We both experienced chronic neck pain and TMJ issues from our accidents.
- We were classmates during chiropractic school.
- When we first met, he reminded me of someone from a prior relationship; he even drove the exact same truck as that person and had similar habits.
- We occasionally commuted together while attending school.
- We both were assigned to the same outpatient clinic for our externships.
- We performed adjustments on each other during school, mainly because he was one of the few people who could adjust my neck, allowing me to get better results.
- While in school, we attended many of the same health fairs.
- While in school, we both got married the same year and only one day apart.
- We each expanded our studies into energetic healing; he learned two of the techniques that I always wanted to learn, but never did.
- His x-wife and my x-life partner's birthday fall on the same day.

- His birthday is on the same day as my nephew's birthday.
- He connected with a twin-flame facilitator (I will explain this term later, towards the end of this chapter) whose birthday is on the same day as mine.
- During our 20-plus years of being friends, he always felt like my brother and I have always felt as though I could really trust him.
- Our expanded studies complement each other. I focused more on learning additional alternative therapies and he focused more on the business aspects of how to run a business – together we have shared the knowledge we each have learned.
- I started my own practice with his guidance. He directed me in every area of business, implementing office build-outs, systems and patient management.
- We have always practiced chiropractic within just a couple miles of each other; in the same building at one point.
- He has always been my go-to person when making major career decisions.
- During every business transition, including me keeping my foot in the door and continuing to practice and also aligning with my mission, he has been there for me every step of the way.
- After experiencing a failed business partnership, if it were not for my twin flame, I believe I would have stopped practicing; if I would have done so, I know that I would have not aligned with the mission that I am fulfilling today.
- We have remained each other's primary chiropractors and it is not the same if either one of us get adjusted by someone else.
- Over the years, he would send out energetic signals for me to stop by when he needed an adjustment, and I would usually show up.
- We both have spent many years working on our own personal development. I gave him his first Wayne Dyer book.
- We both went through the "*dark night of the soul*" at the same time.

- While experiencing some deep personal issues, he was directed by his intuition to come to me for assistance, so that he could receive energy healing.
- Together, we opened a Pandora's Box that directed me on a path to discovering who we were: twin flames.
- I never noticed that we have the exact eye color, until after discovering that we were twin flames.
- We became each other's teachers as we progressed together through the Ascension process.
- Helping him with his own spiritual advancement, directed my every step towards discovering the *11:11 Key Codes* that are in this book.
- Assisting him during his transformation activated and expanded my intuitive, physic abilities. It literally encoded me with translation codes that have opened channels and enhanced my spirit guide connection.
- During our energy sessions, we experience a telepathic connection, either having similar or the same visions.
- We both feel a strong connection to the pyramids of Giza, in Egypt.
- I became his messenger and the facilitator for delivering Divine messages to him from the Universe.
- The times that we have experienced silence were necessary to make the music that we generate together.
- Without conscious awareness, he has always been a catalyst for my career and this has directed me towards my soul's purpose – and the mission that I am now fulfilling.
- It was a shift in direction and deciding to not follow through with a joint business venture that was not only the catalyst — it literally shoved me into alignment with becoming a twin-flame expert.
- This book is part of our joint mission.

I think these parallels give you a good idea of what twin-flame synchronicities really are and a better understanding of what it means to be a true twin flame. You can see in my example how our relationship has revolved the entire time around a mission to serve others — it has not been about a relationship that is romantic in nature.

An Understanding of Other Types of Soul Relationships

I frequently am ask about the difference between a twin flame and other soulmate relationships. I will give a better explanation of each. I will also use examples of my own experiences and observations with these types of relationships along my journey.

Soulmate Relationships

According to ancient wisdom, after each soul splits into two twin souls, they then join their own individual soul groups which consist of their soulmates. Each twin soul has their own soul and their own group; they do not share the exact same soul. It is in our soul group where we spend all eternity — until it's time to reunite with our other half. Each time an individual twin soul incarnates, it returns to this same soul family within this same group or Monad, which is known as the – I AM presence. This group is made up of 144 souls; this comes from multiplying 12 over souls (a direct conscious connections to the Creator) X 12 branches or groupings – representing the 12 tribes of Israel. We read about this in Mathew 19:28 (NIV) - *Jesus said to them, "Truly I tell you, at the renewal of all things, when the Son of Man sits on his glorious throne, you who have followed me will also sit on twelve thrones, judging the twelve tribes of Israel.*

We connect with our soulmates on a very deep level and within multiple dimensions. This is because we spend many lifetimes together in this same family of 144 souls. The family consists of the same twelve facets or tribe — each are part of the colors rays from which we spark. Not all 144 souls in our soul group are incarnated at the same time. *The purpose of these deep connections are to create deep bonds so that each twin soul can use their soulmates to help prepare to connect with their twin flame and release deep karma.* Soulmates tend to experience many life cycles that will help each twin soul grow, clear karma and evolve. You can usually recognize a soulmate quickly since you have shared many lifetimes together. Soulmates can also be of various types of relationships – romantic, spouse, siblings, parent-child and even best friends. Similar to twin flames, soulmate connections tend to be life-long connections.

My last relationship was a very deep soulmate connection. Through experiences we shared, I discovered I had been his mother in a prior lifetime. His mother in this lifetime and I both have birthdays on the same day. This became part of what caused a disconnection in our relationship in this lifetime. Towards the end of our relationship, we both were exhibiting the behaviors of a mother-son relationship. However, it took this deep connection to produce such deep pain for me to later experience the greatest amount of compassion that I would have never known otherwise. I needed to experience this deep pain to heal not only my past life with him, but to also let go of the karmic attachments that I needed to release in this lifetime. The depths of this relationship was exactly what I needed to experience to force me into the "*dark night of the soul*" and to shift my life into the direction that it was intended to go. He taught me such great compassion, not only for him but for others. My twin flame had a similar experience to this. He also experienced deep pain while going through a divorce. He also had a very deep connection with his wife, and it took this same deep connection for him to also identify and break his karmic cycle.

I cannot stress enough that these soulmate lessons were so very deep and they will create much soul pain. But we must experience it on multiple planes and in all dimensions in order to feel the depths and duality of emotions. It takes these deeply connected soulmates to help us cleanse the deepest, darkest parts of our souls.

While assisting my twin flame, I experienced this pain all over again as he identified, broke and cleared his karmic debris. I could identify and relate to everything that he was going through. I too had experienced such great pain and sorrow; this process and his presence helped me to continue to clear the layers of my own karmic debris. It's important to note that my prior deep relationship also helped me to identify and break my karmic patterns, but I still had to work through the layers of karmic debris and clear the remainder. My twin flame assisted me as I revisited every aspect of it while helping him identify and clear his own karmic debris. I know that I would not have been able to clear this debris as easily and effectively without the assistance of my twin flame.

During the process of assisting my twin, I repeatedly praised him for doing such a great job of being able to awaken, acknowledge and then clear his karma. He always had such a hard time understanding how he didn't feel like he was doing the work. He always felt as though it should be harder than it was — that he needed to be in control of being able to break free and let go. He could not comprehend that I had paved the way for him so he was able to process and integrate his karma and even bypass some of the pitfalls I had experienced. In doing so, he was able to release at a faster rate than I had. He also felt as though he was not letting go of his patterns — but that was because as we go through the karmic purge, we experience a layering affect (I will discuss more about this karmic purge in *Key Code 4:4*). It was our spiritual connection that put him on this fast-track path – a hall pass, if you will. The Divine goal of the Universe is to shift into the higher energetic planes in order to increase his vibration so that he was able to release his past at a faster rate. He did not have to spend the 20-plus years that it took me to reach the same levels he was experiencing in months. This was always mind-blowing to me because I could clearly see how open and ready he was. This is not to say he didn't experience a roller coaster effect; he hit points of resistance — reaching deeper to the core, the greater resistance he experienced.

Karmic Relationships

Karmic relationships are similar in nature to those of soulmates. However, they appear when it is time to clear karmic debris, rather than identifying karmic patterns that soulmates teach us. Also, the clearing process is quicker than and not as deep as that with soulmates. They are shorter-term relationships. Your karmic relationships are not in your life for long periods of time and you do not experience that lifelong connection. Personally, I have experienced a karmic soulmate connection with someone whom I was indirectly introduced to by my twin flame. I had known him for 5 years before I understood the depths of the connection; he was actually present and helped assist me with many things. He had hovered around my life not only through the "*dark night of my soul*," but when my twin flame and I redirected our paths to work on ourselves, this person re-surfaced to help me release one of my deepest karmic past lives. This person helped me connect to the Divine creativity which provided Universal intelligence — and this produced the outline of this book.

It was imperative that I connect with this person in order to close a final chapter that had been blocking me from going forward in this life. The interaction also helped him open some doorways and clear some of his own karmic past. He and I shared a past life together as husband and wife. Closing this chapter has allowed me to move forward in so many areas of my life.

False Twin Flames

False twin flames closely mimic a true twin flame. However, they will generally come through quickly, and will blindside you like a freight train. They can turn your entire life upside down. Needless to say, it is a very intense experience. Generally, they keep moving and leave a trail of dust behind them. They don't stay in your life for a long period physically, but they can leave a lasting effect on your soul and leave you in despair after the encounter is long gone. The purpose of this connection is to clear any remaining, stubborn deep-rooted karmic debris. It is most often associated with breaking down ego. This extreme intensity is typical because the goal is to quickly hit the root of the problem so that toxic debris can be cleared faster. Typically, this happens in preparation for the true twin-flame union.

Most often, a false twin flame appears after real twin flames have come into physical contact and you both are aware of it. *This also happens most often to the twin flame that is in the so-called "runner phase."* It almost always includes a very deep, intense physical romantic connection, which is necessary in order to assist in clearing the remainder of ego. *Typically, ego is what causes the disconnection between you and your true twin flame, so it becomes necessary to break down this need for chemical attraction before one can then connect on the deeper levels.*

My twin flame had a very intense false-twin-flame experience. It was imperative that I assist him in clearing not only the energetic attachment to that person but also to help him identify his correlation of this relationship with his addictive behavior and the need for a chemical attraction. It was necessary for him to experience this encounter and its timing was appropriate for the karmic clearing he was working on. He had a hard time understanding how I could assist him without letting his actions bother me. He was afraid of hurting me, so it made it hard for him to open up at times, but I knew it wasn't his goal to hurt me. I knew that this was not about me. This was about him and what he needed to experience in order to let go of his past. I showed up with non-judgment and I only offered acceptance of his actions. This was something that he had never experienced before in any of his relationships. But I clearly saw that this is what he needed to experience in order to release such deep karma. With all that said, it was very hard watching him suffer. Seeing what he was doing to himself was the hard part, but it was not hard for me to be there to assist him. I was honored to help. I knew that it was all about helping him and caring enough to be there to assist him without expecting anything in return. That is what a true friend does and that is what unconditional love is all about.

Twin-Flame Facilitators

Twin-flame facilitators present themselves to facilitate forward motion during your twin-flame journey in a variety of ways. First and foremost, they assist in your personal development by temporarily filling the role as your twin flame, including acting as a mirror for you to reflect the things that you need to continue to work on yourself. They usually show up when you are ready to move forward but your twin flame is not present at the time. They can assist you with the process of Ascension. They can also appear during the time you are working on your karmic purge (I will also fully explain what this means in *Key Code 4:4).* They can even help the more-evolved twin advance by keeping the mission moving forward. They assist keeping the higher self evolved, where a false twin helps to clear the lower self.

A twin-flame facilitator also has their own true twin flame, with whom they have not yet united. They are also not a part of your soul group or soul family. You meet them because you are both operating and vibrate on the same energetic plane. This is different than vibrating at the same soul frequency, which only you and your true twin flame can do. In this case, based on multiple factors, the two of you end up spiritually connecting on the same energetic channel. *This connection is also Divinely orchestrated and operates from the higher selves and higher planes.* It is like being two wandering Jews coming together, so that you help each other during a time when it is needed to keep each of your individual twin-flame journeys moving forward.

This is something you will not find readily available online. However, this is something that both my twin and I have experienced. It is what my Divine guides have shown me to be true. The reason two twins who are not each other's twin flames come together during this time period is because of this mass awakening and Universal urgency to accomplish the mission of all twin flames. I will repeat this for clarification: *Twin-flame facilitators are twin flames who are also not united with their own twin flame, yet they are evolved enough to advance their journey toward alignment with their own twin-flame mission, while assisting you with yours.*

My twin flame had an experience with a twin-flame facilitator. They deeply connected as friends, and it was her assistance that prepared my twin flame to be ready to come to me for further assistance with his spiritual awakening. It was necessary for us to come together on a deeper soul level, which we did for the first time. The purpose of our need to connect on a deeper plane was so that we could assist each other with our karmic purge, which requires your twin flame to be in physical form to do so. As we continued to connect on deeper and deeper soul planes and I began remembering our identity, discovering we were true twin flames, she continued to facilitate the process by sending missing links to the "*Key Codes.*" These were the missing links that I needed in order to shift me in a direction that led me to finally discovering that we were twin flames. My twin would always call her part of his team, but at the time he was not sure exactly what her role was.

I have also experienced a twin-flame facilitator. Throughout "*Twin-Flame Code Breaker*," I will share more about my many experiences with my twin facilitator and what he has taught me during some of the more recent parts of my twin-flame journey. He presented himself at a time I was ready to carry out my Divine mission. He taught me things that my own twin flame could not have taught me during this phase of my journey — especially things that I needed to understand to connect to the heart of a couple of "*Key*" areas. He taught me to open my heart and to be more sensitive to my own emotions and the emotions of others.

During this phase of my journey, he has generated experiences and understanding of what it feels like to participate in a true twin-flame union. This is also a two-way street; this process has sent him on a voyager mission back in time, forcing him to complete a full life review of every past experience that he has not dealt with yet. That means that I am also his twin-flame facilitator, helping him prepare to clear his deep karma so that he too can continue to raise his energetic frequency. We have discussed that it could be preparing him for physical alignment with his own true twin flame.

We quickly jumped on a very intense fast track, forcing us to cram 20 years' worth of information into two months. It left both of our heads spinning as we began to process and then integrate pieces that revealed our identities. Just as with a twin-flame experience, we quickly began mirroring everything back to each other. He hit the core of my being, and this has made me want to run more times than I could count. The only reason that I didn't is because it was crystal-clear that if I did, I would be responding just like my true twin did at one point during our encounters. In this situation, I could clearly see how my true twin was still teaching me what I needed to do in order to continue to work on myself.

My twin facilitator connected me with a path that mimics the path of my true twin experience. But the most interesting discovery from this experience has been the connection I made by being put in the exact same position as my true twin flame during these interactions with my twin-flame facilitator. It has allowed me to understand and feel everything that my true twin flame feels. And I mean everything, including thoughts and emotions about our own twin-flame experiences during the journey. It is so intense that there are times I feel as though my twin flame is running through my veins. It's as though I have been placed in the middle of both of them — my twin flame and twin-flame facilitator — and being able to see my twin-flame journey from both sides. I observe my twin-flame facilitator and see everything about him that mimics myself and my experiences. At the same time, I can see and feel exactly why and how my twin flame feels about me and our twin-flame experience.

Honestly, this experience has brought me emotionally closer to my true twin flame. I now fully understand him and how he feels. It's so bizarre that words can't even begin to fully express the intensity of the situation. But all I can say is: Wow – I have gotten hit by both sides of the coin here. And let me tell you, it has been an experience, but one that I needed to understand myself, my true twin, my twin-flame journey and ultimately to be able to assist other twin flames.

This encounter with my twin facilitator occurred after my twin and I decided to shift our attention to focusing on ourselves. I had experienced a couple of interesting interactions that were necessary for me to open me up and to be ready. That is when I reconnected with my twin-flame facilitator. We previously had brief social media encounters, but now we quickly connected on a deeper level. As I mentioned, the intensity of the experience was so close to a true twin-flame experience that it began to expand my awareness about what was happening. My spirit guides began showing me that he and I were operating the same as my twin and I had done almost to the day, a year prior.

It was as though I was uncovering the clues to a twin-flame experience for the second time. I even asked for signs to show me if I was reading this correctly. The same exact signs that appeared a year prior reappeared, one after the other. This forced me to have to share with my twin-flame facilitator the idea of twin flames and that we were not true twin flames. I knew that our paths had been a Divine appointment and that we had been brought together for some reason.

I presumed that he had no idea what that was or what that meant, but to my surprise, my twin-flame facilitator had already been told by someone that he was their twin flame. At that time he did not believe them, but he had studied the concept and said that due to his prior experience and understanding, he had already put the pieces together and thought that I was his twin flame! Talk about being smacked upside the head! I had to tell him I wasn't; needless to say, this hit him pretty hard. Another interesting awareness was —and one that I encountered with my own true twin — I would not have picked this person for myself. I also was not physically attracted to him. This has remained an ego battle for me in learning to let down my own barriers that have blocked me from fully being able to release and let go.

The very next day after having this conversation with my twin-flame facilitator, I connected with another twin-flame expert who had contacted me for advice, but she was unable to commit to a time for at least six weeks. I discovered that the delay in our connection was because she too was connected to a twin-flame facilitator. I was now able to quickly identify this, and I may not have been able to do so before. This connection confirmed my discoveries.

In *Key Code 2:2*, we'll explore what the Universal mission is for all twin flames and gain a better understanding of *the "New Age."* This will help twins make a connection between the light rays they incarnate from and how that links to the virtues that are to be carried out during their own twin-flame mission. We will discover how the energetic vibration of individual twin flames connect to the light rays, determining the hierarchy of each twin flame's energetic imprint.

KEY CODE 2:2

Master Your Divine Mission

"Twin flames are the dawning of the new age." – Dr. Harmony

The 2012 Phenomenon – Age of Aquarius

TO BETTER UNDERSTAND THE PURPOSE of your sacred union, let's first review what is known as the *"New Age" – an alignment of transformational spiritual development that is really only comprised of old-age doctrine.* In doing so, let's develop a connection between the ancient history of twin flames and the 2012 phenomenon.

History has recorded a series of astrological and cataclysmic events that have taken place from the beginning of time and extending all the way to what was believed to be the end of times, when the Mayan calendar ended on December 21, 2012. When added together, 1+2+2+1+2+1+2 = 11. It was during this same time period that we entered the *Age of Aquarius*, an era that most people associate with the 1960's hippie time frame – a time of promoting peace, love, happiness and harmony. *You might relate to this legendary era by remembering the song entitled "Aquarius," which was sung by a band called 5th Dimension.*

It takes one year for the earth to orbit the sun. On a much larger scale, it takes a cosmic or galactic year (approximately 225-250 million years) for the entire solar system to orbit around the center of the Milky Way. As we make this rotation encircling this galaxy, our journey enters each of the 12 zodiac signs for 2,150 years. Thus it takes approximately 25,800 years before revisiting the same side of the Milky Way again. *This indicates that we will be in the Age of Aquarius just over a couple of thousand more years.* Studying these topics, it made sense to me. The

Mayans understood that as we exited the year 2012, we would be shifting into a new era, a new age – a new timeline of our existence – moving from the old masculine, hard ways that we experienced during the *Age of Pisces* (the zodiac sign we just shifted out of after the last 2150 years) into a more feminine expressive way of living with ease and grace. Now is a time of being more receptive, a time of loving unconditionally and a time of letting go of our old masculine ways. It is a time of letting go of the hardships and struggles, the pain and the suffering and putting to rest an era that not only caused self-destruction but worldly destruction. This 2012 timeline also parallels the Ascension process that also started in 2012. *The dawning of this New Age of Aquarius (this is where the term "new age" comes from) allows us to learn a new way to live, love and experience life.* Twin flames have agreed to the assignment of reuniting during this time frame. They will merge with a joint mission to restore inner peace, happiness and harmony that every soul longs for – once again creating bliss – known as heaven on earth.

Count of St. Germain and Lady Portia

St. Germain is an Ascended Master, Lord of the 7th ray of violet light. He is most commonly known for being a Master Alchemist, but he has also been known as Merlin, the master magician, a mystery man who has visited this earth many lifetimes in many forms – each time creating spiritual transformation and producing expansion in the evolution of souls for all humanity. His transmutation has been tracked all over Europe, where for nearly 300 years he created massive shifts during the 18th century. He has been given the title: "*The man who knows everything and never dies.*" He was said to be a powerful healer and High Priest during the time of Atlantis. It was there that he first introduced the Violet Flame of transmutation as "*The Gift*" to humanity. Today, St. Germain continues to make a huge impact on the world, making occasional earthly appearances, visiting twin flames and appointing them to assist on the earthly plane in this *Age of Aquarius*, in the acceleration of the Ascension process.

My twin flame and I were paid a visit by St. Germain during one of our chakra energy sessions. It was my first introduction to the Count and my twin was given access to the violet flame. He had visions of the violet color all around him. During the same session, I received a direct message of his presence and also drew a picture of the Egyptian ankh cross, which I had never seen before then. The next day during my own personal energy session, I had a vision in which my twin flame handed me a torch with this violet flame burning bright. Together we held hands up towards the heavens with the earth sitting in our palms. Together we Ascended towards heaven. Having no knowledge of the existence of St. Germain or the Violet Flame prior to these encounters, it set me on a personal quest to research St. Germain. In doing so, I discovered the Violet Flame and its association with St. Germain – its purpose was for healing and transmutation. I also discovered that he and his twin flame Lady Portia held virtues of freedom and justice, which directly correlated with a world mission that I was connected with. Since that time, I have continued to work directly with St. Germain. He has become head of my council, directing me towards the mission of my personal twin-flame journey: to help assist other twin flames throughout the world on their personal journeys. I help them to remove energetic blocks that have caused them to stay stuck both personally and in their physical union. I also offer assistance with the Ascension process, as well as facilitating personal development to remove barriers preventing twin flames from coming into physical union.

This book and the pages that unfold before you are directly guided through the Alchemy of St. Germain. "*Twin-Flame Code Breaker*" would also have not been possible without the personal assistance of my own twin flame and the silence and separation that we both needed to work on our own individual journeys that has been necessary to complete our Divine mission. My twin flame and I incarnated from the 7th violet ray – we are of the highest-frequency ray. The fewest pairs of twin souls incarnate from this ray because of the personal mastery that one must achieve to reach this level of energetic frequency.

Saint Germain and his twin flame Lady Portia reign as the leaders of this *"Golden Age,"* the *Age of Aquarius*, where the energetic frequencies of our planet earth Ascends from 3rd-dimensional energy (3D) into 5th-dimensional (5D) frequencies. *These new frequencies started downloading new energetic earth grids in December 2012 and have continued with a complete shift to 5D on 8/8/2015 – the lion's gate, where 2015 represents an eight year, making it the rarest and most powerful lion's gate of all time: 8/8/8.* The number eight represents a twin-flame code because it is symbolic of the infinity sign. These higher frequencies have set the pace for time and space to speed up. This began in 2012 and will continue to significantly increase in speed, generating a fast-forward track as the 5D frequencies continue to rise through 2017. At that time, all mankind will have physically adjusted to the shift in the higher dimensional energetic frequencies. Then, even though time will continue to be on a fast track, humans will not seem to feel the extreme intensity because they will have become accustomed to these new 5D energies by then.

This "Golden Age" that started in 2012 will continue to raise the earth's vibration into the new 5D existence – the purpose is to create a higher state of Christ consciousness in all mankind. There will be a 25-year transition period with a purpose of eliminating the destructive behaviors that have occurred during the lower vibrational energies. This will force humans to let go of their old selves and their old ways; all the negative karma can no longer exist on the new earth. Once we have shifted into this higher state of Christ consciousness and higher vibrational energies, we will have begun living in a higher state by connecting to our higher selves, which is the purpose of the Ascension. *This will also create the new way in which we live on the new earth – the new heaven on earth.* During this transition, old karma will be eliminated and introducing the new Christ consciousness of the planet. Newborns entering the new earth will come with minimal karma to clear. Indigo, crystal and rainbow children will have minimal to no karma to clear; they will have already connected to their higher selves, carrying a higher vibrational energy upon incarnation to the new earth.

Twin Flames are "The Chosen Ones"

The following are a few of the many biblical references demonstrating why twin flames are *"The Chosen Ones"* and I believe that the messages in these verses speak for themselves:

> Isaiah 42:1 (NIV) – *"Here is my servant, whom I uphold, my chosen one in whom I delight; I will put my Spirit on him, and he will bring justice to the nations.*
>
> Matthew 22:14 (KJV) – *"For many are called, but few are chosen."*
>
> Colossians 3:12-17 (NAS) – *"So, as those who have been chosen of God, holy and beloved, put on a heart of compassion, kindness, humility, gentleness and patience; bearing with one another, and forgiving each other, whoever has a complaint against anyone; just as the Lord forgave you, so also should you. Beyond all these things put on love, which is the perfect bond of unity."*

I would like to repeat the last sentence in the verse above in Colossians 3:17 (NAS) – *"Beyond all these things put on love, which is the perfect bond to unity."* This unveils the true mission for all twin flames – *"The Chosen Ones"* — that have signed up for this assignment to become one. Uniting and loving yourself, your twin flame and then honoring your agreement to share this biblical unconditional love blueprint with the world – this is the mission of all twin flames – *"The Chosen Ones."*

I was processing some very intense awareness's that my twin flame facilitator had reflected back to me. While in search of answers, I found a journal entry that I had made just before my true twin flame appeared, in need of my energetic assistance. Until reading this journal entry, I had forgotten that I had been told that I was *"The Chosen One."* The message reminded me that I had awoke at 3 am hearing the voice of Wayne Dyer saying to me that I was *"The Chosen One."* I found this to be a startling message, especially being that I had forgotten about the details. So, needless to say, I was floored when my twin facilitator said these exact same words to me after I had asked for his assistance with proofing this book. His response was, "That must make me" – "*The Chosen One.*" He had no idea of its meaning to me. Another reason this experience was so daunting was because my twin facilitator's voice sounds so similar to Wayne Dyers' voice. About 70 percent of the time, I have to shake my head and bring myself back to reality, reminding myself who is speaking to me.

Prior to this, my true twin flame and I were paid a visit by Archangel Metatron during one of our energy sessions. While performing a chakra-clearing and balancing session, I felt a presence come in and take over. I saw star patterns being drawn over my twin while using a crystal pendulum to clear the energy. I asked for the Spirit to reveal itself. It identified as Metatron and said that my twin flame was to draw an angel card from a specific deck when we were finished. Upon doing so, he drew an Archangel Metatron card. This entire deck of cards had only two Metatron cards in it.

During that same session, he also felt like he was drowning; he could feel water in his mouth and it made him have a hard time swallowing. Unbeknownst to him, I had heard that I was to wash his vocal cords with holy water to open his throat chakra so that he could learn to speak words of wisdom. As always, during our energy sessions, my twin would teach me so many new things that I would act like Inspector Gadget — I would investigate to learn more. During my research, I discovered that the patterns that were drawn were a six-point Star of David, which is made up of the perfect balance of masculine and feminine pyramid energy. An eight-point star represents regeneration and interestingly enough, a ten-point star has the same molecular structure as water. Metatron, the Archangel who is in charge of clearing our chakras, also clearly stated that my twin was "*The Chosen One.*" That is another reason I tuned in closely when my twin facilitator said that he also was "*The Chosen One*" – I began to ask my guides to show me the meaning of this. Being that all three of us were clearly connected to being *"The Chosen Ones,"* I wanted to know the importance behind the trinity – the pyramid that we created. In my understanding, our combined energy created the same energetic forces found in the trinity.

The Twin-Flame Trinity

Soon after, I was shown exactly how important our three-way energetic connection was. I was performing an energy session on a client who has had breast cancer four times. I was drawn to an area where she was experiencing some emotional retention in her physical body. Without conscious awareness, I felt both of my thumbs and index fingers form a triangle. I began to place the pyramid formation of my hands over the area to which I was intuitively drawn. Keep in mind that I never physically touched her. I then closed my eyes. As soon as I did, I clearly saw my twin's face at the base of the pyramid structure on the right side and my twin facilitator's face at the base of the structure on the left side. An image of myself was at the peak, the top point of the triangle. Each corner of the pyramid lit up very bright — so bright that I felt my head shift backwards and I could feel a strong presence. The force caused me to jolt and open my eyes. Upon doing so, I saw my client's arms being lifted into the air. She lay there with both hands open as if she was open to receiving.

At the end of this session, I mentioned to my client how her arms and hands had went up into the air. She told me that at the time this happened, she was really in a deep state. She had really shifted within and had drifted off, but she felt a strong presence that brought her back to a semi-aware state. *She could feel a force come over her that was so strong, she felt it take over and lift her arms up and open them so that she could receive.* I asked her if I could share her experience in this book, and she agreed. Immediately following this session, I had a chiropractic patient come into my office, telling me that she was leaving the next day for Girl Scout camp. When I asked her where she was going, her response was "Trinity" camp!

After this experience, my guides started directing me to use the same pyramid energy, which interestingly enough seems to be generated from my energy combined with the energy of my twin flame and my twin-flame facilitator. Since that time, I have seen this powerful energy force be used for healing purposes. I have noticed that my energetic frequency has risen and that the healing abilities I offer are producing results that are faster than ever before in my entire career. Since then, I have been instructed by my guides to perform this pyramid energy during many of my remote energy sessions with clients. I am always directed as to where and when to use it. I no longer see any faces attached to the pyramid, but I'm quite sure that it is being produced from the energy generated from my twin-flame trinity.

Spirit has shown me how the energy from this trinity is produced. I am the head of the triangle and the one who directly administers this force of God and apply it to my clients' needs. It is one example of how God works through people. My twin being to the right of the pyramid is my true physical-form twin flame; his energy acts as the generator (I will explain this in more detail in *Key Code 10:10*) producing the masculine energy of the trinity. And my twin facilitator to the left is emanating the Holy Spirit, a feminine expression of God's energy. He facilitates the electric portion of the flame (which I will also share more details about in *Key Code's 8:8 and 10:10*). This also demonstrates how my twin flame facilitator plugs the leaks within my twin-flame union being so that all the components are there for me to carry out my twin-flame mission.

THE NUMBER SEVEN LINKS TO THE RAYS, VIRTUES, ARCHANGELS, CHAKRAS AND MISSION

The number seven directly links to the mission of twin flames, and it plays a very important role in making the connection between the heavenly virtues, the Archangels — the highest-ranking angels —and our earthly bodies, and the seven major chakras. It also plays a significant role in the Bible, where it is used 735 times and 54 times in the book of Revelation alone. The number seven represents completion, wholeness, balance and harmony.

Revelation 1:4 (NIV) – *"John, To the seven churches in the province of Asia: Grace and peace to you from him who is, and who was, and who is to come, and from the seven spirits before his throne."* Here we can see the connection between the seven *"thrones"* or chakras and the *"seven spirits"* or spiritual energy rays of light.

Revelation 4: 1-5 (NIV) – Verse 1: *"After this I looked, and there before me was a door standing open in heaven. And the voice I had first heard speaking to me like a trumpet said, "Come up here, and I will show you what must take place after this."* Translation: After clearing the lower chakras and letting go of the lower self, it is time to open up to the higher chakras and connect to the higher self.

Verse 2: *"At once I was in the Spirit, and there before me was a throne in heaven with someone sitting on it. 3 And the one who sat there had the appearance of jasper and ruby. A rainbow that shone like an emerald encircled the throne."* Translation: The rainbow of colors emanates from the lower seven thrones, or chakras.

Verse 4: *Surrounding the throne were twenty-four other thrones, and seated on them were twenty-four elders. They were dressed in white and had crowns of gold on their heads."* The connection of the thrones or chakras of the lower self (7 chakras), higher self (upper 5 chakras- creating *"The Twelve Chakra System"*) and cosmic self (*The 12 Chakra System* of higher self plus the 12 cosmic-self chakras = *The 24 chakra system*).

Verse 5: *From the throne came flashes of lightning, rumblings and peals of thunder. In front of the throne, seven lamps were blazing. These are the seven spirits of God."* The seven blazing lamps or chakras connect to the seven spirits of God or light rays, the spiritual energetic force that connect all souls directly to the Source.

When we look deeper at the meaning of the number seven, it helps us to connect to our intuitive abilities and gives us the desire to become lifelong seekers of the truth, which creates wisdom. Seven also demonstrates the absolute perfection of God. The mission of a twin-flame union is directly correlated between the seven rays, the heavenly virtues, the Archangels and the seven chakras. This is because the missions of twin flames are broken down into seven hierarchies. The Archangels serve on these color rays of God. These rays are infused with Spiritual energy which flows in and through our seven thrones or energetic stars – or chakras.

The Seven Hierarchies of Twin Flames or Twin Rays

The seven hierarchies of twin flames are determined by the frequency of the energetic vibration of each twin-flame couple. This hierarchy is directly related to the seven rays, with the seventh ray being of the highest in vibration and the first ray being of the lowest vibration. Because twin flames come from the rays of light, you will sometimes hear the term "twin ray." However, it is just another name for twin flame. *It is the ray from which twin flames incarnate that determines which of their heavenly virtues they are meant to connect to in this lifetime.* And it is the virtue that links to their mission. Which ray that twin flames come from also determines which Archangel has been appointed to help assist them with their mission. As I mentioned, Ascended Masters are also appointed to assist; however, there is typically more than one per ray. And the rays are also indirectly connected to the chakras.

The First Twin-Ray Hierarchy

The first ray is connected to the blue twin rays. This ray carries the lowest energetic frequency. Their heavenly virtue is Divine Will. This means that twin flames from this ray are on the planet to become leaders and pioneers. They are here to create and protect. Archangel Michael is their direct Archangel assisting them with this their mission. Archangel Michael is in charge of all the angels and Archangels. He is associated with the third eye or brow chakra, which is indigo in color. He is in charge of protecting all twin souls. Twin flames from the blue ray predominantly carry a heavier masculine energy and have a strong will. They know how to get things done. They tend to speak their truth. They are overcomers, overachievers and are here to master the Divine Will of the Creator. The mission of a blue-ray union is to master these concepts both individually and together in your twin-flame union.

THE SECOND TWIN-RAY HIERARCHY

The second ray is connected to the yellow or golden twin rays. Their virtue is Divine Wisdom. This means that twin flames from this ray are on the planet to become scholars. They are here to seek and understand the truth. Archangel Jophiel is the overseer of the second ray and is associated with the violet or crown chakra. These twin souls predominantly carry a balance of the masculine and feminine energies. They have a balanced temperament and always search for the understanding of knowledge, the Divine wisdom of the Creator, so as to share it with others with love and compassion. Their mission is to share their knowledge with others by increasing their sensitivity and intuition, both as an individual and within the twin-flame union.

THE THIRD TWIN-RAY HIERARCHY

The third ray is connected to the pink twin ray. Their virtue is Divine Service. Twin flames in this hierarchy are here to share unconditional love, to be compassionate and to serve. Archangel Chamuel is the overseer of the pink ray and is associated with the pink or heart chakra. These twin souls predominantly carry feminine energies; they are patient souls with the ability to be empathetic, sensitive and creative. They have great faith and they trust others. Their mission is to be caregivers helping others emotionally connect to them self and teaching them examples of Eternal love. They have genuine nurturing abilities and they are compassionate. The pink twin-ray mission is to be of service, generally as care givers in health and wellness related fields.

The Fourth Twin-Ray Hierarchy

The virtue of the fourth or white color ray is Purity. Twin rays in this hierarchy are here to share harmony. This means that twin flames from this ray are on the planet to find inner stillness and balance in the eye of the storm or zero-point field, and find harmonic balance with self and others. Archangel Gabriel is the overseer of the white ray and is associated with the sacral chakra. These twin souls connect to their emotional energy plane and this helps them let go and surrender with ease and grace. They connect to the higher realms. They are here to share with others the harmonic balance of the Creator. If you are a twin flame incarnated from this ray, your mission will be to teach others the art of stillness, how to BE and how to connect to the present moment, both as an individual and within your twin-flame union.

The Fifth Twin-Ray Hierarchy

The virtue of the fifth ray is Divine Healing and is emerald or orange. Twin rays in this hierarchy are here to share their spiritual healing gifts with others. Archangel Raphael is the overseer of the emerald ray and is associated with the solar plexus chakra. These twin souls connect to their mental body and seek to teach others the art of being a healthy human — body, mind and soul. These twin souls are logical thinkers and usually become doctors, nurses or scientists. The mission of the emerald ray twin flames is to master these concepts of healing both as an individual and within the twin-flame union.

The Sixth Twin-Ray Hierarchy

The virtue of the sixth ray is Peace, and is ruby or purple. Twin rays in this hierarchy are returning to share the feminine energy of the Universe. They ultimately gain alignment with their own higher self. They connect to the Christ consciousness and share a loving connection with others. This means that twin flames from this ray are on the planet to help spread inner strength. Archangel Uriel is the overseer of the ruby or purple ray and is associated with the root chakra. These twin souls connect to the spiritual plane. If you are a twin flame incarnated with this virtue, your mission is to be gentle and share your desire for tenderness, peace, and tranquility. These twin souls have a great influence on others. The mission of these twin flames would be to master these concepts both as an individual and within your twin-flame union.

The Seventh Twin-Ray Hierarchy

The seventh ray is connected to the violet ray. These twin rays carry the highest energetic frequencies. The fewest number of twin souls are incarnated from this ray. It takes great mastery of many lessons and virtues before reaching this level of personal mastery. Their Divine virtue is Freedom. This means that twin flames from this ray are on the planet to gain redemption and justice. They are here to rectify past pain and suffering. They are teaching others to forgive not only themselves for making wrong choices but also to forgive others. Archangel Zadkiel is their direct Archangel and is associated with the throat chakra. Twin flames from the violet ray seek to balance their masculine and feminine energies. St. Germain is the head of this violet ray; because of its high frequency, he shares "*The Gift*" of the Violet Flame for transmutation so that it can help to transmute toxic energies and recycle them back into the light of the Creator as positive energies.

We incarnate from different rays over multiple lifetimes with the intention to learn different virtues throughout the soul's evolution. One might identify with characteristics and the feeling of being connected to multiple rays. However, you will always have a stronger connection to one and it will be the reason you incarnated during this lifetime. For instance, my twin flame and I are both healers, and we both carry a very strong emerald ray connection. However, because we have been healers over multiple lifetimes, it comes as second nature. Hence, we have already mastered that virtue. However, during this lifetime, I know that I was sent here to rectify judgment from a past life. I also spent most of this lifetime with a feeling of being trapped and stuck. It was not until

I started breaking my karmic patterns that I began to feel a taste of freedom. While training for my personal mastery transformational life-coaching certification, I experienced past life regression, and I uncovered a particular past life that was significant in order for me to identify what my purpose was this lifetime. Once I knew my purpose or virtue, I could relate to the idea of how that particular past life was holding me back. It was after uncovering this lifetime that I started writing a book entitled, "Personal Freedom Unleashed."

A couple of years after this, my twin flame and I had several encounters that triggered a voyager journey. Without conscious effort, I was sent back in time with a series of visions and dreams that sent me on a scavenger hunt. I was pointed in the direction of answers to why I was experiencing so much bondage in this life. It helped me make a deeper connection to that past life, and I uncovered more details that explained my lifelong search for personal freedom. This connection came full circle after St. Germain passed the Violet Flame to my twin flame, who passed it to me the next day during my own energy healing session. Because of this, I did much research on the Count and discovered that his virtue was Freedom; his twin flame Lady Portia's virtue is Justice. It helped me to develop a better understanding of my Divine mission and develop a relationship with the St. Germain. Over time, I realized that he was head of my Divine counsel and I began having direct communication with him. We must remain open to be able to identify the presence of a specific energetic force. This is done by experiencing a series of encounters, which allows a person to fully understand which Ascended Master or Archangel is present during direct communication with these Divine entities.

Under the direction of St. Germain, I perform twin-ray hierarchy readings for clients all over the world. I place their twin-flame unions on a global map, creating a grid. Mapping out these grid-point energies help to maximize the energy of each twin soul and anchor their energy as they transcend through the Ascension process. Coming together as a collective will raise the energetic vibration of the planet. As twin flames move into reunion, this energy will continue to magnify, sending the higher vibrational love signals back to the Universe. By helping twin flames identify which energetic ray they incarnate from and who their direct guides are, they will be able to make a direct correlation between their Divine virtue and Divine mission. This helps to speed up the process of the merger of twin flames, so that the mission of this planetary movement will come to pass faster.

A Channeled Message from St. Germain for All Twin Flames:

Dear Beloved Ones:

I, St. Germain, the head of the Age of the Aquarius and leader of all rays, represent transmutation and Alchemy of all light rays and twin flames from the present through the Age of Aquarius. My wish for you and all twin flames of this era is to be the leaders of light workers and to perform your own individual personal mastery and then the personal mastery of your Divine mission. I ask that you trust your intuition and release all past karmic experiences that have held you back up unto this point. Releasing these past negative experiences and awakening your own spiritual gifts will be a "Key Code" for you to learn how to love yourselves as well as your twin unconditionally. This process will teach you to trust your own intuition and follow Divine guidance so that you can continue to activate your higher consciousness, which will expand the evolution of your twin soul. This will be important for you to fulfill your karmic agreement with each other and then to participate in this worldly mission of being active light workers for others to follow your examples. Please release all self-doubts and fears that you have had in the past. This is a necessary part of your own soul transformation and it will enhance your own sensitivity. You will need to master this skill so that you can become more sensitive to your needs and the needs of others, creating compassion for all humanity. Practice the Violet Flame meditation to protect you and your mission. Doing so on a regular basis will help "unlock" you and your twin flames' joint "Key Codes." They will direct you to the necessary tools that you will need to follow as you go through such purification of your soul to prepare for the merger of your union. Consistency will be "Key" for you to come into full "spiritual awakening" and alignment to connect with your Ascended Masters and Archangel that have been appointed to your Ascension ray, they will be your direct guides during this process. In addition, please call upon the Violet Flame as needed to heal and protect your soul during your Ascension process and your connection between you and your twin flame. Visualize a lotus flower which will represent the growth of your union. I have housed it in a unified field of pyramidal energy that will reflect the harmonic frequency of energy set to vibrate at the same vibration of all twin souls. This will generate the call signal for each of you to raise your own individual vibration and will open the pathway for your twin to follow, raising the energetic vibration of both of you. I would like to remind you that all you need to accomplish your mission is encoded within the DNA of your soul, and that you can do this. You will prevail and when you feel weak, call upon Archangel Michael for strength and he will assist you to stay strong. It is my blessing that you and your twin flame shine beyond the Universe by not only performing your Divine mission but that you become one again.

And so it is.

Much Love and Blessings from

Me, St. Germain and my Twin Flame Lady Portia

The Return and Mission of All Twin Flames

Today, more twin flames than ever in the history of all time are "*The Chosen Ones*" returning to honor their soul agreement that they made, which is to help restore the Christ consciousness of our world. They have agreed to take on not only their own karma, but to clear the karmic patterns of the Universe. *Their purpose in this mass uniting, which began in 2012 and will continue to occur through 2027, aligning with the "Age of Aquarius," preventing self-destruction of our planet once more.* Twin flames have chosen to become the facilitators of what man knows today as the second coming of Christ. They have been appointed the same burdens of poverty, struggles, bondages, pain and suffering and have made the same self-sacrifices that Christ chose to take on by cleansing the sins of the world. *Twin flames bear the same burdens represented by the crown of thorns.* It is this same act of unconditional love that will raise the energetic vibration of our planet so that together we can restore heaven on earth – returning to an unconditional love vibration that will produce inner peace and happiness for all mankind.

Let's now review ways in *Key Code 3:3* that will help you understand the importance of identifying and breaking your karmic vows, contracts and all negative attachments. These old ways and acquired belief systems hold us back not only in our personal lives, but also in our twin-flame union. So let's acknowledge what we need to let go of so we can start moving forward – so we can find our way home!

KEY CODE 3:3

Discover Why You Should Break Your Karmic Vows

"Once we have identified and broken our karmic patterns, we continue to have debris to integrate and process creating higher conscious awareness that gives us clarity for our future spiritual progression." – Dr. Harmony

MANY OF YOU MAY HAVE HEARD of the term *"dark night of the soul."* It is a time in one's life that forces them to experience what feels like a negative or dark season. But going through these pitfalls of hell is a required part of a twin-flame journey. We must face our fears head-on. This consciously brings about our awareness of that which no longer serves a purpose in our life – the things that are keeping us stuck and holding us back from our fullest potential. This awareness produces a karmic purge of all past negative emotions, experiences and even people. We are forced to go through very intense challenges and circumstances that forces us to consciously experience our dissatisfaction of the old ways. As these negative events arise and our awareness expands, we begin to acknowledge and clear them. They are also known as karma or karmic patterns. As we break these karmic patterns and release the debris, we begin to seek inner peace and happiness. Sending our souls on a journey in search of personal freedom, which is required before finding our way home.

Just like Jesus, all twin flames have agreed to take on the karmic patterns of the world. This is part of the agreement that twins signed up for during this phase of their soul's evolution. They accepted the assignment of helping the world release these past karmic patterns that caused extreme amounts soul trauma, created during the past generations of self-destruction. It is imperative to identify and acknowledge these karmic contracts and to identify which vows you have agreed to during this lifetime. That allows you to break these karmic vows and let go of the attachment to these negative energies. Through my experience of working with twin flames, I have seen a common thread in the karmic contracts that twin flames took vows for to be poverty, struggle, pain, hardships and suffering.

I have helped many twin flames not only identify their past karmic vows but also cut these energetic karmic cords that they are subconsciously attached to in past, present and all future contracts and in all energetic dimensions. I have found this to exponentially accelerate the transformation process as twins begin their *"spiritual awakening." That is, when they are forced to experience "The Wake-Up Call" – a desire to shift out of the darkness and connect to a higher consciousness.*

It is very important to know that if one or both twins are in a relationship at the time of physical connection, those karmic agreements must be fulfilled and completed with their existing partner before it is possible to fully reunite with your twin flame.

Release Your Karma by Letting Go

Have you been feeling stuck — not only in your twin-flame relationship but in every area of your life? Being that twin-flame souls have a lot of karma to release, it can feel like one is creating repetitious patterns. This is because they can only consciously process and integrate a certain amount of their hidden, subconscious, or energetic memory at a time. Sometimes, they subconsciously hang onto it in fear of letting go. It becomes an extraction process as the soul releases layers of the underlying energetic toxins. They have to repeat the process of letting go because of multiple lifetimes of fears, self-doubts and conditionings. Each layer brings up even-deeper thoughts, feelings and emotions that must surface in order to be released. Thus, each time creates a higher state of awareness as they move through the depths of the debris. Therefore, be prepared for the journey home to be continuous.

Breaking karmic vows such as; pain, suffering, poverty, hardships and so on, must be released so that we can gain personal freedom. This includes our past, present and future vows that we have agreed to in all lifetimes and in all dimensions. *Once we have identified and broken our karmic patterns, we continue to have debris to integrate and process creating higher conscious awareness that gives us clarity for our future spiritual progression.* It is imperative to release karmic bondage that has been keeping you a hostage to your circumstances, allowing you to find your way home.

Letting Go of My Own Karma

Many of my first childhood memories are of me trying to understand and process my inner feelings about why people tend to judge others. I didn't understand how people could be so opinionated that they believed their way was the only way and the right way. I grew up in a home of organized religious beliefs; my parents, who have been great and loving and have always supported me, they are actively involved in their religious community. As a child, however, I felt that I was not accepted for what it was that I felt was my truth. I experienced feelings of being judged for things like wearing makeup, jewelry, or watching certain television programs. There was a time when I was not allowed to go to the movies, get my ears pierced, or watch television on a Friday night because it was the Sabbath. I had to abide by rules that did not resonate with my own inner truth, and this felt very constricting. I did not feel any limitations inside; I had a desire to think outside the box.

These early experiences set the tone for an inner battle of self-criticism and brutal self-judgment that put me on a path of overachievement and perfectionism. I tried to comply with the expectations from not only others, but from myself. This set the precedence of a feeling of not being good enough, which has taken me a lifetime to change. While attempting to break these patterns, I continued to be reminded of the untimely deaths of my uncle and cousin. In 1997, they were both killed in a plane crash. They have taught me the importance of living a life of no regrets. It was as if a never-ending mental movie was playing in my head, reminding me that my uncle was always going to take a vacation, build his dream home and start dating, but these things never came to pass. He never got a chance to smell the roses. It hit me hard that I was living the same way. That became the defining moment in the start of my own spiritual journey, but the inner battle seemed endless, and I continued to have more karma to release.

For most of my life I have been a raging Type A personality who equated "doing" with success. I graduated chiropractic school with honors, creating a business that brought in a six-figure salary and a great car, and had what appeared to be the all-American dream life. But I was always unhappy, exhausted, overworked and overwhelmed. There was a dark hole forming inside me and nothing seemed to fill it. Sound familiar? I felt as though I had sold my soul to the devil.

Several years later, many other challenges had presented themselves. I had divorced. I had a failed business partnership that cost me a twelve-year practice in exchange for a magnitude of financial issues. After picking up the pieces, I started a new business with a new life partner. When our dreams fell apart, and we ended our relationship, we sold that business. All of this transpired as I continued my own private practice, which meant that I was running two businesses for a few years. And when I finally woke up and became aware of the insane torment I was creating for myself, I began to desire to shed my skin by letting go as fast as I could. I raced to the finish line only to be told that I had uterine cancer! I finally got it! Or at least I thought I did at the time.

Importance of Stepping Outside Your Own Circumstance – The 100-Day Smile Challenge

A couple of years ago, I found myself repeating the same patterns in my life, I had hit an all-time low and found myself once again revisiting the "*dark night of the soul.*" Only this time it was much darker and deeper. But I noticed that on the days that I ran with my dog Champ, who is my partner in "*spiritual crime*" and a deep soulmate, something happened. He is an energetic magnet. He always has a way of putting a smile on everyone's face – this dog, a Staffordshire Bull Terrier with *"bully-breed"* lineage from England, that was supposed to be so scary! People always want to know what kind of dog he is; we frequently heard comments like, *"Dude, that is one good-looking dog."* Because I was not at a happy place in my life at that time, I experienced first-hand what it felt like to step outside of my own sad emotions and how I could also, like Champ, affect another human being in a positive way. Running with Champ became so rewarding and gratifying that I began to smile, even bigger on the inside. But I questioned why I was yet again trying to learn these life lessons that appeared so simple on the surface. It felt like I was letting go of the same lessons over and over again and for the 100th time. And now, like Champ ripping his blanket in the process of burying his bones (letting go), my blanket had become shredded. I was starting to understand that these were some deep-seated subconscious karmic patterns that needed to be excavated from the dinosaur age, from other lifetimes. These ancient memories were appearing so that I could become aware of the changes that I needed to make in order to release the old patterns I had been holding onto. I was no longer that little girl being judged so harshly. It felt as though it had taken what felt like eternity, but I was finally beginning to let go of what no longer served a higher purpose in my life.

Around that time and in response to Champ's magnetic smile, I had the idea of starting a 100-Day Smile Challenge! I wanted people to stop judging my dog by his breed and I knew that this would help make it happen. We set a goal to run 100 days in a row. Whenever anyone paid special attention to him and he made them smile, we would stop that person, gently educate that person about his breed, and then post that person's picture with Champ on his social media page. Not in my wildest dreams could I have imagined the impact this gesture would make around the world! In no time our smiling challenge was picked up and re-posted by seven of the leading dog magazines around the world. An overnight superstar, Champ Avalon, my 32 lb. fur-baby, became known for his smile. He made people around the globe smile while they tracked our smiling challenge. To this day I am floored at the way in which the small seed of an idea and the simple gesture of making another person smile could create *"bully-breed"* awareness — and changed my life in the process.

I began to realize that I had much more to learn from this dog. This set me on another mission and created a passion that I could never have dreamed possible on my own. I began to read story after story of dogs being euthanized just because of their breed. I found this to be similar to the way we judge each other as human beings, which causes discrimination and division within society. The story of Lennox from Ireland, who was euthanized for merely looking like a pit bull, really struck a chord. I knew I wanted to educate people and become the voice of these innocent creatures that are nothing more than a reflection of the Divine and demonstrate the Christ-like characteristics of humanity – the same as twin flames do.

This process inspired me so much that I became the founder of a non-profit organization, *Global Paws For Peace*, an organization dedicated to creating unity among all breeds. Yes, you might say that I'm on a mission to live up to my nickname of the *"Mother Teresa of Canines!"* This mission is also how I developed a connection to a past life in England which stemmed around the concept of being judged. Understanding this allowed me to release it and break the barriers it was creating. Making this global connection, especially with many of Champs fans in the UK, really helped me identify and realize that part of my contract as a twin flame was coming here to rectify the judgments with a burning desire to create freedom and justice. I had to become a voice for these creatures. This experience not only facilitated closure of the past life in England that consisted of being persecuted by others, but helped me make a connection to St. Germain and Lady Portia — representations of the virtues of freedom and justice.

Why Do Humans Judge? – A Survey

One of my favorite quotes by my longtime mentor, the late Dr. Wayne Dyer, is, *"When you judge another, you do not define them, you define yourself."* We know people judge, but why? This is the question that I have spent most of my lifetime trying to answer because, as I mentioned, it has taken me many years to release from my own self-judgment and self-imposed expectations. You've probably guessed by now that I couldn't let this question go unanswered, so I sent out a survey. I posted it not only on Champ's Facebook page, but also on my own. In addition, I surveyed anyone I came in contact with. I wanted to hear it straight from the mouths of anyone interested enough to answer. There were 101 responses! Here are the top five reasons people gave for their inclination to have a biased opinion:

1. Belief Systems – conditioning and what they were taught
2. Ego – the need to be right or the need to control
3. Fear – afraid to let go and afraid of change
4. Protection – putting up walls in order to not let their own guard down
5. Holding Grudges – the inability to forgive

While working with twin flames, I have discovered that these are also the top patterns of action that are holding twin souls back from gaining personal freedom, which in turn energetically blocks their connection to their twin flame union. So, let's explore the weight of these judgments we carry around that make our load in life so heavy. Let's try to gain a greater understanding of each of them so we can bury them and let them go. Let's find out what new and exciting treasures we will uncover — just like Champ, who is always thrilled about the treasure he finds hidden in his blanket after he has let go and buried his bones.

Letting Go of Old Belief Systems

It has taken me much of my lifetime to realize that I am not my mother's fears, nor my father's beliefs. As I mentioned, old patterns of thought and prejudices tend to be passed down from generation to generation.

These thoughts sit deep within the subconscious memory. The "*Key*" to understanding our thoughts and patterns of action is to become aware of our belief systems, learn to accept them and then release them, for they no longer serve our higher selves. By letting go of these old ways of thinking, we can start to think for ourselves. I am an accumulation of my own knowledge, experience, wisdom and understanding. Just like Champ, this is the treasure that I uncovered by letting go of the opinions, thoughts and energies of other people that had been imposed upon me. This helped me to create the space to discover my own individual, unique set of beliefs – my own identity, if you will.

Sometimes it may be necessary to revisit the past in order resolve the conflict that is holding us back from reaching our fullest potential. *Our past experiences become an accumulation of imprints that are not only stored within our subconscious memory and in the cells of our mental, physical, spiritual, emotional, energetic and etheric bodies, but that also track all the way to our birth and past lives.* Releasing our old habits is a loving way to cleanse and detoxify mind, body and spirit. During my years as a holistic chiropractor and transformational coach, I have often compared this cleansing experience to cleaning out a closet and getting rid of everything that no longer looks good on us. Once we decide what we really love, it is easier to let go of what we no longer need. Getting rid of what no longer serves a purpose becomes a purification process on a very deep level. The new space we open allows us to view our life in a way that feels lighter and brighter, because the space we have cleared helps us to see better. It offers us the clarity to affirm a new way of thinking; to form new and healthier habits that also add to the feeling of joy and happiness in our life.

Letting Go of Ego

In order to let go of ego, we must first understand that ego is a false sense of reality, a false illusion of what we each believe ourselves to be. It is that inner voice embedded within the mind that speaks to us, telling us what it thinks we should have in life as well as defining who we are. "*We are*" meaning the cars we drive (like the really great one I had as I was crashing and burning emotionally), the clothes we wear, the houses we live in and/or the physical appearance of our bodies. The specific definition will be different for everyone, depending on their own individual experience and conditioned belief patterns. Ego is the byproduct of our external world and the society we live in. A healthy ego is one that helps us to maneuver daily through the physical world. We are not born with an out-of-control ego center, but we develop this "lower self" that identifies us as what we desire.

We have all heard the saying, "*Me, myself and I.*" I like to interpret it this way: Me, my physical body. Myself, my spiritual being. And the "I" is the control center of the mind that can become the "*know-it-all*" if we allow it to. As our "I" center develops over time, this is where our inner drive for the need to be right comes from — along with our perfectionism, competitiveness, and all the other expectations that we place on ourselves. As our ego grows, it can become hungry, greedy and self-serving. The more we feed our ego, the more influence it has over every decision that we make in life! Ego likes to remain in control and know that it is "I" alone who is responsible for my actions, my achievements and my success. Our "*Myself*" spiritual being, on the other hand, knows that you are here for a higher purpose. "*Myself*" knows that everything happens for a reason; that if we choose to rise above the ego by surrendering to a power greater than ourselves, and if we allow assistance from our Universal intelligence, that tends to make our journey through life easier. This battle between ego (lower) self and "*Myself*" (higher) self can create chaos – an inner battle that plays tug of war on our emotions, thoughts, feelings and decisions. This war can cause paralysis, preventing us from moving forward with our dreams and aspirations or accepting the treasures that are presented to us, because they may come clothed in a different fashion than what the mind's "I" sees.

We have to become aware enough for our spiritual Being to prevail and to break down the layers of our "I." Once we allow this process to take place, we begin to realize that our uncovered treasures may come to us in a different form or fashion than what we originally asked for. While they may be exactly what we are asking for, we just can't see it until we let go of enough of our past. The space we create by letting go leaves room for our souls to expand, which creates the necessary clarity we need in order to see the path towards our destination. In order to find your way home, it is imperative that you follow this process and connect to your higher self. Over time, this process allows us to tame our ego. Many times we ask for what we want in life, yet we're not receiving it. We may in fact just be receiving what we asked for, but we have to learn to search a little deeper and let go of deeper layers in order to recognize this.

How Do We Transcend Ego?

How do we transcend ego, connect to our higher, spiritual self and start to live from a place of Divine order and acceptance of the hidden treasures that we want to discover? Here are a few suggestions:

- Let's try to approach every conflicting situation from a place of peace. Let's try to rise above every circumstance, and view it from a place of trying to understand where the other person is coming from.
- Let's try putting ourselves in someone else's situation. Maybe that person is only having a bad day.
- Let's let go of the notion that everything is personal or that any conflicting encounters are directed towards us. As we have all heard, contrary to what the ego might be telling us, "it's not always all about you!"
- Let's vow to remove all competition from our lives. Impossible, you say? Life is not a race and we don't win by getting to the finish line. It's more important to have meaningful interactions with people and sometimes have the grace to allow the other person to be "right," even if they aren't.

- Let's take a step back when placed in tough situations and practice keeping our opinionated thoughts to ourselves. The reality is that we have nothing to win by trying to prove that we are right.
- Let's try to remove the need for superiority from our thoughts. The need to be better than someone else serves no one; in the eyes of the Divine we all come from the same place and are equal. Trying to be better than someone else really only pulls you apart from that relationship or encounter and causes a disconnect from who you really are — a spiritual Being.
- Finally, let's try to overcome the need for major accomplishments that originate from a place of desire or greed and pulls us out of alignment of our higher purpose. Things that cause us to disconnect from being able to go within and discover our authentic self are usually not for our highest good.

Letting Go of Fear

What does it mean to let go of inner fear and walk safely in the world? If you ask many people what they are most afraid of, at the top of their list would be fear of change. We don't always like our circumstances. But we are not always willing to make a change, because we are too fearful of having to let go of what our ego wants and surrender to what our soul knows it needs. Letting go of fear is nothing more than a decision to let go of an illusion that is produced in ego. Many souls have a hard time with this. *So, let me say that again: Letting go of fear is nothing more than a decision to let go of an illusion that is produced in ego.*

Ego likes to trick us into believing that bad things will happen in order to keep us attached to outcomes that have not even occurred. When we try letting go of fear, ego scares us into falling back into old patterns. When we allow fear and ego to take over in our life, we hear the voice that tells us lies: e.g., we are inferior, we are not worthy, we are not good enough. I recall my grandmother telling me as a child, "*Don't borrow trouble.*" Today I completely understand the meaning of her message.

Are You Stuck and Ready to Let Go of Your Past?

Most people are afraid of the unknown, of all the *coulda, woulda, shouldas*. This prevents us from making the choice to choose something different. Often we are stuck in a rut because we are busy looking at all the external circumstances that we think are holding us back, and not willing to take personal accountability for our own choices. I recently had fear creep back into my mind, reminding me once again of how letting go is progress, not perfection. I had to make a decision about moving forward with the process of writing a book last year. I had a couple of options. One was safe and comfortable, but the other presented itself with more risk and involved getting four months of work completed in four weeks! My first instincts were to not put pressure on myself — but it did not take me long to realize that fear was a factor in this situation. It was not about the pressure. It was about how I handled the pressure. I could do this in a fashion that was stressful and operate out of my lower self and old habits, or I could choose to go beneath the anxiety and realize that all this meant was that I had some additional inner work that I needed to learn from. When I asked my twin flame for advice, I was reminded that I needed to meditate on my decision and go deeper within to find what resonated with my soul. I immediately did just that, and within fifteen minutes, I had my answer. I realized that how I handled the project was really my choice. I could allow fear to control my decision or I could shift my perception and realize that I had some deeper inner work that needed to be done in order to move below the anxiety to find the peace within the situation. I could hear the voice of Wayne Dyer saying, "*Do not place attachments to outcomes. Do what it is that you came here to do and the rest will take care of itself.*" My take-away from this experience was to go forward with peace. Our experiences are nothing more than the perception that we choose for them.

Hanging onto the fear of what we are lacking or what might happen to us produces physical responses within the body — just as if the thing we are afraid of has already happened. This keeps us living in a place of uncertainty. It creates a sense of lack in our mind that may translate to feelings of something missing in our life. Identify your fears in order to meet them head on. Translate their meaning and see what may be lacking in your own self that might be causing the fear to begin with. Fear in the mind will become real in the body, paralyzing not only you, but also the life you are trying to live. It only makes you vulnerable to illness.

Letting Down Your Guard and the Need for Self-Protection

We often put our guards up in order to avoid conflict. A good example is the notion that because we have to confront someone about a situation that is not acceptable to us, we automatically believe that conflict will occur. In reality, if we can learn to approach that same situation with the idea that no conflict has to occur, then we can usually defuse it. Sometimes we have been hurt repeatedly; we are afraid to try something again or to reconnect with the person or situation that hurt us. We start protecting our emotional state of Being. We put up guards and emotionally block ourselves from receiving the unburied treasures in life that the Divine has in store for us. In order to move forward, it's very important to start learning how to heal from the inside out. Sometimes emotions can be too painful to handle all at once, and we have to step away from a situation and process the information in a way that helps us get clarity about it. By becoming aware of our "*shielding*" habits, we can take the first step towards recovery and begin to walk a path of self-discovery, opening new doors of opportunity. Learning to take the next step and the next step and the step after that leads us towards a life of peace and happiness.

This process teaches us to trust our new decisions and ourselves, so that we start to learn when and how to stand our ground and set appropriate boundaries. Now we feel confident in speaking our truth and we no longer allow others to rob us of our own inner strength and empowerment. We learn to choose our battles wisely and carefully. We learn we can even skip some of those battles and walk away. We learn that holding onto the issue will only rob us of peace and joy.

Letting Go of Grudges – Learn to Forgive

Too often people hold onto past experiences in which they have been hurt. They put their guards up and then harbor unspoken words and feelings that never get resolved. The important lesson to learn about burying this bone is that this behavior will hurt only you – body, mind & soul. Not only does holding onto grudges prevent us from living from a place of self-acceptance, but grudges also keep us from being able to release judgments and accept others. In order to let go of our grudges, we have to practice forgiveness. Looking beyond fault, blame and resentment is an opportunity to look at the person in the mirror – you! Let's try to set the person who has harmed us free, and see them happy. Most of the time, what we see in others is what we need to work on within — and also what we don't like about ourselves. Use these situations as an opportunity to observe what is taking place with the one in the mirror. Let go and heal that situation with the other person as well as healing yourself. This will give you a chance to release your old negative patterns of behavior and bury your bones, creating a space that will raise the vibration of your soul. By creating peace and compassion within, you will no longer feel the need to judge.

Now that we have a better understanding of the top five most common reasons given in the survey for why we judge, we can start to practice letting go of these negative behaviors that keep us attached to our karmic past.

Lighten Your Load and Unlock the Personal Freedom in Order to Find Your Way Home

Over an eighteen-month period, I moved from a house I had lived in for seventeen years, sold 95% of everything I owned, ended a relationship and we sold a business that we jointly owned. This was followed by a notice that the landlord of my chiropractic office would not be renewing my lease. With the help of my twin flame, I then moved my office and downsized my practice in order to shift into alignment with my soul's calling to write, teach and inspire others to find personal freedom. Right at the time I thought I had reached a place of settlement and was ready to start my Divine purpose — that's when I received the diagnosis of uterine cancer.

My twin flame was there for me during this time. With his assistance, I uncovered our identities; however, I did not know at that time that my real mission was being a twin-flame expert. With my background of working with cancer patients, I had no fear of taking a natural approach to my cancer treatment. In fact, I was more fearful of having the surgery. The thought of releasing a part of my body scared me, and I was horrified of the nightmare hormonal stories that you hear about as part of having a total hysterectomy. Night sweats, hot flashes — the list goes on. Quite frankly, that scared the hell out of me! After some deep contemplation and connecting with my inner spiritual guidance, I realized that rather than trying to be the "fixer" I had been my whole life and trying to hold onto my uterus — and hanging on to the notion that I could be the healer of my own body — I needed to become the patient and not the healer. I decided to face my fears and have the surgery and bury my bones once and for all! This was a way for me to physically release all the pain of my past and let go of the toxicity that had filled my life up until this point.

Since that time, I have worked with several twin flames that have also experienced having uterine cancer. Cancer is always about letting go of anger and resentment and therefore, learning the power of forgiveness. Cancer is related to stored emotions; in the uterus, it represents our home life and relationships.

While recovering from my surgery, I quickly discovered that this process taught me how to learn to ask for help. My twin flame helped me experience this. He taught me how to ask for help and the importance of allowing someone to assist when in need. He would have me make to-do-lists and he would come by and help with the things on the list. He also attended the initial doctor visit when I received the initial diagnosis, and he patiently listened as I verbally processed the pros and cons of having surgery. There is something about his patience while listening that mirrors back my answers, without him having to say much.

Slowly, I began to look at this opportunity as a whole new way of living. The excitement of starting a whole new life in a whole new way is so empowering! I can feel the bliss running through my veins and my heart bursting with such love and compassion that I would never have understood at this level had I not learned from the lessons of my past. I am well aware that I will have future circumstances to release in my life going forward, but I am quite confident that I will have no problem identifying, processing and releasing future toxicity.

I can tell you without a shadow of doubt that letting go, releasing and surrendering to a higher power has allowed me to unlock the *"Key Codes"* to finding my way home – inner and happiness – heaven on earth. I am quite certain that if you can learn the art of letting go that you too will find your way home.

Letting Go of Codependency and Need for Addictions

I have found addictive behaviors to be very common occurrences in a twin-flame journey. Most often, this is found in the male or the twin with the heavier masculine energy. I have confirmed this while working with some of my gay and lesbian twin-flame clients. Typically, the male energy has a codependency need for addictive behavior and connects it to the highs and lows of manipulation and control in relationships. I have also seen an association when the masculine Being has been raised by a very controlling mother by emasculating the twin soul as a child, or an association with the energetic imprints that carried over from addictive personalities in past lives. Either way, this causes emotional immaturity and creates a need for external stimulus to fill an internal void – creating codependency. Codependency is being addicted to someone or something that only robs you of your sense of inner confidence and strength while stifling your inner drive to build a life on strength and happiness — a loss of personal empowerment. A person tends to seek outside themselves for something that is missing on the inside. Learning to be happy with yourself is the first step to recovery for a codependent person. Having an additive personality will affect all your relationships and experiences in life.

Another common sign of an addictive personality is the need for chemical attraction. It is the expectation of an immediate burning desire for another person during romantic relationships. This is quite common in twin flames, being that the goal of releasing twin-flame karma includes releasing the ego's desires — developing meaningful relationships that reside deeper than the bubble love phenomenon. These instant sparks sets relationships up for failure, because when the initial attraction wears off and day-to-day reality sets in, most often the couple will have nothing in common.

Letting Go by Releasing Your Story

Over the years, I have seen people who become so attached to their story that subconsciously they don't have a desire to release their negative experiences. They hang onto their story, dwelling on and treating it as if they are *lucky* that these things are happening to them. You have heard the term, "*if I didn't have bad luck, I wouldn't have any luck at all.*" This idea keeps you stuck in a belief system that everything always happens to you. The truth is, it is happening because you are attracting it on all energetic levels. For you to release these reoccurring negative attacks, you must learn to release and rewrite your story. What you focus on expands, and so if you don't like what is happening in your life, it's time to let the past go! Realize that only you can change your external circumstance by changing your mental perception and energetically letting go of the miseries that you are attached to. The bottom line is: only you can choose to be happy. If you don't like where you are, only you can change it by changing your choices in life!

It is also important to start letting go of toxic relationships that no longer serve your higher purpose. That could mean friends, family or even a significant other. I personally never recommend ending relationships. But being that I help facilitate transformation in the lives of others, I have seen repeatedly and I have personally also experienced relationships that have become toxic. Hanging onto toxic relationships will only keep you feeling held back from connecting to your highest purpose. I have learned to look at every past relationship as part of my journey. I have managed to reconcile past differences and continue meaningful relationships. I have experienced this with both my previous x-husband, and my prior x-life partner. I have chosen to want to release the past. I cannot stress the importance of letting go – it will only hurt you in the long run. Through a lot of letting go, forgiveness and allowing the lessons to become teachers, I have maintained very good relationships with both of these life teachers who played very important roles during my journey this lifetime.

In closing of *Key Code 3:3*, I would like to offer you the challenge of finding the blessing in all your situations. I encourage you to ask yourself what you can learn from each experience. When we start seeing experiences as teachers rather than obstacles, we can let go of the need for control and release all that no longer serves our purpose. I would also like to encourage you to find a way to step outside your circumstances, find a need, and fill it. Focusing on the positive aspects of the service you are providing will fill you up on the inside; your perception will shift away from your own obstacles. Here are some thoughts to ponder as you let go of your own karmic debris:

- Let go of the need to resist change and begin to go with the flow moving down stream.
- Cut the cords of all negative thinking – the same thing you would do if you were to cancel, edit or delete a computer file.
- Find the innocence in the behavior of others and let go of the need for control. Life is not a fight and there is nothing to gain by winning.
- Learn to forgive those who have offended you — and above all, remember to forgive yourself!

- Stop clinging to your past and decide to take back your inner power.
- Choose and then commit to making the necessary changes in your life that will free your soul.
- Give yourself space by lightening your load and allowing yourself to become a happier soul. In doing so, the greatest uncovered treasure that you will ever discover is an inner feeling of safety, security and protection that can offer peace of mind. This will begin to resonate throughout your soul.
- Now go do a life review and take an inventory of what you need to release — and then take action by starting to let go!

In *Key Code 4:4*, you will gain a full understanding of the meaning of Ascension. It will paint a mental picture of the process of letting go and shifting from the *"dark night of the soul"* as we transcend to the higher self. It will give you a better idea of what is going on behind the scenes, and help you to learn to trust the process so that you can let go and go with the flow. It will make the transition process easier as you shift from your old ways, creating an increase in your energetic vibration as you transform into a better version of you. This process will enable you to carry out the mission that you came here to accomplish!

KEY CODE 4:4

Trust the Ascension Acceleration Process

"The Ascension process creates soul expansion, which occurs as we transcend from our lower self to our higher self." – Dr. Harmony

ASCENSION BEGINS THE MOMENT WE SHIFT beyond our illusion of being a hostage to our circumstances by changing our perception and shifting out of the *"dark night of the soul"* into the light of day. The Ascension process creates soul expansion, which occurs as we transcend from our lower self to our higher self. It enhances our energetic receptivity, which is necessary to raise our energetic vibration and allow us to tap into our Divine creativity and Universal intelligence (I will present a greater understanding of this in *Key Code 10:10*). As twin souls near the end of their journey, they begin to experience an inner knowing and seek change. As we transition through the process, we become the best version of who we were meant to be, while aligning with our soul's purpose.

Ascension Acceleration is the process of purifying twin souls on a fast track to union in physical form. *It activates the karmic purge phase that is triggered by the mirroring effect, where each twin soul becomes the reflection for the other.* The process will continue until they reach the deepest core of their being and eliminate all of their karmic history. Connecting to the higher self is a requirement of all twin flames in order to purify their souls, which must be done prior to completing their soul's mission.

Nearing the completion of Ascension, we experience a unification phase. We master the idea of becoming one with our self while creating harmonic balance as we shift into our higher, more radiant self (I will explain further in *Key Code's 8:8 and 9:9*). Both of these stages are necessary before reconciling with our twin flame and aligning together into a full reunion.

Layering Through the Karmic Purge

Most often, the karmic purge leaves a person feeling as though they are repeating old patterns, negative thoughts and limiting behaviors. Once we let go of all that no longer serves our purpose, we create room for expansion of our soul. This increases our receptivity because it heightens our energetic vibration. As we evolve through this transcendence process, we tap into our higher self, which involves connecting to "*The12 Chakra System.*" (I will review this in more detail in "*The 12 Chakra System*" in *Key Code 5:5*)

Once the lower seven chakras are energetically cleared of all the karmic debris, it activates our higher-self chakras. *We create soul expansion by increasing our receptivity and raising our sensory system, which creates "crystal-clear conscious awareness."* This helps us to gain clarity and an understanding of our purpose. This is where the term "enlightenment" comes from. Once we connect to our higher selves, we begin to view our circumstances with more clarity. This increases our energetic vibration, creating visible breakthroughs in our life. Now we process and integrate the pieces of our karmic debris. This purging process repeats itself, each time taking us deeper and deeper within our soul until we get to the core of our karmic patterns, so that we can energetically cut all ties to our karmic past, including vows and agreements that we made at the beginning of our souls' evolutionary journey.

Frequently, twin flames tell me they have been working on letting go of their past experiences, but they feel they are repeating the same old patterns. I explain to them that this layering process will continue until they get to the core root. I am notorious for giving action-oriented assignments that help them release karma at a faster rate. I use the analogy that purging is the same as shaving through layers of karma, rather than waxing it by the root. It gets straight to the point, helping to eliminate energetic attachments that have been keeping them stuck in life and in their twin-flame union. When twin flames better understand what feels like repetitive patterns, they learn to trust the process. They start shifting beyond their illusions at a faster rate.

Thus, I am seeing years of work being accomplished in months, months of processing and letting go in weeks, and weeks of releasing taking place in a matter of days. *Being an energy healer for has long as I have, I find these accelerated transformation results to be quite profound.* It amazes me to watch people transition through the same process that took me 20 years to release, process, integrate and then execute. I have assisted some of my highly vibrational twins through this process in a matter of a few months. I observed my own twin flame jump on the fast track to his higher self. *He progressed quicker than anyone I had ever witnessed, taking close to a year to shift from his spiritual awaking to the rebirth stage, which is the hardest and longest stage.* He has remained in this stage while mastering the final stages of the Ascension process.

As we transition through Ascension, we continuously process and reprocess our conscious awareness by integrating information that creates new awareness viewed with a higher state of perception. As we move through each cycle, we reprocess the information, continuing to create new awareness. Each time we revisit the concept, we review it from a higher state of consciousness. Eventually, we connect all of our dots and we begin to see the bigger picture with clearer vision. I experienced this in an eye-opening way. First, while processing and integrating my own experiences, I revisited my experiences while assisting my twin flame — only this time, my own understanding and knowledge was reinforced at a deeper level. Then I revisited those same experiences while assisting other twin flames, creating new awareness and viewing the discoveries from a higher state of consciousness. Things really hit home after revisiting many of the same experiences with my twin-flame facilitator. And I revisited the entire process while writing this book. This became the moment of completion where all my dots collided and I could see the final image before me. I realized that I had found my way home and was in full alignment with what I came here to do. I could see where I had been in training for this Divine mission my entire life. The *11:11 Key Codes* within "*Twin-Flame Code Breaker*" are an accumulation of wisdom that took an eternity to experience. I had been preparing my entire life to serve others, giving them an opportunity to fast-track their own Ascension process so that they might bypass some of the challenges that I have had to experience.

Comparing Ascension with the Christmas Tree Star

I share this Ascension analogy with clients: It's the same process as placing lights on a Christmas tree every year. We repeat cycles of our lives as we revisit particular areas multiple times. If you can imagine stringing a strand of lights around the Christmas tree, you most likely would start at the bottom, taking longer to go around the tree. As you move up, each time around becomes smaller.

Similarly, each time we repeat the process of reviewing the same information, we process and integrate the information faster and with heightened awareness. Eventually, we make it all the way around and up to the top of the tree. Then everyone can stand back and admire the star placed on the top. As we layer through past experiences and release the negative karma, our awareness heightens. We repeat the cycles until we have electrified every dimension of our soul. Just like the star at the top, we begin to radiate and view everything from a higher state of Being. Now, we too become the North Star, shining bright for others to admire and follow.

Understanding the Nine Stages of Ascension

It is important to understand that the stages of Ascension are not linear; we advance from one to the next. However, some of the stages do parallel each other as we continue to Ascend. They also co-exist, meaning you may experience more than one stage at the same time. As we evolve, we weave in and out of the paradigms of each stage. While doing so, we release the negative karmic patterns until we get to the core of the karma. This creates space for our souls to expand. The following are the nine stages of Ascension and a brief introduction of each:

- **Beyond Illusion** – Spiritual Awakening – Gain Spiritual Understanding – Awareness – Shift or Be Shifted
- **Receptivity** – Raising Energetic Vibration – Recalibrating Your Vibration
- **Transformation** – Battle of Head vs Heart – Transform & View Life with Your Heart
- **Breakthrough** – Processing the Pieces of Karmic Debris – Creates Expanded Consciousness
- **Clear Karmic Debris** – Integration – Heightened Awareness – Layering Effect
- **Rebirth** – Letting Go of Old Self – Connecting to Our Higher Self – Transcending –Recreate Who We Are – Take Action in a New Way
- **Unification** – Become One with Self – Balance Masculine-Feminine Energies – Expanding Consciousness – Blossom Like a Lotus Flower
- **Harmonization** – Getting in the Vortex – Alignment of all Possibilities – Abundance – Become Radiant – Personal Freedom Unlocked
- **Mission in Motion** – We are the World – Paying Forward – You Are Ready – *"The Gift"* – Honor Your Agreement and Share Your Mission with the World – Divine Creativity – Sacred Sexuality – Connecting to Universal Cosmic Intelligence

Stage 1: **Beyond Illusion** – This is the start of heightening our conscious awareness and marks the beginning of our *"spiritual awakening."*

As we continue expanding, we gain an understanding that there is more to life than our challenging circumstances. We begin to seek an understanding of who we are and what purpose we serve along our journey. We wake up and find ourselves "*unhappy*" with our current life status. This gives us the burning desire for a connection to all that is; we long for inner peace and happiness. We are ready for change in life, but we are not exactly sure where to start, or how.

Moving beyond our illusions happens once we acknowledge and accept responsibility that the choices we have made up to this point are the reasons for our current situations. We begin to realize that if we desire a shift in our lives, we must move beyond our illusion that we have to stay stuck. We no longer have to accept victimhood. We can choose to take responsibility and choose to rise above our circumstances. We let go of the old perceptions that we acquired through our old belief systems. When we change our perceptions, we can change our reality.

Stage 2: **Receptivity** – Once we open our energetic channels of thought, we realize that we can take ownership of our own lives. We begin to connect with ourselves on a higher energetic level. Our senses heighten and we become more receptive to the signs and signals that are directing our lives. We become more in tune with our own intuition by going within. This teaches us to trust our own inner GPS systems. We begin to realize that we are more than just a body with a soul. We are a soul that is merely housed in a physical body and if we get out of our own way, it will direct us towards our mission in life.

We begin aligning with the people, places and things that show up in our lives to guide and direct us. The more receptive we become, the greater our shift in life will become. We may not always know the exact destination, but by being receptive, we begin to open up to the idea of receiving and allowing. This gives us the necessary faith we need to trust that we are on the right path.

As we start to see visible breakthroughs in our lives, we begin to let go of the need for control and our struggles begin to fade. Our receptivity continues to heighten, opening up even more energetic channels for expansion. During this stage, it is important to learn to let go of analytical thinking, which only creates constriction of receptivity. When we try to make things happen and we focus on lack, we create more of what we don't want.

Stage 3: **Transformation** – Now we can see beyond our illusions and begin to trust the process. We begin to open up and allow things to flow through and around us. Miracles begin to unfold. In the beginning stages of our transformation, this can be challenging, because the heart becomes more receptive to the desires of the soul, but the head continues to question with logical thinking. *It creates a battle between head and heart.* This will block a person's mental awareness and slows down the transformational progress. This becomes the start of the layering affect, or karmic purge that I mentioned. We have to let go of the things that makes a negative impact on our energetic receptivity.

As we review our circumstances, some of the decisions we have to make may consist of thing such as: ending a relationship, changing careers, moving or just forgiving your past and yourself. By letting go of these things that we hold onto, we accept more strife and struggles until we have matured enough to speak our truth and express ourselves in a new and more evolved way.

Going through this produces emotional highs and lows. The heart knows what it desires. The head second-guesses the process. In the end the heart will always win. So, how fast a person moves through this process is dependent on their own abilities to surrender and let go. Because of free will, we get to choose whether we move forward with ease and grace or by creating resistance which only prolongs the process.

At this stage of the game, there is NO turning back! A person has evolved and expanded enough to feel the process and they begin seeing their reality shift. They realize that the uncomfortable change taking place is necessary and they become aware of the lessons they are learning. Over time, they continue to grow, expand and to shine. Shifting creates empowerment that becomes embedded within the soul and continues to heighten the desire for change. A person now sees physical transformation occurring in their life, not just themselves! This motivates a person to continue the soul's journey toward greater evolution.

Initially, this can be one of the toughest phases to be in because it feels like a make-or-break point. It will make a person want to run because the amount of shift that it takes in order to change is more uncomfortable than remaining stuck in their circumstances. However, the soul's evolution always wins, so how long it takes for you to shift is up to you! Up until this stage of the Ascension process, a person continues to weave in and out of these first three stages, until they finally realize that circumstances no longer have to be issues. Now a person can see all of their obstacles as teachers that enhance our awareness in order to let go of the negative energy attachments associated with each experience.

Stage 4: **Breakthrough** – Our breakthroughs occur once we have let go of enough of our baggage. When we release the bondage, we begin to feel lighter, which enhances our clarity. It also creates personal freedom which produces a feeling of inner peace and happiness. We can now look around and see things actually transpire that we could only trust were taking place while we were in the middle of the storm. A person's resistance to their circumstances and situations are directly dependent on the extent of their personal breakthrough. Therefore, the greater the resistance, the greater the breakthrough. *Personally, I found my greatest breakthrough on the other side of my greatest resistance.* In addition, the greater a person's mission, the greater their breakthrough will be and therefore, their greatest resistance.

This process involves cleaning up toxic debris within our souls and the external circumstances in our life. During this stage a person may begin feeling freedom in progress, but in reality we may still have things to address before we can close certain chapters of our lives. This stage is rewarding because as your awareness expands, you begin to seek more of a connection to your higher self. The desire to be in control of our outcomes fades away. Challenges will still occur, but a person begins to shift how they view experiences as they become more consciously aware, and they learn to go below their moments of fear and anxiety to find inner peace.

Stage 5: **Clear the Karmic Debris** – Integrating and assimilating fragmented pieces of understanding generated through our "conscious awareness" is like a baby learning to walk on two feet. We realize that it does not matter how many times we may fall; we will get up, dust ourselves off, and keep walking toward our aligned path. We begin to integrate everything that we have discovered up until this point. This stage is similar to the cocoon phase of the metamorphosis process. During this stage, a person goes within and starts to ask for inner guidance and understanding. They begin trusting their selves and their decisions and they can look back at the progress they have made and know that everything in life that they have went through was for the benefit of their Being. We continue integrating the gold nuggets we learn along the way. Eventually, we become a balanced Being — our yin-yang or masculine-feminine energies move into harmonic balance while our conscious awareness continues to expand beyond measure.

Stage 6: **Rebirth** – The rebirth phase is like a resurrection or a shaman's death. As we let go of our old habits, beliefs and self, we eventually come into full alignment with who we are and who we were meant to be. Our hearts' desires start overriding the logical thinking that comes from our heads. We also begin to understand our purpose as our hearts expand with a Christ consciousness of unconditional love for everything in and around us. We use logic when necessary, but we have learned to allow our lives to unfold by gaining an understanding of why we came to earth. This prompts us to search for our mission. We continue to release the layers of our old habits and beliefs, which facilitates the act of transcendence to our highest self and connecting to our highest potential; we are being born again.

Life now has meaning. As we look around our external world, we have a desire to shift every area of our life so that it matches who we are on the inside. In addition to discovering that our old ways and the things around us may no longer serve our purpose, the way in which we use to process or handle things may no longer work. We realize that we cannot put a square peg in a round hole and so it becomes necessary to re-create our life to match who we have become. Letting go of the deepest parts of our Being can feel like a death of who we were, but at the same time it celebrates what we have become. As tough as it might be, it's really a beautiful experience. You are now a butterfly being granted your wings, and without conscious effort you will learn how to fly. You are now experiencing personal freedom!

Stage 7: **Unification** – Flowering. I describe this stage as akin to the lotus flower. The root system took a long time to cultivate the Universal intelligence by creating a foundation with everything needed to provide for the beauty that is to follow. Eventually, the root blossoms and pure perfection begins to display. You now look at yourself, your life and the world with your heart. This level of bliss allows your light to shine and you become a magnet attracting your desires; your possibilities are endless. You are an example of unconditional love and you begin to show up as love, lead with love and share love. Your passion is contagious and others want what you have.

Stage 8: **Harmonization** – Radiance and Abundance –You are magnetic! You are now in full bloom and your thoughts, actions and feelings fully align with your heart. You attract the right people, places and things that help you accelerate your journey towards connecting to your soul's mission and purpose in life. You have let go of all the shields that once blocked who you were. You fully express yourself and speak your truth, while living a life of ease and grace. *You have* *unlocked The Secret to discovering personal freedom.* You have let go of ego and so you don't try to take on life by yourself. You have entered the vortex of the higher realms of wisdom and understanding. *All you have to do is show up, because when you are in full alignment everything that you need for your journey will appear.* You are able to manifest and use the law of attraction principles at a higher level of vibration. You found your way home!

Stage 9 – **Mission in Motion** – We are the World. Finally, you have learned how to fly as an earth angel, helping others attain personal freedom. By stepping outside of yourself, you discover your soul's purpose and your Divine mission. The final stage is honoring your agreements by completing your Divine mission, which generates a state of bliss, connecting you to everything and everyone. Now you see the bigger picture as you make meaningful money and have meaningful relationships. You found your way home to heaven on earth, experiencing inner peace and happiness!

As we weave in and out of the last three stages of Ascension, we gain an understanding of who we are becoming and how we should go forward on this planet. Transitioning through the process of recreating ourselves can be an intense process. That is why my Divine guidance has directed me to share expanded knowledge on the last three stages of the process. I assigned them their own chapters, each becoming part of the *11:11 Key Codes.*

Ascension, Acceleration, Activation of 12 Stranded DNA

As we Ascend, we transition from a lower energetic vibration into a higher energetic frequency. We are Divine light Beings. The higher frequencies not only affect the physical body, but it also activates changes in the DNA within every plane of our Being — etheric, energetic, spiritual, emotional, mental and physical. This means that as your lower chakras come into balance and you shift into the higher vibrational realms of multi-dimensional consciousness, you tap into your higher five chakras. The higher your energetic frequency becomes, the greater amount of DNA that is activated within the body in order to support it. Therefore, you will experience changes in your physical body. These Ascension symptoms can cause real discomfort in the physical plane. Typically, one might feel these symptoms while going through extreme personal challenges. The same holds true as we go through the Ascension Acceleration process, transforming dense and lower vibrations into a high vibrational crystalline light form and producing 12 stranded DNA.

Scientific research has documented such changes within the DNA structure of higher vibrational light beings. DNA are the genetic coding passed down from our hereditary ancestors, and creates our genetic blueprint. The production of DNA is generated and controlled by the pineal gland, which is a photosensitive organ. It uses crystalline light structures to produce DNA, and it is housed between the right and left hemispheres of the brain. As we shift through Ascension process, the pineal gland begins to produce more mitochondria, which is used to make chromosomes. This then generates chromosomal chains that make up a double-helix structure that coils up, forming a double-stranded chain of DNA that mimics a spiral staircase. As a person raises their energetic frequency the pineal gland produces additional mitochondria which in turn makes more chromosomes, which then generates a twelve-stranded chain of DNA verses two-stranded.

Research has proven these physical changes have occurred as planet earth moves into a higher vibrational energetic frequency from 3D (third dimension) to 5D (fifth dimension). Thus every human Being on the planet is going through these physical changes in order to support the higher light frequencies of the Universe. That is raising the "*conscious awareness*" of the planet. This shift is forcing everyone to seek a connection to the higher realms and the higher consciousness, thus stimulating a more "*awakened*" planet.

Ascension Symptoms

The following are a list of Ascension symptoms that I personally have had and have also seen my clients experience while shifting from lower vibrational energies to a higher energetic consciousness.

- Changes in behavior
- Changes in eating habits
- Desire to stop eating or drinking toxic foods
- Desire to release anything in life that is toxic
- Trouble sleeping
- Body aches & pains
- Weight loss due to loss of appetite
- Brain fog – dimmer switch on the brain
- Memory loss
- Vivid dreams
- Blurred vision
- Ringing or buzzing in ears
- Loss of Identity – rediscovering who they are
- Extreme fatigue
- Out-of-body experiences
- Chills
- Increase in internal body temperature – A burning sensation
- Extreme hypersensitivity to surroundings, noise, crowds, etc.
- Isolation – a feeling of going within
- Changes in relationships – Releasing toxic relationships
- Depression and anxiety
- Feelings of being homesick

The Ascension Voyager's Journey

It is imperative that we release ALL the karmic past, so it is very typical of one or both twin souls to revisit past lives that have caused them to remain stuck in their present life. These negative experiences remain embedded in the DNA of our souls, which creates energetic blocks during our present lifetime. *Therefore, the past must resurface within our conscious awareness, so that one can move forward in life – karma free. The voyager's journey is activated and stimulated without conscious effort.* Situations or circumstances triggers a response that links to past negative experiences. This will send twin flames down a path of revisiting the traumatic soul trauma so they can heal.

Going back into time may occur in a variety of ways. Most often they are vivid dreams, but sometimes visions, experiences, emotions and being are directed towards revealing information that creates the connection between the past and current situation.

I experienced this firsthand during my own karmic purge. As I previously mentioned, a couple years ago, I experienced making a connection to a very significant past life in England. At that time, I only uncovered the big picture of that life understanding enough to make a link between freedom and justice via my dog, Champ. But it was not until my twin flame and I connected on a soul level that I began a much deeper voyager journey; it happened without conscious effort. The journey started just after discovering we were twin flames and having a conversation about a band from Germany that we both liked. This prompted me to listen to an old CD. Immediately following that, I started having visions and I could feel myself in England. It was during the medieval era, and for two straight days I visually saw things and could feel everything happening around me as though I was really there. These visions were followed by other unexplainable experiences that helped me connect every dot and very specific details of that life. Information I received included exactly what happened, the year it took place and how it related to my feelings of being held hostage to my circumstances in this lifetime. Understanding my previous life experience helped me release the soul trauma that I had experienced. It was imperative that I release the pain from that lifetime in order to experience the freedom I was seeking and to align with my Divine mission.

Since this impactful experience, I have had multiple *voyager journeys*. In one, I was a refugee in Germany; I could hear everyone talking in German, but I knew exactly what they were saying. I have also discovered 3 past lives that my twin and I have led, each time being brother and sister. One of them plays a very significant role in our mission today, and explains our deep brother-sister bond during this lifetime. I have worked with other twin flames who have had brother-sister past lives together. These past experiences need to be cleared in order to release the energetic imprints of prior past life memories. For instance, in this case, it is important to release the incestuous feelings that remain in the current lifetime.

The Ascension Process Connects You and Your Twin Flame

Ascension is a purification process that all twin flames must go through individually before reuniting together in full union. I am continually reminding twin flames of this when they shift their focus onto each other. Too often, the higher-vibrational twin will repeat old patterns and try to fix their twin by focusing on what their twin is not doing for themselves. However, if the higher-vibrational twin stays in alignment with their own higher state of Being, they continue to raise the energetic pathway for the lower-vibrational twin. So, if you want to help your twin flame, I would suggest you stay focused on your journey and work on yourself. This self-discovery journey takes much devotion and mastery; I see twins all the time want to give in, and blame their twin for their pain. If this is you, I want to remind you that you signed up for this mission and you have everything inside of you that you need to continue and finish this journey. You can do this — it's not about your twin, it's about you becoming the best version of you that you can be.

This becomes what your twin flame is attracted to, from their higher state of Being. Energetically, like a magnet and with no conscious effort you will draw your twin flame closer to you. If you shift into the lower vibrational energies and push towards your twin, they subconsciously feel it and this only makes them pull further away from you. Now you are the one slowing down the process. If you want to help your twin, keep your vibration high and focus on yourself!

Understanding the Seven Stages of the Twin-Flame Journey

As I have mentioned, both twin flames must experience becoming the star on the Christmas tree before experiencing the ultimate relationship. The entire process is preparing the twins to become great light workers and to shine brightly for others to follow as they implement their joint mission. Therefore both twins generally parallel the Ascension process, with one twin being more evolved than the other. But in addition to that, the joint twin-flame journey also has a series of stages that you go through together. Let's review the seven stages of the twin-flame journey.

Stage 1: **Soul Recognition** – Twin souls connect and energetically communicate on the same plane through their higher selves, or the higher chakras. The higher consciousness is encoded with the akashic records, which connects to a Universal database containing all the information of every soul. This is where the agreements are energetically stored between the twin-flame couple. It is through these higher chakras that the twin souls unconsciously stay connected at all times. When it is time to start communicating in the physical plane, the souls seek each other out. Their higher selves recognize each other through these higher frequencies by energetically sending sonar signals to each other — the same way they communicate throughout their evolution.

My experience with soul recognition is a perfect example. My twin and I were in very close physical contact, but it was not until we were both ready to be fully awakened that we connected on a much deeper soul level. This occurred when my twin was intuitively guided to reach out to me, in need of my assistance in helping him heal and remove energetic blocks so that he could break his karmic patterns. I also needed him to create a reflection for myself so I could release some of my deep debris before putting the mission in motion.

Stage 2: **Soul Merger** – Soul merger occurs upon initial physical-soul contact. The twin souls have recognized each other on the higher level and now the energy between the two of them connects, merging the two souls. This process can be so strong that it can cause a dizzy or drunken state that can last a few days to a few months. This happens at the exact timing when the energy between the twin souls merge, creating the term "twin flame." It is important to note that once these cords of energy merge, you cannot cut the energetic bond between you and your twin flame. I have worked with several clients who have tried running from their twin; the more they try, the stronger their twin attaches to them energetically. As the twins connect on a deeper level, this energetic bond grows and connects in every plane — the etheric, energetic, spiritual, emotional, mental and physical. Over time it magnetically pulls the twins together in spite of their conscious decisions to run.

I have had twins ask me to help them cut the energetic cords. I explain that it is not possible. However, I have helped them release situations where one twin will intentionally try to energetically enter the space of the other with attempts to force them to connect. Doing this is bad karma. That is why there is free will. It is better that you remain working on yourself. I have helped them release the intentional negative attachments and teach them how to shield and protect their energy. I have also seen cases where one twin may have been energetically attacked by someone attached to their twin flame. That person's energy can filter through the energy of their twin flame and causes them to emotionally and physically feel the experiences of that person. I have also helped these twins to release that third-party energy.

My twin and I experienced this merger after connecting during our first chakra-clearing session together. Even though we had known each other for over twenty years, it was the first time we had come together on a soul level. Our energy merged, causing us each to feel an intoxicating and out-of-body state for a couple of days. As we continued sessions, this energetic bond became stronger. Just before discovering that we were twin flames, I was energetically pulled into one of his sessions, and I saw visions of being with him on his journey. I knew I was not just the messenger during that session; I was a part of the session. Afterward, my twin said that he could also feel me with him during that session and that I was his teacher.

Stage 3: **The Karmic Purge** – Most people refer to this phase as the "*runner*" phase. This is what I refer to as a push-pull phase. It is during this phase that twins are brought together, creating the mirror effect — each reflecting back to the other twin what the other needs to work on within themselves. Then they go apart to work on their own selves by processing and integrating awareness's that surface. However, the Universe always has a way of bringing them back together to continue the process, until all the karma has been purged — not only that of their individual souls but also the karma that exists between the two of them. Everything that needs reconciled between the twins must surface in order to be released. This is what creates the need for confession between twins, where nothing can be hidden. Once again, I would like to remind you that when your twin pulls back to work on themselves, and you shift your focus on your twin, your twin is teaching you to let go. *If you don't, that makes you the runner – running from yourself.*

Stage 4: **Surrender** – The surrender stage occurs after enough karma has been cleared and both twins realize that they need each other present to help facilitate their own journey. In the beginning phases of this stage, twins must surrender to their own personal progression and learn how to let go and allow. The Universe has a way of way putting us in the corner until we become aware, which only makes us repeat the process of letting go. This occurs until we finally let go of ego and analytical thinking. *This opens us to the idea of letting the heart lead us through life.* Only then can we surrender to the idea of a twin-flame relationship coming into full union.

Stage 5: **Integration** – Once twins process and integrate their own experiences, they start processing and integrating their experiences together, now from a higher state of consciousness. One or both of the twin flames begin to realize that it was necessary for their other half to assist them with the process. They finally see the bigger picture and understand the importance of having their twin flame present.

Stage 6: **Harmonize** – Harmonization or balance of self is mandatory for one or both twins before they can reunite. After being in separation, they come together to work out all final differences before they can merge into full energetic union. Up until this point it has been an individual journey; now they harmonize together.

Stage 7: **Full Union** – Full union is brought into physical form once both flames have recognized their identity and advanced spiritually. This is not to say that everything must be perfect before union occurs. Nor will everything be perfect after. I have helped twins come together in full union, clearing any remaining ego and still raising their vibration in order for a physical relationship to stay in harmony. Just like anything in life, we must work to remain in harmonic balance, and what you put into the relationship you will get back. The important point to remember is that both twins must be mature enough to work out any differences they have together, just as any couple.

Over the last few months, I have continued to assist twin flames as they shift into full union. I had one twin contact me just a few days ago, giving me an update that she had been doing the forgiveness work with her twin by energetically releasing the past abandonment and soul trauma that occurred in Atlantis. She reported that her and her twin are now engaged to be married. I have also worked with someone whose twin showed up after three and half years. Now they are fully awakened to their identity and finally believe that they really are twin flames. Others report seeing the signs and knowing it's time to be together. Another twin contacted me yesterday, informing me that she was heading out of town to spend the weekend with her twin, after being separated for several months. Also on multiple occasions, twins have received text messages from their twin flame during our energy release sessions.

Ego remains the #1 reason why twin flames do not unite in the physical form. The personal mastery required for one to work on oneself can be so intense, that until recently, less than 1% of twin flames would come into physical reunion. As I presented in *Key Code 2:2*, the Universe has a collective plan for twin flames to unite in full union. Over the next five to seven years, more twin flames in the history of time will reunite in full union as a collective, conscious effort to create the unconditional love vibration of the planet.

In *Key Code 5:5*, I will present ways for you to learn to survive your shift. I will share my "*Reboot Your Twin Soul*" blueprint, giving you some action steps to help you build a bridge as you transcend from your lower self into higher self. It will assist you during your Ascension process.

KEY CODE 5:5

Learn How to Reboot Your Twin Soul

"Choose to release your past, raise your vibration and reclaim your life!" – Dr. Harmony

REBOOT YOUR TWIN SOUL is a three step blueprint designed to facilitate soul transformation by building a bridge that helps one to survive the shift from the *"dark night of the soul"* through transcendence to the higher self. The first part of this blueprint is learning to let go of the past, or present life situations that no longer serves a purpose. Such situations include negative emotions, thoughts, relationships or even physical clutter in our home. Secondly, expansion of our souls raises our energetic vibration and enhances our clarity, which allows us to view everything about our life with a whole new perception. We now attract positive things in our life — thoughts, feelings, people, relationships, job and physical belongings. Lastly, we are now able to reclaim our life and manifest at a higher energetic frequency, what I also call *"getting into the vortex."* We love the new life we created because we start attracting into our energetic field that which matches our new higher energetic vibration.

Over the years, one of the biggest challenges I have heard both patients and clients mention is, *"I'm not happy and I want to change my life, but I don't know where to start making the necessary changes to cross the abyss to get from where I am to where I want to be."* This is where my experience and expertise enhances my ability as a twin-flame expert. The following is the exact three-step approach I teach my clients, helping them to reboot their twin soul and activate the *11:11 Key Codes* found in this book.

- Release Your Past – Creates Space
- Raise Your Vibration – Conscious Clarity
- Reclaim Your Life – Connect with Your Twin

Of course, letting go of the past sounds easier than it actually is. However, identifying your negative patterns of behavior and committing to the idea of allowing change is 75% of the battle. Acknowledging and releasing the negative patterns of behavior is imperative before you can shift into alignment with personal freedom, which is necessary to direct you towards your Divine mission. Most of the time, people feel held back by their circumstances and remain stuck because staying where they are is more comfortable than shifting. Once you reach this level of awareness, the Universe will not allow you to get too complacent. We either get to decide to shift, or we get shifted. The stronger we are and the more we resist change, the harder the slap we receive when being forced to change. This is why our circumstances sometimes have to be life-jolting — we are smacked into becoming spiritually awakened enough to connect to our higher consciousness.

Recalibrating your vibration also raises the energetic vibration of your twin flame. Due to your energetic connection, the lower-vibrational twin gets a "*hall pass*" and can jump on a fast track to recalibrating their energetic vibration. The higher-vibrational twin paves the energetic path. Conversely, your energetic blocks can create an energetic block for your twin. *So, if you are the higher-vibrational twin, which most likely you are if you are reading this book, then it is your responsibility to continue to focus on your personal path.* Let your twin flame follow the energetic trail.

When it comes to being happy, we could all use a few lessons learning how to get out of our own way so that we can climb out of the messes we create. If we take action and let go of our past, we can find that inner heaven that our souls long for. Instead, we tend to look outside ourselves for something to fill a void on the inside, yet we refuse to let go of the things in life that no longer serve our purpose. This lack of personal accountability while searching for something or someone to blame has become a global problem. It has resulted in prejudice and conflict that only produces more conflict, and stems from an inner battle of *"head versus heart"* in the souls of most individuals. This worldly dysfunction is merely the reflection of our individual internal soul dissatisfaction. *The sooner we decide to look within and change, the sooner we will become the change we want to see in the world.*

Awaken Your Twin Soul

As the soul awakens, we raise our energetic vibration, allowing our inner light to shine brighter upon our path toward our mission in life. Most people fight this process because of their analytical minds overriding their hearts' desires. Using my own experiences as an example, let's take a look at how old behaviors and coping mechanisms that cause us to shut down our senses and prevent us from being fully present and connecting to our inner self.

You might say that I learned a deadly lesson when my 40-year-old uncle and his son were killed in the plane crash! Talk about waking up! As I mentioned, this experience started my own spiritual transformation. I was in the *"dark night of the soul"* and because I'm a strong-willed person, with the spirit of a wild horse, it took more than a few times putting a saddle on me before I decided to let go enough to make it a smooth ride! I opted for an intense ride before learning how to fully release and surrender to a power greater than me. It was not until I was diagnosed with uterine cancer that I learned how to be vulnerable and ask for help. I had to learn how to get out of my own way.

Once I got out of the way, I understood that if I just showed up and got into alignment, I was presenting life with the best version of the person I wanted and was intended to be. I stopped resisting and swimming upstream; I started going with the flow. Once I finally let go, I discovered I had built a bridge connecting the gap by shifting from a life of misery to a life of bliss. With the effortless assistance of my own twin flame, I have found personal freedom – and I have connected to my Divine calling and am becoming the best version of myself. Shifting did not happen overnight. My patience was tested beyond belief, but I now view life from the other side. That is what fuels me to teach others how to survive the changes that come with a shift of this magnitude.

Shift or Be Shifted!

Let me say this loud and clear – SHIFT OR BE SHIFTED! You either get to choose to make changes in your life, or —because of your soul's agreement to align with your Divine mission — you will be shifted into alignment. Either way you will end up on your Divine path, but the choice becomes yours as to whether you choose to do it with ease and grace or fight the process — which only causes more self-inflicted pain and suffering and only prolongs the process. At any given moment, you have the power within you to stop and say, *"I choose to change. I agreed to my current reality, and if it is my internal state of being that creates my external reality, then only I can choose to change it."*

Clients all have shared similar stories of how things have really been shaken up in their lives. Each had some major decisions to make regarding jobs, careers and relationships. This mass shift in the conscious awareness of all souls is a *"wake-up call"* that marks the beginning of a *"global spiritual awakening."* I will say it again – SHIFT OR BE SHIFTED! It is never easy to make life-changing decisions — but when we can shift our thoughts about the process, we can shift the way in which we go about processing the shift.

Building Your Bridge and Surviving Your Shift

In this section, you'll find six tips to help you build your bridge. When practiced, these ideas will create energy rather than exhaust you, giving you fuel for your journey towards finding inner peace and happiness:

Tip 1: **Living in Present-Time Consciousness.** This is the importance of living in the NOW – what I refer to as PTC or (Present-Time Consciousness). When we can stay in the present, it teaches us how to consciously stop zig-zagging from past to present to future. *What does living in the Now really mean?* I discovered this the hard way after the plane crash. I saw first-hand what it means not to have the opportunity to fulfill your dreams. This sent me searching within, asking myself, "*what do I really want out of life?*" Because of my uncle, I made it my mission to "*live a life with no regrets.*" This really hit home for me several years later when I found myself once again waking up after feeling like I was drowning in misery. I was so unhappy with the life I had re-created. I realized that my circumstances became my spiritual teachers. *However, I was sick and tired of being sick and tired!* My soul longed for that peace-like presence, patience and kindness towards myself.

Personally, I have practiced and taught visualization, meditation, breathing exercises, and positive affirmations to support clients in learning how to redirect their conscious awareness into PTC. They start to live moment to moment; they stop during the day and take a few minutes to review its moments. This simple action helps us to redirect our thoughts and make more out of each moment and each day. When practiced over time, this will create a new pattern in the quality of life. It is our birthright to find joy and inner peace — the kind of peace that resonates within our souls, allowing us to let go of the mental chaos that blocks peace. We can now enjoy "*The Gift*" of the present moment!

Tip 2: **Speak Your Truth and Learn How to Express Yourself.** When it comes to expressing ourselves, we have a lot we can learn! Most people try to avoid conflict and run from such situations by assuming responsibility for the actions of others, which only produces guilt. To learn to fully express ourselves, it's important to learn habits of effective communication and start speaking your truth from your heart – not your head. I have worked with many clients who say they are expressing themselves. I often have to remind them it is not what you say – it's how you say it. Body language, actions, energy and feelings behind the words – these speak louder than the words. When we allow our spoken words to come straight from the heart without hesitation or expecting resistance in return, it frees us up to speak our truth – the truth that only our souls knows. By doing so, we gain confidence that opens the doorway to receptivity from another person.

When we learn to have patience and tolerance of others, we also gain an understanding of the importance of being able to deeply listen to others with acceptance. This kind of energy exchange will neutralize all conflicting situations. It is also important to understand the difference between using passive, aggressive or assertive speaking skills. Learning assertive speaking skills to get our point across, without the fear of hurting another person's feelings or holding back to avoid conflict, allows us to express our inner truth. It becomes a reflection of your own self confidence. And communicating truthfully, in a heartfelt manner, doesn't have to include "*claiming*" the perception that conflict will arise from speaking honestly.

Tip 3: **Trust Your Instincts!** Follow your inner GPS system! It will never lead you in the wrong direction! People tend to have a hard time trusting their own instincts — and sometimes for good reasons, such as past negative experiences that can cause a person to question their choices in life. So they continue to make fear-based decisions and worry that they will make the wrong choices in the future. When we let go of the past and start with a clean slate, it is important to develop and trust our own inner guide. Once we learn how to determine whether our thoughts, feelings and emotions are being guided by our newly-awakened consciousness, that helps us align with our highest good. But if our feelings are coming from fear and lower energetic thoughts, that produces a need for control and power of the egotistical mind. Learn to listen to your gut. Unlike google maps, it will never send you down the wrong path. Spending time in meditation and journaling will help you develop this skill.

Once you release your past, raise your energetic vibration and connect to your higher self, you will discover how to tap into your own sixth sense. You will develop a stronger connection to your emotions and feelings, and begin to know where these feelings are coming from. Most people block their own ability to be open to these inner, energetic signals, so they are far less sensitive than they were wired to be. I have helped many clients learn to view their intuition as an inner guide, with an accumulation and wealth of knowledge. Tapping into this Divine knowledge increases a person's sensitivity, which creates balance between a person's emotional state and their mental perception. They then can become the leader of their own life by taking charge and becoming accountable for their actions and responses to all situations. This will offer a person the power to redirect their course in life and begin making better choices without second-guessing themselves.

Tip 4: **Become Your Own Best Friend**. It is very important that we become our own devoted Being and learn to nurture our inner child. We need to practice, self-love, self-worth, self-acceptance and self-patience. We are worthy of becoming devoted to ourselves. You become your own best friend through practicing self-care, learning the art of delegation, and being open to receiving so you can let your inner diamond shine. When we take care of ourselves on every level – body, mind and soul – and practice regular self-care, we are treating ourselves like first-class Beings. As spiritual Beings, we should expect nothing less! We deserve to treat ourselves like royalty. Like the Kings and Queens we are. It is our accumulated belief systems and our attempt to meet the expectations of others, along with the expectations we place on ourselves, that create a false illusion of not feeling good enough.

For many years, I have taught people the art of learning how to practice gentleness, compassion, acceptance and honesty, as well as, the importance of being loyal, faithful, and quick to forgive ourselves. It is important to learn how to dismiss false guilt and be accepting that it is okay to take plenty of naps and to play – yes, play! –on a daily basis. When we do this, we gain insight into why we no longer have to take life on by ourselves, and can ask for help. We learn to stop blocking our blessings, no longer robbing others of the joy of giving to us. In addition, we will gain an understanding of the importance of not being a people-pleaser and giving away our own power. We set loving boundaries without guilt and understand the difference rather than putting up walls that blocks us from receiving.

Tip 5: **Live Life with Purpose and Passion**. You should be loving yourself, loving others, loving life and loving what you do. We should be waking up every day with enthusiasm and excitement just to be alive and to have a chance to start fresh. Each day is a day to take full advantage of, finding passion in everything we do and looking at life as an adventure. Thriving rather than surviving. I cannot stress the importance of living a simple life by putting into practice simple yet powerful tools such as daydreaming, starting a bucket list, and setting an intention (e.g., to take a dream vacation). I encouraged you to choose a happy attitude, show passion with gusto and even learn how to smile. Make it a point to learn, as I did, to stop numbing your senses due to worry, fear and being afraid of what others will think of you. *Explore the importance of living a life of no regrets – living every day as if it were the last.* Make it a practice of getting outdoors and connecting with nature, often. Take walks and go barefoot in the grass or sand. Remember how it was like to play as a child – not being afraid to get dirty or play in the mud. These are fun behaviors that also keep us grounded and connected to the earth. For those who can't get outside – open those curtains and windows as often as possible! Stay connected and have fun. Even sunbathing and daydreaming every day keeps us in an emotional state of balance, and refreshes and renews our soul.

Practice looking at life through the "eyes" of your heart. Each day, create a new picture of the new life you want. Over the years I have practiced the process of starting with a clean slate by becoming the artist of my own life: *Paint It ~ Own It ~ Love It ~ Live It ~ Share It!* Stir some passion by listening to music or dancing or laughing, which really is the best medicine for shifting our energy. If we are not having a gut-wrenching laugh now and then, we're not vibrating at the frequency we were meant to. All that blocked energy becomes stuck and stagnant, lowering our productivity in life. It is time to connect to yourself and bust wide open!

Tip 6: **Find Harmonic Balance – Zero-Point Field.** No matter how many challenges we face, it is important to overcome our adversities and find our zero-point field. We must learn to live life in balance, tapping into our infinite possibilities and purpose, and using the talents we have been given! We can move below the anxiety in all situations and learn how to find the stillness within, regardless of what our circumstances are. It teaches us how to access our infinite potential by finding harmonic balance, or zero-point field. This zero point is the exact point at which stillness occurs within and balance is created. When we find this same inner peace, we learn that all obstacles in our life are merely illusions. The only limitations we have are the ones we see through the "eyes" of our mind.

The secret in finding this stillness originates in the symbolism of the balance in the Yin/Yang, our masculine and feminine energies. It give us the ability to create oneness between our lower self and higher self. When balanced, this creates a solid foundation that helps us transmit this inner peace and harmony outward into all areas of our life. A strong foundation is necessary for us to strengthen our bridge as we connect the pieces needed to fill the gap between where we are in life and where we want to be. Once you learn to find and balance this internal place of stillness from within, your external life and worldview will improve, and this will support you in using your talents to the best of your ability. Even while living in a world of chaos, or trying to escape our reality, we can find balance if we choose to see it that way.

In addition to finding ways to build our bridge, here are seven suggestions that will help you change the perception of your reality, helping you learn how to survive your shift:

Suggestion 1: **Ask: "What is the lesson in this situation?"** Remember that every circumstance that occurs in your life is always attached to a lesson. The sooner you can identify your lessons, the faster you can move on and let go of what it is you are to learn from that situation. In doing so, it no longer has to feel like a negative event. More importantly, let go of everything but the lesson!

Suggestion 2: **Release and Surrender.** What our minds conceive and what our hearts believe can be two different things. When we don't listen to our heart and our soul, we fight the experience of allowing a shift of our consciousness into new paradigms. When you can release and surrender and believe that there is a greater power than you, you no longer have to carry the load by yourself! What a relief!

Suggestion 3: **Let Go of Control**. Many times we become attached to what we believe to be the way, or how we want things to occur in our lives. We allow ego to consume our reality and we hold onto the illusion that our minds perceive to be the way we think things should be, rather than the way they could be. When you release the need to control all situations, you free yourself from the need to be attached to thoughts, or things that no longer serve you purpose. Every ending is only the opportunity for a new beginning! As scary as it can be to let go and let God, in doing so, it gives you the freedom and peace that you so desire.

Suggestion 4: **Divine Plan and Divine Timing.** Don't forget that there is a Divine plan. Because of your soul agreement, you are to align with your mission. When you are in this vortex, everything you need for your journey will appear. If you fight this process and don't allow it to happen, you will be shifted into directions that send your soul spinning out of control. When we get out of our own way, things have a way of unfolding and showing up at just the perfect time!

In *Key Code 7:7*, you will gain an in-depth understanding, but here I would like to remind you that your entire twin-flame journey is in the Divine order. There is no need to try to fix your twin flame. If you do so, you operate from the lower vibrational behaviors that will prolong the process. Ultimately, how long it takes for your twin to shift is up to you.

Suggestion 5: **Be Grateful for the Lessons.** Give thanks to everyone and every situation that causes you to shift your thought processes in a new direction. When you begin to trade your expectations for appreciation, you clearly see the purpose and reason for why that situation needs to change. You understand that these things are present to teach you something. It now becomes something to be grateful for.

Suggestion 6: **Watch for Teachers.** When the student is ready, the teacher appears. Treat everyone and every event that happens in your life as a part of your personal journey. If your teacher has appeared, then you are already ready to embark on a new concept or idea; this is the Universe giving you what you need during this time. This means it is time to pay attention and take notes. This is the answer to what you have been asking for!

Suggestion 7: **Embrace "The Gift":** Shifting your life in a new direction is never easy; it takes a lot of courage and letting go. However, when you treat every experience as an opportunity to be open and receive, you open yourself up for better opportunities. Once you let go of ego and your lower self-desires, what shows up in your life is even better – better than the lower self could anticipate! The Universe knows this. Once you let go and become open to receiving from the heart and not the analytical mind, "*The Gift*" becomes something better than you could ever have humanly asked for. Sometimes it might come in a different form, but when you get out of your own way, you quickly realize that it's actually better than what you asked for to begin with. It is a reward from a Source greater than you!

Now we have a better understanding that we are granted free will, but we get to choose the path of least resistance or continue our path of hardships and struggles. *Now let's set the intention to shift our reality.* I challenge you to take a look at some ways that you can physically shift your internal energetic environment to change your external reality.

Reboot Your Twin Soul – Reunite with Your Twin Flame!

If you are wanting to reunite with your twin, you MUST first *"Reboot Your Twin Soul!"* So when it comes to changing your life, think about these questions: *Are you tired of feeling stuck? Are you seeking connection, searching for your Divine purpose? Are you ready to energize your life? Do you desire inner peace and happiness?* If your answer is yes, then it's time to take charge and accept responsibility for your own self — stop running from yourself by focusing on your twin flame! Once again, I cannot stress the importance of this! I am repeating this thought because this is the number one reason why twins stay stuck in their twin-flame journey. *They expect their twin to shift and change, but they are not willing to change some of the deepest parts of themselves.* Usually, the person focusing on their twin is the one having trouble "letting go" and the one who needs to "practice patience."

Remember that soul purification and raising your energetic vibration is imperative to reclaiming your life by making you the complete, whole and loving person that you need to be in order to experience a true twin-flame relationship. When you recalibrate your vibration, it will energize every area of your life, helping you to become healthy – body, mind and soul.

Previously, I have given a thorough description of how energy works on a much deeper level, but here I would like to introduce some practical concepts of energy so that you get a better understanding of our energetic connection with the external world. The following list consist of energetic sources that can affect your energetic frequency in a positive or negative way, some of which you may be familiar with:

- Radio – TV – Cell Phone – Microwaves.
- Acupuncture – Meridians – Channels in the body. Needles act as an antenna to redirect blocks.
- Vortexes – Energy portals in the earth.
- Prism of Light.
- Energetic Field – Aura.
- Magnets – Masculine-Feminine – Opposite polarities.
- Lower to Higher Frequencies – Negative to Positive,
- Thoughts and Words are Energy,
- The Silent Elephant – Enter a room and you can feel the negative energy and emotions, but no one will talk about the issue.
- Toxic and Harmful Environmental Factors,
- Global Energies – War – Everything destructive arises to clear and heal.
- Solar Energies – Moon Cycles – Water/Tide,

Understanding the Layers of Your Energetic Light Being

The following list will give you a better understanding of energetic layers that comprise your energetic light Being, also known as your internal energetic world:

- **Energetic Body** – connection of the physical body and emotional Being.
- **Spiritual Body** – energetic field or aura.
- **Mind Body**
  - Subconscious Thoughts – Stored memory such as birth – Keeps your heart beating.
  - Conscious Thoughts – Right/Left brain thinking patterns – Connected by pineal gland.
  - Higher-conscious Thoughts – Connects to higher self and cosmic Universal intelligence.

- **Emotional Body** – Thoughts become things and then creates feelings – Feelings attract.
- **Physical Body** –Action - Energy in motion.
- **Etheric Body** – Stores the energy between you and your twin flame and other relationships.

Our thoughts, feelings and emotions all create energetic vibrations. Depending on whether they are positive or negative, they correlate with the frequency at which their signals vibrate – negative ones carrying the lower vibrations and positive ones carry the higher vibrations. Thoughts generate our feelings, which create emotions; if these emotions get stored in the body, (for instance, you do not express your feelings) these energetic imprints create energetic blocks that need cleared on every level. Our Being operates like a computer; it stores every type of feeling and emotions in files. For example, if every time you are angry you do not clear the emotion, it becomes stored in an angry file. Then each subsequent time you get angry, you have pulled up all the suppressed emotions. It is important to cancel – edit – delete these files, so that they don't cause energetic blocks and keep you stuck. Basically, it's time to empty your cache. Our emotions are what generates the vibrational synchronicity of our mind-body connection. If this connection becomes blocked or out of sync, our thoughts and body will disconnect energetically. Then our Being will become distorted and that in turn creates mental distortion – hence, a lack of clarity.

The Law of Attraction

There are many resources available explaining the law of attraction, and most people have heard of the idea. But few really comprehend the science behind the external reality and how it's comprised of your internal rate of energetic vibration. The frequency at which we energetically vibrate becomes an energetic magnet and connects to everything we attract in life, whether positive or negative. Our bodies are comprised of 72 percent water. This becomes the sonar and sound waves that send out signals to the Universe, generating our connection to everything we attract in life.

Here is an example of how this scientifically works. Because we are primarily made up of water, it becomes a conductor for all electrical impulses. This same concept is used in many medical devices such as ultrasound, which measures the frequency of the energetic impulses in the body and the pattern of these signals. The machine uses the signals to reflect an image of the internal body and can be used to diagnose health issues, or monitor the progression of an unborn child.

These sound waves are generated through the rate at which our chakras energetically function and are then filtered through the aura, or energetic field, around our physical bodies. Therefore, one of the most important things to understand about the law of attraction is that once our thoughts generates feelings and emotions, it is the feelings —not what you are thinking — that become the primary magnet to our reality. The energetic frequencies of emotions create the physical manifestation of what you are attracting. Lower vibrational thoughts and feelings will attract lower-vibrational people, things and experiences into our lives. Therefore, the higher our vibration, the higher the energetic frequency channel that we tap into. Then we are able to attract other people, things and experiences that operate on that same energy channel.

Dr. David Hawkins gives and excellent explanation of this concept in his book, "Power vs. Force." He thoroughly explains how frequency channels work in terms of energetic vibrations. He presents a chart with a list of our emotions, assigning them each an energetic frequency rate at which each emotion is calibrated. For example, joy is one of the highest vibrational emotions and fear is on a lower vibration frequency. Interestingly enough, according to Hawkins' list, unconditional love is calibrated at a frequency of 500 — which is right in the heart of the Consciousness scale ranging from 0-1000, with 1000 being the highest energetic consciousness. This is a good example of how our sonar signals generate a specific sound frequency or rate. That affects whatever we are attracting, positive or negative, into physical form or shape.

Hawkins also gives an example of how the healing powers and presence of Jesus energetically calibrated at 1000, the highest frequency humanly possible. I have heard Dr. Wayne Dyer mention that having the St. Francis of Assisi Prayer on paper in your physical presence produces a calibration of 600. For years, I have carried this prayer with me. I placed a copy of it on my bathroom mirror to read upon arising every morning.

The second-most important thing to understand about the law of attraction: It's the Universe's desire to give you not only what you need, but also what you want. Truly enough, your wish is the Universe's command — but to receive your wishes, you must be able to clearly answer the following question, "*What do I desire?*" This is where the block usually begins, because most people don't know what they want. Until we set *crystal-clear intentions*, we cannot attract or manifest what it is that we desire. I teach my clients to do this by performing a life review and making two lists. *One is a list of the things that no longer serve a purpose, and the second list includes what is it that you desire instead that is the same, better or different.*

What you focus on expands, and if you are focusing on the lack of physical union with your twin, then you are actually creating more lack and prolonging reunion with your twin. So, rather than focusing on what is lacking, shift your focus first and foremost to what no longer serves a purpose. Second, once you have connected to your higher consciousness, focus on making a list clarifying the question, "*What do I desire?*"

The Seven Dimensions of Vibrational Harmony

Being that your internal vibration becomes the mirror for your life, what do you need to change on the inside to change your life? (This is the same concept that energetically explains how your twin flame mirrors back to you what you need to work on.) There are seven vibrational dimensions that can affect your soul's Being. Recalibrating your vibration and staying in vibrational alignment in every area of your life, also known as harmonic energetic balance, and is The Secret to finding a place of joy, harmony and inner peace. The following seven dimensions are part of my *"Reboot Your Twin Soul"* blueprint, which focuses on starting on the inside of your Being and working outward. These dimensions are affected in the following order from top to bottom starting with your internal energetic Being, expanding outward to your external life:

- Reboot Your Chakras & Stop Feeling Stuck
- Reboot Your Soul & Find Inner Peace
- Reboot Your Mind & Gain Mental Clarity
- Reboot Your Life & Live Your Soul Purpose
- Reboot Your Space & Clear Your Clutter
- Reboot Your Mission & Love Your Livelihood
- Reboot Your Twin Soul & Reunite with Your Twin Flame

Are You in Harmonic Vibration?

The rate at which your energetic Being vibrates can be determined by performing a life review and identifying what is no longer serving your purpose. After making a list for every area of your Being, then prioritize that list and pick the top three things that no longer serve your purpose. Rewrite those areas by writing down exactly what you do want, or *"What do I Desire?"* As you accomplish freedom by letting go, keep prioritizing and checking off that list. *Make sure to keep your focus on the top three areas at all times.* Creating and writing these lists generates action and makes an energetic statement that it has already happened. So I recommend you get that list out of your head and out of your life.

Think of this question as you ponder the idea: *"How could I soulfully expand by performing a life review?"* Taking the time to put some thought into these questions will not only help you recalibrate your vibration, but help you reclaim your life!

1) Energetic –
   a. What energy vampires are in your life — people and things that rob you of your energy?
   b. Do you experience constant fatigue?
2) Spiritual –
   a. What can I do that would help me personally develop, making a connection to my highest good?
   b. Are these thoughts coming from my head or my heart?
   c. I know that I can trust my inner guidance because…?
   d. As I let go, I shift my vibration; in doing so, it activates my intuition. Am I listening to my inner GPS?
3) Mental –
   a. What negative thinking patterns do you have that need reframing?
   b. What negative emotions do you need to release?
   c. What are you affirming in your life on a daily basis?
   d. Are you speaking your truth to others?
4) Physical –
   a. Are you operating at optimal health?
   b. What do you eat?
   c. How do you exercise?
   d. How do you sleep?
5) Space –
   a. Do you need to clear the clutter?
   b. Do you love where you live?
   c. Do you like your personal belongings, or have you settled for less than what you desire?
6) Life –
   a. How are your current relationships?

   b. Do you set loving boundaries?
   c. Are you having fun?
7) Livelihood -
   a. Have you connected to your purpose and making meaningful money?
   b. What is your why?
   c. What is your mission?

Before you know it, you will begin to attract into your reality only things that both serve you purpose and also things that you love!

Recalibrate Your Vibration

In addition to letting go of what consciously no longer serves your purpose, it's just as important to energetically release the past subconscious energetic imprints that have been holding you back in life and in your union. Use the same principle of Cancel – Edit – Delete, cutting all ties to the karmic debris on every plane of your Being. This is the only way to heal soul trauma that occurs from past negative experiences that have occurred in past lives, present life, and future soul contracts that have been made — and in all dimensions and on every plane your Being. I am frequently asked how to release these things so that one can raise their energetic vibration. The following are six steps to take in order to recalibrate your vibration:

Step 1: **Cut Energetic Karmic Cords** – Visual Meditations and Energy Healing Sessions.

Step 2: **Clear Karmic Contracts** – Verbally Release & Visually Cut All Ties to Past, Present and Future Life Contracts and In All Energetic Dimensions.

Step 3: **Clear Etheric Body** – Visually Clear and Release All Negative Energies.

Step 4: **Aura Cleanse** – Let Go of Energetic Walls – Sound Healing – Salt Water Baths.

Step 5: **Pineal Gland Activation** – Facilities the Connection to the Higher Self.

Step 6: **Chakra Clearing and Balancing** – See Tips at the End of this Chapter.

Understanding the Importance of Clearing and Balancing Your Chakras

"Chakra" is derived from the Sanskrit word meaning wheel or disc. The human body has seven major chakras and also many minor chakras. These seven major chakras start from the base of the spine and end on the top of the head. Basically, those chakras possess the wheel of continuous revolving and rotating energy. The root (1st chakra) has the slowest revolving speed while the crown (7th chakra) rotates the fastest.

These seven major chakras function as a vortex of spiraling energy that energetically exchanges our internal and external environments. Both energies are filtered through the aura or energetic field with the purpose of creating a harmonic balance. When the energetic exchange between our body and its aura become blocked or stagnant, it creates an imbalance that causes the frequency of one or more of these chakras to spin at a lower and sometimes higher vibration, frequency or speed. These blocks can affect every area of a person's life and on every level of body, mind and soul. Not only will these energy blocks keep you personally stuck in life but they can prevent your twin-flame reunion from manifesting into physical form.

The 1st chakra starts at the base of the spine extending upward to the 7th chakra located at centrally atop the crown of the head: The following is a list of the seven chakras and their associated color, location, Sanskrit name and their affirmative connection to our feelings, emotions and understandings.

1st chakra (red)	Root Chakra (Muladhara)	I AM	Survival
2nd chakra (orange)	Naval Chakra (Svadhisthana)	I Feel	Creativity
3rd chakra (yellow)	Solar Plexus Chakra (Manipura)	I Do	Power
4th chakra (green/ pink)	Heart Chakra (Anahata)	I LOVE	LOVE
5th chakra (blue)	Throat Chakra (Vishuddha)	I Speak	Expression
6th chakra (indigo)	Third Eye Chakra (Ajna)	I See	Clarity
7th chakra (violet)	Crown Chakra (Sahasrara)	I Understand	Awareness

I would like to point out that the heart chakra is in the exact center, becoming the facilitator assisting in balancing between our acquired characteristics in the lower-self (lower-chakra's) and our higher-self (higher-chakra's) knowledge and wisdom, which creates enlightenment.

The Seven Major Chakras – Our Connection to Our Twin Flames

As previously mentioned, ALL things are made up of light or energy. Everything emits electromagnetic frequencies, creating an energetic field around everything. Chakras are energetic magnets that connect you to every element of your life. Twin flames energetically connect with each other through these energy portals, because their energetic blueprints have the same electromagnetic imprint. Their energetic vibration functions at the exact same frequency and their vibrations send out the same sonar signals back to the Universe. That is the reason the Universe wants twin flames to be together in physical union. The power of two is greater than one; as they raise the love vibration of their union and send out higher vibrational sonar signals, that collectively shifts the planet into a higher vibration.

The importance of understanding this concept is that when twin flames initially merge on a physical plane, their energetic frequency may appear slightly different. This is due to the amount of karma that still needs to be cleared. *Initially one twin has cleared more karma than the other, which automatically creates a higher energetic vibration.* But on a spiritual level, they quickly get on a fast track and work together to raise both energetic vibrations. The one who usually has the higher vibration tends to help assist the other twin flame in raising their vibration.

Are Your Chakras Vibrating at Optimal Frequency?

Personally, I have been a recipient of energy healing and done extensive research. I have been an energy practitioner with combined experiences of nearly 30 years. My energy healing abilities, also known as vibrational medicine, are why I have been able to have such huge success helping other twin flames reboot their own twin souls. *There are a variety of healing tools that can help recalibrate these blocked or lower vibrational frequencies, converting them into higher vibrational energies.* In each lifetime, we experience different life lessons and create different mental, emotional, spiritual and physical experiences – the collection of these experiences become the expression of the soul's DNA makeup and leaves an energetic memory imprint that follows us throughout our soul's journey. Therefore, you might not have a conscious memory of past life experiences, but these past experiences can have a direct impact on your present energetic functionalities. These energetic malfunctions can cause a person to be stuck in their present life. This is why it's so important to release all energetic cords to all past, present or future lifetimes and sever all karmic vows in all dimensions. There are many techniques available to assist you with this process and to help you keep this internal and external energetic exchange in balance.

The energy techniques can vary due to individual training and abilities of each practitioner. Keeping these energy channels open and clear helps you to practice the energetic laws of giving and receiving and to function better in every area of your life — because you are now energetically in harmonic balance. Chances are, if you are feeling stuck in any area of your life, you have energetic blocks.

The Higher-Self Connection - The 12-Chakra System

The lower seven chakras represent our physical Being and lower self; they are highly governed by our physical plane and logical self. *The lower chakras must be cleared of karmic debris before one can advance through the process of connecting to the higher chakras or higher self.* Once you have broken your karmic patterns, the connections to the higher five chakras begin to open up. *These five upper chakras become the genetic makeup of the higher self.* Activation of the higher chakras will help you to connect to the cosmic Universal intelligence through what is called "*The 12 Chakra System.*" Twin flames must be in physical connection before their higher chakras and their higher selves can become fully activated. The purpose of opening this portal is to be granted Divine intelligence and to manifest at a greater level than we do when we operate from the lower self or lower chakras. Twin flames are encoded with "*The 12 Chakra System.*" Once these chakras are fully activated and opened to the cosmic level, twin flames are able to tap into this Universal intelligence. It will give them all the wisdom that they need in order to accomplish their mission. Twins can consciously connect on the galactic level once both twins have connected to their higher selves.

THE 5 HIGHER-SELF CHAKRAS - CREATING *"THE 12 CHAKRA SYSTEM"*

Below are the higher five chakras, their associated colors, and their connection to our higher selves. I would like to point out that you may see these chakras presented in a variety of ways and colors. It's also important to know that we have hundreds of secondary chakras in and around our Being. However, *"The 12 Chakra System"* is something that is activated within all twin flames, but must stay energetically cleared in order to keep open lines of communication with your twin.

8th chakra (pearl)	Soul Star	Gateway to Cosmic
9th chakra (blue/green)	Akashic Records	Karmic Contracts & Agreements
10th chakra (pink)	Divine Creativity	Mission & Soul Purpose
11th chakra (silver)	Cosmic Connection	Universal Intelligence
12th chakra (gold)	Galactic Connection	Direct Communication with Your Twin

The following are seven benefits to staying in harmonic vibration by keeping your chakras balanced:

1. A more positive outlook in terms of your thought processes and in your perception and by gaining wisdom and understanding of events and behaviors.
2. Increased concentration, awareness and even memory.
3. Heightened creativity and resourcefulness are enhanced once you shift your perception.
4. Better and deeper sleep; one might awaken more refreshed in the morning; overall health will also benefit.
5. Reduction of stress in all areas of your life because you will have better control over your emotions with greater tolerance and patience.

6. Improved overall health and well-being. It helps to lower blood pressure which in turn can help prevent strokes and even heart disease. It will also alleviate the stress effect on people suffering from chronic illnesses.
7. Finding balance and vibrational harmony of the major chakras helps to keep all biological, emotional, and spiritual aspects nurtured and can help release physical debris from the body by cleansing physical, emotional and spiritual toxins.

7 Tips to Help You Keep Your Chakras Energetically Cleared and in Harmonic Balance

Energetic blocks in your chakras, or improperly aligned chakras, will prevent your energies from flowing throughout your body, causing interference that can result in negative moods or lower-vibrational thinking patterns. As you remove these energetic blocks, you will restore balance in your life, which is critical to healing on every plane and in every dimension. It will not only harmonize your soul's vibration, but will create harmony throughout the seven dimensions of your soul's Being. The steps involved are fairly simple; it is important to focus on one chakra at one time. Here are five general techniques that can help you remove energetic interference:

Tip 1: **Visualization through Meditation** – a B12 Shot for the Spirit! A very effective technique that clears your mind, as you focus on each chakra and visualize its associated color spinning counterclockwise to remove energetic blocks, then clockwise to restore balance. While doing so, set the intention of what you would like to release, followed by an affirmation of what you would like to restore. Use the Release, Rebalance & Replace concept.

Tip 2: **Sound Therapy** – There are a variety of ways to use sound to shake up the lower dense energies. Binaural beat sounds or crystal singing bowls are good techniques in addition to mantras that generate a vibrational sound within our throat chakra. It enhances the energetic vibration of our energetic channels and aura.

Tip 3: **Crystal Connections** – Stones or crystals carry energetic frequencies based on the type and color. Each are encoded with their own energetic frequency. Thus each type of stone can help to shift different types of energy blocks. Hold the crystal directly on the chakra or right over the chakra. You can even place it directly on top of the chakra which also helps to rebalance or absorb negative energy.

Tip 4: **Exercise – Physical/Breathing** – Exercise is needed to keep healthy and have an energized body, especially in your chakras and aura. Rebound therapy helps to keep energy circulating. Stretching and Yoga helps to keep the chakras in alignment. Deep breathing techniques are another way to remove, shift or balance energy. Here is an exercise – roll a towel up and place it down the center of your spine from the base of your neck downward. Lay on it with arms out to the sides for 3-5 minutes. This will help open your heart chakra. You can also use a Swiss ball by doing a back bend. Lie over the ball on your back for 3-5 minutes.

Tip 5: **Eat Live Foods** – Eating live, organic and wholesome food helps to promote proper pH balance within the body. Detox the body with a gentle 7-10-day full body cleanse and add organic green alkaline foods to your diet. To get your body in an alkaline state, use organic barley. Changing the pH of your body will raise your energetic vibration.

Tip 6: **Keeping the Spine Aligned** – Chiropractic adjustments and soothing massages will help to keep your energy channels open and your chakras vortexes in proper alignment. A full-body massage is an effective way to remove blocks not only from the seven major chakras but many of the minor chakras as well.

Tip 7: **Clear the Clutter** – Eliminate clutter in every area of your life: body, mind, soul and space. This will prevent chaotic external energy patterns from distorting your internal energy by preventing negative interference. Feng Shui is a great way to work with your external energetic spaces. Here is an exercise challenge: Move 11 things around in your home and watch your energy shift.

For additional information and assistance to *"Reboot Your Twin Soul,"* visit my website: www.TwinFlameExpert.com

I have designed this blueprint to help you take action so that you can release your past, raise your vibration and reclaim your life! This program is beneficial for everyone looking for their other half, twin flame or not. We must all pave the energetic pathway tapping into a higher vibrational state of Being and harmonize in unconditional self-love before shifting into any ultimate relationship.

Let's now explore the purpose of connecting to our higher consciousness. We will see in *Key Code 6:6* that the Ascension process is necessary to raise our unconditional love vibration and gain a deeper understanding of *"The Gift"* of unconditional love. We will discover the importance of practicing self-love, so that we can become complete individuals finding harmonic balance in the unconditional Christ consciousness. It teaches us to become an imprint of the Holy Grail vessel as we open our hearts and find balance in giving and receiving unconditional love — not only with our twin, but with the world.

KEY CODE 6:6

Raise Your Unconditional Love Vibration

"Love shrinks or expands according to one's vibration." – Dr. Harmony

YOU MAY BE FAMILAR WITH the renowned *"unconditional love"* Bible verses: 1 Corinthians 13:4-8 (NIV) – *"4 Love is patient, love is kind. It does not envy, it does not boast, it is not proud. 5 It does not dishonor others, it is not self-seeking, it is not easily angered, it keeps no record of wrongs. 6 Love does not delight in evil but rejoices with the truth. 7 It always protects, always trusts, always hopes, and always perseveres – Love never fails. But where there are prophecies, they will cease; where there are tongues, they will be stilled; where there is knowledge, it will pass away."*

The *"Key Code"* takeaway is this: When you learn how to view life through your heart and not your head by letting go of expectations and conditions that are placed on others, it creates harmonic balance and raises our unconditional love vibration. It infuses our lives with compassion. In order to share *"The Gift"* of infinite Divine love, we must keep our energetic love channels open and clear, free of past pains. *Then our lives can vibrate at the same frequency that our hearts desire.* We are now open to sharing our love vibration with others through our radiant hearts.

Most people ignore the wounded child within. Letting go of our painful emotions creates room for expansion of our souls. It allows us to experience love in a new way, while allowing our hearts to speak the new earth-heart language. We become representations of the Christ-conscious voice of the Creator. We become expressions of Divine unconditional love, to be shared between twin flames and then with the world.

Becoming energetically one with ourselves is how we stay connected to the Creator. We produce the same Christ consciousness seen in the imprint of the Holy Grail vessel, which helps us find balance in giving and receiving.

Learning to love without walls keeps our energetic love channels open between self and the Divine. Disconnecting ourselves from our energetic Source only blocks our blessings. When we release emotions and express who we are it keeps us from building walls of protection around our hearts.

We are energetic Beings made in the image of the energetic Creator. Some people have a hard time putting themselves first, but in doing so, you are really putting God first. When we pay attention to ourselves and our needs, it prevents us from stuffing the pain inside, which only creates more pain and suffering.

Learning to take care of myself has taught me to *"see only love"* in others and view life with my heart and not my head. It makes life a more beautiful experience. Those who view taking care of the self as a selfish act look outside of themselves to fill a void within. When we give ourselves away, it depletes our souls and lowers our energetic vibration. There has to be balance to remain connected to ourselves and our Source. *Once we master the art of self-love, sharing that unconditional love becomes our spiritual gift to others.* Now the laws of unconditional love remain balanced with the Universe. Giving unconditional love is the exhale of our soul; receiving unconditional love becomes the inhale.

The art of nurturing the inner child helps us to blossom within, and then we radiate into our lives and then the world. *When we release "old" toxic feelings and emotions and surrender to our ego battles between mind and our heart, it helps us to forgive the past, others and ourselves by creating freedom of the soul.* Now we express the highest form of compassion — experiencing unconditional self-love, self-respect, self-worth and self-acceptance.

What is a Radiant Heart?

When people refer to love, they automatically reference the heart. The heart is a vital organ that supplies blood and oxygen to every other part of our Being. It is the strongest organ in our bodies and it was designed to sustain life. A radiant heart lies deeper than the physical heart. *It is the energetic life force deep within our souls that infuses every cell of our Being with an infinite expression of the Creator.* Keeping an open heart prevents disruption in our life energy and allows us to achieve inner peace and harmony.

The heart chakra is the energetic control center for our love vibration and our feelings. It is the fourth chakra, in the center of the seven chakras. Its primary role is to connect our spiritual Being with our physical existence. When our heart chakra is energetically blocked or imbalanced, it produces a feeling of pain or restriction and is caused by anger, resentment and hatred and so on. This is why a person will say that their heart hurts. They can really feel this restricted energy and it produces real physical pain. These emotional blocks prevent the flow of love and compassion.

When your heart chakra is open, it allows you to feel the love vibration within. The energy that flows through your heart is infused with Eternal love. You are feeling love come to life and put its energy in motion. *Many times I see clients who do not see themselves as being worthy of being loved, and so they block the Holy Grail exchange that prevents them from giving or receiving love.* Keeping these love channels open also raises your unconditional vibration and you can now experience the highest form of Christ-conscious unconditional love — compassion.

Once we let go of the lower self and connect to our higher self, our heart chakra becomes the root chakra of our energetic Being. This is the first step in fully activating "*The 12 Chakra System*" and serves as the base for our higher Being. This opens up the high heart chakra, which is located in the area of the nasal cavity, becoming the gateway of our Christ consciousness.

A Radiant Heart is an Expansive Heart

Due to suppression and creative avoidance, most people block their painful emotions. This numbs our emotions and prevents us from being able to express how we feel. However, if we do not know how to feel the bad, we cannot experience the good emotions. We become wounded children who never healed from the past. Building walls of protection prevents us from experiencing Divine love. It takes the duality of love and hate to experience the balance of positive and negative emotions that follow the energetic laws of the Universe. This means that if we want to experience love, we have to know hate. *Then to expand outward, we have to dive deeper within the depths of our emotions. So, in order to experience great love, we also have to experience great sorrow.* As we expand our emotional range, our souls continue opening up and raises our heart energy, which increases our love vibration. These heightened levels of feelings now allow us to express our souls on a deeper level, creating an expressive radiant heart.

How I Shifted Into Heart Radiance

Several years ago, after my divorce, I decided it was time to heal the wounded child within. I could see repeating patterns of failed relationships and I knew that going forward, I didn't want to take those issues with me. So, I spent four years focusing on me. Even though it didn't always feel like it at the time, it was four of the best years of my life. I got to experience me on every level. I immersed myself into recreating myself, which allowed me to find inner peace and happiness at a level I had not experienced before. I was so complete that I did not need anyone to be responsible for my happiness.

Moving forward, I was ready to experience the ultimate relationship. I no longer needed anyone to complete me — I was ready for someone to complement me. However, I remained closed off, not sure I was willing to open up to giving or receiving great love. It took the Universe to show me I was ready by giving signs and signals that I was ready to share what I had with someone as equally and emotionally stable. Once

I opened up, I did not go searching for love. I simply agreed with the Universe, saying, "*If it's time, then send me the partner I am to experience.*" I even wrote a soulmate letter. I knew nothing about twin flames at the time. I just sat back and waited for the right person to appear.

I already knew that person — he was present in my life and was waiting for me to open up. I just didn't recognize him because I had not been open to receive at the time. We had met on an online dating service and exchanged messages for a few months before actually meeting in person. When we finally met, I was not physically attracted to him. Physical attraction had always been a prerequisite for me — I always wanted to make an explosive connection creating a chemically intoxicating relationship. I needed sparks, and I didn't experience that during our first meeting. We remained friends for a few months after. Then one day he contacted me to get together and the instant I saw him, I said to myself, "*Where has this guy been?*" I seriously took a double take. It was not because he had changed but because I had opened up.

We immediately connected and bonded on a very deep level. It did not take long before we experienced a connection on every plane of our Beings. We shared everything I had wrote in that letter to my soulmate. When the time was right, I read that letter to him. Our relationship was so deep that I thought it was the forever connection that my soul was seeking. We were the envy of everyone and we experienced four years of heaven.

Then after I experienced a failed business partnership, my life-partner (soulmate) and I started a business together. The strain and stress took over — not only of our relationship but of our lives and our souls. Soon after we both became completely exhausted and depleted. At first, I thought our relationship could survive the challenges. But after reaching the pitfalls of hell for an additional three years together, I realized that it was not because of the business that our relationship failed. It was because the core of our Beings were being tapped into, and we each were hitting some deep karma. These areas had to be broken into, digging up the skeletons of our past. He hit a spot inside my soul that no one had ever touched and it hurt — it broke me down to the pit of despair.

I began feeling things I had never experienced in my life. I had never known what it was like to hate anyone before. And he had his own resentful feelings about me. We each ended up not being what the other wanted. I could not understand how this happened. *This was when I reached the "darkest night of my soul."* I spent an extra two years in hell trying to make sure I was not running from myself or things I needed to work on. It was my goal to make this relationship work. I was becoming the "fixer" like I had been in every area of my life. I knew what we had before and I knew we could find it again. I gave everything, my heart, soul and almost even my life. The life force had been completely taken from me. I became so sick and exhausted that I didn't have anything left. I knew I was "unhappy" and even mad at myself for allowing myself to end up in such a situation. Not to mention, I felt trapped. We had built a web together that was so strong, I didn't even know how to get out.

At this point, I was working at my chiropractic office part-time to pay back all the debts that I inherited from my previous failed business partnership. I had sold my vehicle for us to live on while starting our business; I had even sold my house to him. I had no resources of my own and I did not know how I would financially survive if I left. But the longer I stayed, the more exhausted my soul became. Finally, I woke up in the middle of the night and heard a voice that clearly said; "*You have to get out of here; this is killing you.*" I immediately knew that it was time to go. I didn't know how I would survive; I just knew I was already dying inside.

I was forced to trust and to listen to my wounded inner Being that I had ignored. I left, even knowing that the only thing I could count on to support myself was a $3000 line of credit. Sure, I had all kinds of fear of how I would survive, but I had more fear of knowing that I was in a relationship that was killing me. Within a few days, I located a furnished condo that didn't require my having to take care of much but myself. Then I notified him of my decision to leave and moved out 10 days later. There is nothing worse about being alone than being alone in a failing relationship!

My wounded heart felt as if it had been stabbed with a knife. But as I began healing, I realized that he had expanded my heart. He took me from the depths of the greatest love to the pit of hell and I realized that was what I needed to experience before being able to know the greatest unconditional love — something he didn't know how to give me. But I understood that he was the catalyst I needed to break my karmic pattern. I vowed to no longer be the "fixer" anymore. I didn't want to take care of anyone else anymore. I wanted to take care of me. And as I continued to heal and began seeing him as my teacher, I realized that he taught me the greatest amount of compassion that I had ever felt in my life.

God knew what he was doing by making sure I would not forget this lesson. We jointly share custody of our beautiful fur child, Champ and we both deeply love that dog. And so we have managed to heal our pasts; we each work on ourselves, in our own way. Just prior to my leaving, I gave him tie-dyed roses, thanking him for teaching me to color outside the lines. We also managed to work through untangling our web in a respectful way. I know that somewhere in his heart, something has changed for the better so that he can experience life in a better way.

During the healing process of letting go, I also discovered that we had a mother-son relationship in a previous life. In the last two years of our relationship, that was exactly how it played out. On multiple occasions I would state: "*I am not your mother.*" And I could tell that emotionally, it was his own inner child that was hurting; he had lashed out at me in the same way he had always done with his parents. Later, when I was diagnosed with uterine cancer (the uterus emotionally represents home life), I relived many of the same emotions and anger. I didn't think it was fair that he could move forward and I was left to clean up another mess of his. Holding onto hate and resentment will manifest inward and surfaces in the form of cancer. I thought I had forgiven him by that point, but it surfaced again. Then I realized I had not forgiven myself for giving myself away. I vowed to never do so again. Relationships must have a harmonic energetic balance creating the Holy Grail exchange or our Being becomes depleted. It shifts us out of alignment with our energetic Creator.

It took being dragged through the pits of hell before I could surrender to the deepest layer of my karmic debris. When you reach the bottom of that pit, there is no one left but yourself to reconcile your own differences between head and heart. It took the assistance of my twin flame to help me clear the pit, and to clear the deepest part of myself. You have to reach the core of this pit before it breaks open your heart, releasing everything that has been stuffed from the outside in. It is imperative you fill yourself up on the inside with self-love so that you can experience a radiant heart and then share unconditional love.

The Secret to Raising Your Unconditional Love Vibration is Loving Yourself First

"When we experience loving ourselves it is our opportunity to experience God's eternal love firsthand." – Dr. Harmony

Every human being has experienced pain and suffering at some point in life and those emotions leaves open wounds within our energetic Being. These past negative experiences become locked inside the memory of the DNA of our soul. Then when we unconsciously connect to those past negative feelings and experiences, it creates heightened emotional sensitivity. *This causes us to lash out at others, making another person responsible for what we haven't been willing to accept accountability for within ourselves.* The past now plays a part in our current emotional status by triggering fears, anxiety, turmoil and dismay. Fragments of these past imprints remain within our energetic makeup at the beginning of our incarnation and throughout the soul's evolution. The wounded child within is in pain and asking for attention, but usually gets ignored and unnoticed. Now your suffering that shows up in every area of your life becomes a reflection of the status of that inner child. *When we reconcile the wars of our past, it breaks the bondage that has been holding us hostage in all areas of our life.* Then we can find inner peace and happiness!

The secret to healing your life is honoring and embracing that inner child. The following are six suggestions to help you start treating yourself like a first-class Being!

Suggestion 1: **Be Gentle with Yourself.** There is no such thing as perfection. Learn to nurture your soul by watching everything you think, speak or do. Time to release all guilt that only creates self-sabotage which will rob you of your inner peace.

Suggestion 2: **Compassion.** Learn to be kind to yourself in all situations and remember that you are human and you will make mistakes. Use those mistakes to learn and grow. By giving yourself permission to honor your emotions in all situations, you begin to become your own best friend and start treating yourself like a first-class Being.

Suggestion 3: **Self-Acceptance**. Try seeing yourself through the eyes of others with no judgment and only unconditional love. When you can become accepting of yourself, you become more tolerant of others and learn to accept them too.

Suggestion 4: **Be Honest with Yourself**. It's often easy to try to justify certain circumstances or rationalize a situation with your mind. This causes the idea to become tainted or twisted to match what the mind believes, rather than how our heart truly sees it. Look inward and listen to your heart and soul — it will always tell you the truth in every situation. Then make it a practice to stay in harmony with your soul. This will help you to feel safe with your own actions and build strength and courage that will support you during times of change.

Suggestion 5: **See Only Love**. Shift your perception by looking at the positive attributes and actions that you engage in. A shift in your consciousness will allow you to heal and embrace every mistake, your faults or errors. It only creates confusion when you focus on the negative, which gives you a false sense of being imperfect. That does not honor your soul as a spiritual Being and takes you further away from the Source.

Suggestion 6: **You Get to Choose**. Allow yourself the opportunity in every situation to take responsibility for your choices and actions in life. If you don't like where you are in life or how things are going, only you have the power to change your choices and your reality. There are no bad choices — there are only occurrences creating a series of lessons that connect your steps to a higher place of thinking. That allows you to make better choices next time. Let go of blaming yourself and others. Start fresh with a clean slate and paint a new picture. Watch your life begin to change.

The following are suggestions to help you gain self-respect, self-worth and self-acceptance.

Self-Respect

Suggestion 1: **Treat Yourself Respectfully**. If you want respect, start by treating yourself with respect. Don't down play your own abilities. Imagine that you are all that you want to be. Even if you are not where you want to be, continue treating yourself as if you are already there. Watch yourself blossom.

Suggestion 2: **Change Your Thoughts**. Negative thoughts have a great impact on how you view yourself. Pay attention to those negative thoughts; notice when you tell yourself you are not meeting your own expectations. Replace that negative thought pattern with positive self-talk. It takes 100 positives to cancel one negative thought, so it is important to feed the mind with positivity on a regular basis. Use positive affirmations to help you achieve your goals.

Suggestion 3: **"Who Am I?"** Get to know who you are and honor your emotions and feelings. Learn to appreciate your good qualities. Spend time reviewing everything that is positive about yourself. I can promise you that you will begin to notice that you are worth more than you give yourself credit for! Make a journal of your characteristics, talents and abilities and create a good relationship with yourself.

Self-Worth

Suggestion 1: **Keep Your Promises to Yourself.** Make time to make yourself matter! Perform regular check-ins, reviewing your emotions, feelings and interactions in life. Make sure that if you have set goals for yourself, to keep those commitments. Remember that it is progress, not perfection.

Suggestion 2: **Create Personal Empowerment**. Building self-confidence is important for you to gain that inner fulfillment. Find ways to educate yourself with knowledge that supports your desires. Creating inner strength starts with finding activities that set you up to win – not fail like you have previously done. Do things that will give you a sense of self-accomplishment and before long, your inner child will be standing up with muscles flexed!

Suggestion 3: **Let Go of the Idea of Rejection.** Especially self-rejection. Fear of rejection is one of the primary reasons that people do not follow through with their aspirations in life. Learn to stand tall with your chin up and don't take things personally. More often than not, when a situation feels like rejection, it's really coming from within, leaving you feeling the void. Don't allow someone else to rob you of what is missing, because most often it is not the other person rejecting you, it's you rejecting yourself. Look in the mirror, because that is who you are running from. Learn to face the reflection in the mirror and you will quickly see your fears dissipate.

Self-Acceptance

Suggestion 1: **Forgive Yourself.** Let go of the notion of regrets and see your mistakes or your quirks as an opportunity to grow and expand. Let your inner child speak up, and listen. Be patient with yourself. After your inner child has been heard, apologize to that inner child, let it go and move on!

Suggestion 2: **See Your Inner Child's Point of View.** Take a step outside of your situation and look inward. Detach yourself from the pain of the emotions and decide that it is time to let it go. Now you can begin to see yourself with only love and that inner child will be beaming with joy.

Suggestion 3: **Let Self-Acceptance Crack Open Your Heart.** Find the deepest part of your Being. Stop worrying about trying to change yourself. Focus on your feelings and connecting to that inner Being that lets you get in tune with you. Play music that touches your heart. Do things that will make you feel again; it will help you to open your heart chakra. Allow yourself to feel your emotions, embrace the feelings and then fill yourself up with the essence of your energetic Being.

I challenge you to take a moment right now and review your level of self-respect, self-worth and self-acceptance. Take note of your level of self-love. Now, over the next 11 days, focus on just one main area within your heart that needs attention. *Then over the course of the next 11 days, do one thing each day to nurture that inner child.* Then re-evaluate again at the end of the 11 days and see how much your inner child has blossomed.

Now that we have a good understanding of ways to raise your unconditional love vibration by nurturing your inner child and creating a radiant heart, let's take a look at how that relates to relationships outside of ourselves.

How Do We Love Unconditionally?

You have mastered the heart language of unconditional love once you can express your love and stop withdrawing it. Withholding only blocks your blessing of being able to receive *"The Gift"* of unconditional love. *But when you can truly love without walls, it will give you freedom in all your relationships.* It is a choice to believe in the magic of love, and a choice that will make all your fears fade away. Release the fear of losing or being hurt, and the reality of having a romance with life will begin to resonate with your heart's desires. This will create a dreamlike state and a life you no longer have to imagine. Your dreams will become a part of your reality.

When we let go of all judgment and predispositions, we let go of these notion that we have to hold onto past hurts and pain. We begin to feel that it is safe to learn to love again. When our hearts are filled from within, producing radiance that reflects outward, it serves a purpose. Then our unconditional love vibration becomes *"The Gift"* to ourselves. *Once you can comprehend and understand love that comes directly from the Divine, you will be ready to share that same feeling of unconditional love with others because you no longer need it for yourself.* Your soul was intended to feel a blissful state and it helps you be in the present moment. By enjoying the language of true love, everyone and every experience along your journey becomes an opportunity to experience harmony and balance in all areas of your life.

At What Love Channel Do You Vibrate?

More often than not, people operate on two different love channels. This is primarily because neither person knows how to express themselves effectively enough to understand what the other is saying. *One person will tell the other what they want and what their needs are, while the other is trying to meet those needs.* The second person becomes frustrated by giving and giving; no matter how hard they try, it is not good enough. It leaves both feeling frustrated and confused. They feel there is no hope and ask themselves, "*Why bother to continue?*" What neither one realizes is that they are operating on two different love channels. Usually, it is the Divine feminine that has a history of abandonment, where lack of commitment becomes a repeated pattern that creates feelings of not being good enough. They are trying to fill that void with love from the other. *Typically, the Divine masculine is trying to give what the Divine feminine has been asking for, but they have been emotionally emasculated by control issues at a young age and never experienced or exercised the skills it takes to do what is being asked of them.* So, no matter how hard they try, they don't know how to follow through. The efforts they are putting out are perceived as not good enough. The only way to break this cycle is for each to work within themselves, releasing their past and learning self-love that creates self-worth, then allowing them each to tune into the same love channel.

How to Identify Abandonment

Feelings of not being good enough will produce feelings of rejection, leaving people feeling as though they don't matter. Feeling abandoned generates anger and resentment, causing people to withdraw. Expecting someone outside themselves to fill this void not only sets up the other person to fail but creates pain that causes you to energetically push away the person you are seeking to fill your void. *You react to not only the present situation, but to every past emotional pain and trauma that has never been healed.* This pain can only be healed from within. Abandonment issues derive from childhood abuse, divorce, lack of love at birth, a history of being ridiculed or teased, along with many past life imprints that remain in the DNA of our energetic souls. Most often, those dealing with abandonment issues are givers. They give themselves away; as much as they want love from another, they are not open to receive it. They have built walls of steel trying to protect that wounded child inside. Yet, they are resentful for being givers and not receiving in return what they expected.

This is not unconditional love. This energetic imbalance pushes people away, leaving one with more feelings of abandonment, and the cycle continues. Letting go of abandonment starts by letting go of the past and then forgiving every person and negative experience in this lifetime and in past lives. *I see this to be very common with twin flames; many have past pains that are traced back to the abandonment from their other half of their Divine soul during the Fall of Atlantis.* This is why I frequently recommend that twins work on forgiveness to heal their abandonment issues. I can tell you from experience that this is not easy. But identifying the issues and then forgiving others and the self is "*Key*" to healing abandonment issues.

Top 3 Secrets to Having Loving Relationships

Secret #1: **Effective Communication.** If you find yourself in a relationship that is not progressing, be honest and communicate your concerns with that person. Express your feelings from your heart. This will diffuse conflict. It is only your perception that creates anything otherwise. They will respect you for being able to open up and they will naturally reciprocate, which 99% of the time resolves all issues. *The reason why most relationships of any nature fail is because of a lack of effective communication.* Be honest with yourself! Honesty comes from speaking from your heart. If you are speaking from your head, you are not being honest. Learn to express your desires and not be afraid to ask for what you want in all relationships.

Secret # 2: **Compromise.** The second-most common reason relationships suffer is from the lack of compromise. Compromising and cooperating with one another is "*Key*" to any successful relationship. This also follows the energetic laws of harmonic balance between giving and taking. This produces harmony needed to create a healthy relationship. Monitor all your relationships and review if they are out of balance. Are they still serving your purpose? *But do not run away from the lesson, because another teacher will come along and teach you the same lesson — only this time the Universe will speak louder, and again each time until you get it.* Make a conscious effort to practice compromise in all interactions in your life. It is so important to surround yourself with positive influences that lift you up, rather than pull you down. Just make sure you are not the one pulling someone else down.

Secret #3: **Let Go of Lust.** Let go of the need for chemical attraction. There is nothing wrong with passion, but there is a difference in that verses addiction to lust, which is superficial and usually codependent in nature. *People with addictive behaviors tend to also be addicted to a chemical reaction produced in relationships that are built on lust.* Many times a person will stay in toxic relationships that create the highs and lows of drama. When it's really good, it's really good. When it's really bad, it's really bad. Breaking these addictive behaviors can be as challenging as if you were addicted to heroin. It is always that next fix that they need to fill them up on the inside. *Chemical attraction is real; it stimulates neurotransmitters in the brain to produce endorphins and adrenaline that enhances feelings.* Unconditional love is not infatuation, nor does it have anything to do with sexual desires. Relationships revolving around lust always involve being connected to someone who is your type and that you feel physically attracted to. This presents itself at the top of the twin-flame identifier list. In a twin-flame relationship, if you are not feeling a chemical spark, then it is the Universe's way of breaking down ego. I hear this same common theme repeatedly, "They are not my type." Next time you need a fix, try reassessing the situation and determine if it's Lust or Love.

The Secret To Loving Relationships with Parents and Family

Learn to love your family, ALL of your family. Most people run and hide from family. Look at all the conflict that occurs during holidays. All the unresolved issues come to the surface forcing everyone to see themselves while still blaming the others for their pain. Now we have an entire group of wounded inner children having screaming fits! *Every situation offers an opportunity to heal not only your heart but the hearts of others.* Learn to have compassion and tolerance for others. Try seeing the innocence in all situations. When faced with conflict, imagine your love surrounding that person with your highest good intentions. Send them thoughts of love and shower them with blessings, no matter what has happened in the past. Be open to forgiving and let go of any past wrongdoings. *Holding on to any hard feelings only keeps you from loving to your fullest potential.* No matter how difficult it is or how much you feel someone has wronged you, choose to take the high road, honoring yourself by sending the other human waves of love from your heart. This is what a radiant heart does. This kind of love will awaken your own spirit, creating more compassion and a love for life towards all creatures and mankind. You can heal anything with love.

Healing your past family issues will help you create better relationships not only with them but with yourself and others who are in your life for a reason and a season. *Forgiveness of another person is a Divine way to show love and respect for them.* You are setting the example for them. You are the extension of our energetic Source, here on this planet to represent the Creator. We all are human and everyone makes mistakes. *Too often people keep their eye on the problem, rather than focusing on the solution and strategizing a way to rise above the negativity of a situation.* Continuing to focus on the issue will only create more conflict. Be a wise person. Let go and choose forgiveness over the need to be in control. *The need to be right is merely an egotistical desire in the mind's eye and only creates resentment within the heart of the beholder.* Try putting yourself in someone else's shoes. Don't assume. Someone might just be having a bad day. They may even be at fault, but remember, they are hurting. See the good in them and try showering them with unconditional love. This gives you an opportunity to become their teacher while they look at themselves in your mirror. This moment will bring more self-awareness into their life. Don't be the "fixer,"— choose to let them fix themselves!

While we may need to let go of toxic relationships and limit the amount of time we spend in the lower vibrational presence of others, here I am suggesting that you learn how to accept others for who they are by practicing patience and learn how to set loving boundaries rather than building walls that only shuts others out of our lives. In doing so, you are only masking the problem and not creating solutions by learning how to express yourself and speak your truth from the heart.

Release Your Ex

We all try to move forward after ending relationships, but we usually take our old ways with us. The relationship may end but the problems remain. *You must purify your old ways if you don't want to take your Ex with you.* Every relationship creates the ebb and flow of Universal harmony. That means all encounters are equally proportioned; each person is responsible for a portion of the outcome. So even though you want to blame the other person for your pain, you are equally responsible. This is how the energetic exchange in all interactions works. *In order to break these patterns, it has to stop with the last person with whom you were energetically out of synchronicity with.* Spend time reflecting back to when those patterns began, and start clearing those energetic attachments to those relationships. What did you need to learn from your Ex? What did they teach you? Don't blame them, they were your teacher. Let your actions mirror back their reflection and they will heal also.

When I say release your Ex, I am referring to energetically cutting all ties to past painful experiences. Start by making amends, even if just energetically. Receiving energy healing and keeping your chakras in balance is a good way to cleanse your internal electrical system of any short-circuits.

If you have children and there is a need to continue relating to your Ex, you must be able to forgive and be cordial. If you are holding onto grudges and won't let it go, this is teaching your children the same patterns. And for God's sake, PLEASE don't put your children in the middle of something that should be between you and your Ex. Set good examples for them. I know this is a common occurrence, so I feel it is worth reminding you of this. I can tell you from experience using my example, that it is possible to carry unconditional love forward with your Ex!

When my husband and I got a divorce, sure, there was pain and hurtful words. A lot of things could have kept us from choosing to stay connected. However, I knew that I did not want anything negative going forward with me. *My ex-husband and I both have worked on our relationship; his new wife says we have the "fairy tale divorce."* He has always been a strong provider and played an important role in my journey. He has remained in my children's lives and is the only father that they have ever known. He chose to be a part of their lives; he adopted my son at the same time we got a divorce. We remain friends to this day. I am invited to all the functions and holidays and his family remains a part of my life. His new wife has made it a point to go out of her way to send me special messages, letting me know how I have inspired her and that you never know what it takes to bring people together — but that she was glad that I was in her life. I consider her a very good friend. When

I had to share my diagnosis of uterine cancer with family, they were the first two people I contacted. When I asked for help, they didn't even question, they showed up. I knew that I had to be strong for everyone else and I chose to go to them for my own strength.

Now, I will say it again – LET IT GO! The outcome in ALL situations is up to you and what you want out of it. If you are not getting what you want, only you can change it. Don't put blame on the other person or make the comment: "I would, but …" There are no buts! Release your Exes, and make peace with them! You will set your soul free!

Master *"The Gift"* of Unconditional Love – The New Earth Heart Language

Unconditional love is the Divine language of heaven; what we experience in heaven shall be experienced on the new earth. *Loving ourselves helps to raise the unconditional love vibration of the planet as it shifts into fifth-dimensional energies, creating a new earth heart language of Christ consciousness.* When we learn how to forgive we share *"The Gift"* of unconditional love and we demonstrate compassion – not only for ourselves but the world. Make it a point to speak the new earth heart language by making a list of all those that have wronged you and decide to forgive – including yourself!

Write a Forgiveness Letter

I challenge you to review your life and look at every person, situation or experience that has caused you pain. Then choose to see those experiences as teachers. Action speaks loud! There is power in writing things down. For every bit of pain and suffering that you are holding on to, it's time to let it go! Write a letter to each of those people, including yourself, and do whatever it takes to feel those emotions as you write. When you are done, burn the letters and let it go once and for all. You will feel lighter and your soul will feel the freedom it was meant to experience! And for all the twin flames who have experienced deep soul trauma from Atlantis, it's time to let it go so you can go home! *Let it go by forgiving your twin flame, because holding onto this painful experience could just be what is keeping you from experiencing the relationship that you came all these years to achieve!*

In closing, I would first like to point out that *Key Code 6:6* has been appointed the heart chakra of this book. There are 5 *"Key Codes"* before it and 5 *"Key Codes"* after. This infuses *"Twin-Flame Code Breaker"* with an unconditional love vibration that radiates throughout this Divine message. It is meant to help others learn to raise their unconditional love vibrations, so we can all experience the Holy Grail imprint of the Christ consciousness of the Universe — thus, creating heaven on the new earth.

In addition, the number one reason I have heard people say they don't honor their inner child is because they don't have enough time. Exactly! We don't have enough time NOT to nurture ourselves. It is time to start waking up to Being rather than Doing. It is time to STOP making EXCUSES and start taking personal responsibility for ourselves and our actions. While growing up, we had many expectations of others placed on us, not to mention our own. Release the expectations and false sense of not being good enough. Don't let these things rob you of raising your unconditional love vibration, preventing you from receiving *"The Gift"* of speaking the new earth heart language. For once in your life, choose not to block the blessing; allow unconditional Eternal love to harmoniously flow in and out of your heart and your life. Now, go out into the world with a radiant heart and give someone who is hurting a big hug or a smile! I can promise you that if you do so, you will find your way home – a place of inner peace and happiness!

In *Key Code 7:7*, I will show you why you can relax. Everything is in Divine order. There is no need for control of a twin-flame relationship. Everything unfolds as it should. Practice patience and focus on raising your love vibration, and watch your heart shift into radiance.

KEY CODE 7:7

Practice Patience – Everything is in Divine Order

"When we practice patience and learn to listen to our intuition, we begin to translate the language of our Divine guidance, realizing that everything in our lives' unfolds the way it was intended to be." – Dr. Harmony

A TWIN-FLAME JOURNEY CAN BE INTENSE – no doubt! But just like any other adventure or journey, it is nothing more than an individual's perception and choice as to how they choose to experience the ride. Two people can be on the same trip and have completely different experiences. Because of free will, we get to choose whether to move forward along our path with ease and grace — or with resistance, which only creates hardships and struggles. Since we prearrange our lessons to learn during each lifetime, we should trust that everything is in Divine order. By understanding this, we can begin to practice patience, knowing that we ultimately have no control over our final destination. However, we are granted free will, which means we do get to choose the way we go about the journey and how long it takes us to arrive.

Choose the Path of Least Resistance

Everything about life always presents us with two paths, or two decisions to make. As we process the options and decide the direction we choose to go, our decisions come from a place of head or heart. Until we fully develop our intuition, it can be hard to tell which one is speaking and to understand where the answers are coming from. Typically, we tend to proceed in the direction of logical thinking. We often wonder what difficulties we might face during our journey, or we worry about the outcome of a situation. *Most people proceed in the direction that might feel like the path of least resistance based on the viewpoints of their mind, rather than learning to listen to their heart and hearing what the soul is really speaking.*

Processing and interpreting these thoughts, feelings and actions helps us develop our intuition as we begin to understand that the resistance we may be feeling actually comes from the subconscious mind, not our gut guidance. What happens is we run from our fears of the unknown and begin to follow what feels comfortable. Eventually we realize that what felt like the path of least resistance was really only making a comfortable decision, rather than stretching our comfort zone. *Making decisions from the heart are rarely comfortable decisions, because our souls seek to expand and evolve, and that stretches our comfort zone.* Therefore, we end up making a decision based on false perceptions. This only holds us back because we are only running from the shifts that are required for us to change.

It does take practice to understand and reach a level of awareness allowing you to follow your intuition rather than your false perceptions. Only then can we fully observe the fork in the road as an opportunity to choose the path of least resistance, which might create some initial discomfort because it requires change. *In the long run, when we let go and decide to go with the flow, it can actually shorten the time it takes us to reach our destination.* As we develop, it becomes easier to discern between our head verses heart decision making. Becoming more energetically in tune, we begin to intuitively connect to our guidance. Going forward with new decisions, we begin to trust the process. So when we come to that fork in the road, we can clearly see which path will direct us forward with ease and grace rather than hardship and struggles.

Let Go of Conditions & Expectations

Life is a personal journey for everyone, and not just for twin flames. Therefore, choosing the path of least resistance doesn't always mean aligning with your other half. Your twin might have chosen the path of resistance. Remember that everyone learns their own way and in their own time. The sooner you can see them with unconditional love and compassion and accept their decisions, the sooner you can focus on your own journey and keep your attention directed upon what will raise your own vibration.

Clients are always asking me: *"When is my twin coming back?"* and *"How long will it take before they stop running?"* They often state they have no intention of giving in until their twin decides they are going to start giving them what they are expecting. I remind them that a twin-flame journey is all about unconditional love. Such expectations of how your twin should be fulfilling your own needs before you yourself decide to trust the process, is setting your twin up to fail. Yes, I said fail!

Here is an example: I have clients who will send a text message to their twin flame who has been silent. They expect a response, or a certain response. Not only does this create more anger, frustration and confusion for themselves, but these self-serving actions only set your twin up to fail your expectations. *The real issue here is that your twin is teaching you by reflecting back your need to let go of control.* If you are doing this, I suggest you let your twin go and know that everything is in Divine order. Your agreement was prearranged, so you don't have any reason to try to control the outcome. You must practice patience. This is teaching you to focus on yourself.

The Law of Magnetic Forces

In Faraday's law of magnetic forces and magnetic fields, we can see the science behind the karmic purge or the push-pull phase of a twin-flame relationship. This law describes positive and negative polarities of energy. These polarities act as an unspoken language that exist between any two people and their interactions. For instance, resistance equals resistance. *If you approach someone with resistance or someone else comes at you with a negative, resistant attitude, it will put both of you in a defensive mode that will set the precedence for a confrontational interaction.* The opposite is also true; for example, you pull back because you are fed up with your twin. You start to connect to your higher self and by doing so, you feel peace and you feel like you have let go. Then your twin starts contacting you again and you go back into your old lower-self ways by giving your power away. You start redirecting your energy towards your twin, thinking they got it this time. But they feel the direct energy coming towards them, unconsciously this causes your twin to pull back and then they disappear again.

Technically, this is setting them up to fail. Having expectations sets you up for frustration. You reprocess your emotions, then blame your other half for what they have done to you. Sound familiar? The "*Key*" to staying in vibrational alignment is to stay within your own higher self and stay connected to your own path. Your higher self is what your twin is attracted to and what they are energetically searching for, rather than the negative energetic cling that they feel when you direct your attention on them or are always available to them. These direct energetic forces will only continue to push them away. *Because of these energetic laws, when you focus on the lack of your twin, it really creates more lack and more separation.* When you release all the past negative experiences and you learn to practice more self-love, that is when you can stop trying to fill your own void with your twin flame, which then stops pushing them away.

Learn to Trade Expectations for Appreciation

As we now know, unconditional love has NO conditions. When you can grasp this idea, it will allow you to start to trade your expectations for appreciation of not only the journey but also your twin flame. See them as your teacher; allow them to show you what you need to work on within yourself. They deserve credit for that. I sometimes have clients who complain about their twin and are so fed up that they don't ever want to be with their other half or even to see them ever again. This is viewing the journey as a negative experience and blaming the other twin flame. *Try seeing the journey from your twin's point of view and then try to see them with unconditional love and compassion.* Watch your own heart begin to open up and feel the magic happen within your own soul! That in itself is enough to thank your twin for the journey.

Don't assume!

Most of the time, assumptions are made when an outcome does not meet one's expectation. For instance, let's say you don't hear back after texting your twin. Now you have the idea that you know how they feel or that they are off doing something they shouldn't be. You get mad about what they are doing before you even know why or what they are doing. These assumptions only causes you more unnecessary confusion and frustration. So, you feel the need to express yourself, telling your twin off — usually in a text message that can get misconstrued. *This need to express yourself and to be heard by the other person before hearing all the facts is only self-serving.* It becomes another way to set your twin up to fail. It is important to get all the facts correct before speaking your mind.

I would like to add here that I am not talking about allowing someone to walk all over you. You do need to set loving boundaries and become more assertive. There is a difference between this and letting go of expectations and not placing conditions on others.

STOP Focusing on the Outcome!

In addition to letting go of expectations, it's important to let go of the outcome throughout your twin-flame journey. I work with a lot of twins who live in different countries, much less in the same cities. They are already prearranging their life, trying to figure out how it's all going to work in the end. *The reality is, these thoughts not only block you from experiencing the present moment, but it also sets your twin-flame journey up for failure.* You already think you know what is going to happen; now if it doesn't happen, you decided that it was a bad experience and was not meant to be. This way of thinking is another block that will not only hold you back in your twin-flame relationship, it will keep you stuck in life and set your own self up for failure.

When you can let go of the outcome, you can now begin to move into alignment with Divine order and allow your destiny to unfold. That will put you in a position to attract everything you need in your life — including your twin flame. Now you begin to practice the patience that helps you learn how to shift into your own destiny. The following are five suggestions to help you practice patience:

Suggestion 1: **Listen More – Speak Less.** When you allow others to be fully heard, you will have mastered the highest form of self-expression one can achieve. Silence now becomes the voice of God speaking through you. *Why do you think monks go into silence? It is their way of hearing God's voice.* You too can accomplish this same art of silent expression, once you become aware of the power that lies within this form of expressing self. Now, you too can allow silence to become your inner voice, which will then synchronize your thoughts with emotions, while making a connection with another.

Suggestion 2: **Sit Quietly and Just Be.** Many times we find ourselves in the middle of the hustle and bustle of the rat-race of life. Practice bringing some Zen into your life. *Take a few minutes every day to experience the stillness of God by going within and clearing the mind.* This exercise takes time to develop, but eventually, we learn to slow our minds and gain tolerance for ourselves and others in the process. When we practice this form of patience, we begin to feel the inner peace rise up inside of ourselves, eventually becoming inner bliss!

Suggestion 3: **Stop and Breathe.** The lungs are the most under-used organ in the body. A lack of oxygen creates numerous physical complications. I have seen patients over the years holding their breath due to stress, worry and just racing through life. *When feeling rushed, practice stopping, identifying your anxiety and then taking a deep breath.* Feel the presence of peace wash over your body and the tension wash away. Once we learn to relax, we develop an understanding that things occur in our lives at the exact moment they are supposed to, and this teaches us to deepen our faith and let go of the need for control.

Suggestion 4: **Ask Yourself, "Why Am I Being Impatient?"** When feeling the inner drive to push forward, stop and ask yourselves the question, "*Why am I being impatient?*" This question creates awareness that allows us to see that, more often than not, there is no a reason for us to have to feel so rushed in all of our experiences. It is merely an illusion of the mind. When we let go of this control, we can start to go with the flow and enjoy the journey. However, like a muscle that contracts and expands during a workout, this will take practice. But if you do so, before you know it you will be going downstream.

Suggestion 5: **Steps Back are Really Steps Forward.** When hitting road blocks along our journey, it can feel like a step back at first. But usually, it's really just an opportunity to re-evaluate a situation so we can go forward. When you hit these barriers, remind yourself that it could always be worse. Start by asking yourself, "*What is the worst thing that could happen in this situation?*" Then shift your perception and realize your situation could always be worse. Now you are really just re-evaluating and prioritizing your direction. *Take this opportunity to set crystal-clear intentions that will open your energetic channels, creating awareness that will help to steer you in the right direction in life.* I challenge you to practice letting that one step back take you three steps forward.

Watch for Mysterious Messages

Once we grasp the idea of practicing patience, realizing that everything is in Divine order, we can open up our energetic channels that enhance our receptivity and intuition. Learning to get out of our own way opens us up to the idea of allowing things to naturally unfold. This is where the magic happens. *I will share the concept I use: Ask – Listen – Allow.* First, our guides and angels cannot help us until we ask. But sometimes, even if we do ask, we may be either non-receptive to the answers or we may not be listening and watching for the signs. Then we block our blessings. The answers will always arrive; your guides gain great joy by being able to express their presence for you to see and understand. Mysterious messages are indicators that everything is in Divine order.

I have practiced the idea of asking, listening and then allowing in my own life for many years. But it was not until learning to let go on a deeper level — raising my vibration and connecting to my higher self — that I experienced the true meaning of alignment and getting in the vortex of all possibilities. (I will go into this concept in greater detail in *Key Code 10:10*) Despite years of practice, it was not until after I identified my role as a twin flame that I was able to fully exercise the concept of getting in the vortex.

I have found it common for twins to feel that they cannot trust their intuition. As members of society in general, we ask for signs and then question if the messages we receive are real, or if we are just seeking an answer so desperately that we perceive signs to be made up in our heads. I have heard other concerns about receiving "mystical messages" and whether to acknowledge them as good or evil. Due to acquired beliefs and prior teachings, they think the signs may be coming from a negative force and leading them in the wrong direction. *My response is this: our guides and angels transcend all lower darker energies; those lower vibrational energies cannot reach the higher realms.* So, if you are operating at your higher self and moving up through the Ascension process, those negative energy forces cannot enter the higher energetic planes. It is safe to trust your guides and the angels that govern these realms.

This is not to say that during your shift to your higher self that you might not invite in lower vibration thinking such as fear and negativity that can keep you trapped. *With practicing your spiritual gifts, you will shift your awareness, feelings and thoughts into the higher vibrational planes.* Here are a few ideas that can help you learn to communicate with your guides:

- Ask for guidance.
- Ask to make a direct connection with them.
- Learn to understand and feel their energetic vibration.
- Ask for assistance in helping to raise your energetic vibration.
- Ask your guides to help you make a connection to your higher self.
- Ask for signs.
- Ask for assistance to expand your intuition.
- Listen to your intuition.
- Watch for signs.
- Be open to receive your answers.
- Ask your guides to reveal their language and for you to gain an understanding of it.

My Divine guidance has instructed me to share with you a few of my own experiences. I have learned to allow these voices of wisdom to guide my every step in every area of my life. One of the most important things *I have learned about the idea of letting go and listening to my heart is that it's very important to learn the language of the messengers.* So, ask your angels and guides to direct you towards information that will lead you to the answers you are seeking. In doing so, you will learn how to interpret these messages and begin to recognize the presence and identify their energy.

My Mystical Messages:

I have had many encounters with the 11:11 number sequence (I will explain the meaning behind this phenomenon in detail at the end of this chapter), right before, during and after assisting my twin flame with his own spiritual awakening. My twin also saw signs, but he did question them at times with logical thinking. Questioning whether these signs are real or not creates constriction of energy by distorting the perception of a person's receptivity, preventing them from being able to allow and accept the messages. I have seen other twins battle this head-and-heart dichotomy. That is why it's important to learn how to let go of logic and allow.

Once I attended an event at the chiropractic college where my twin and I studied. Upon arriving I was asked to sign in, including time of arrival. I looked at the clock and it was 11:11. During this time, I was playing detective and connecting the dots to every clue that I was uncovering that lead me towards identifying my role as a twin flame. I repeatedly received phone calls from the number 1111. I would answer and no one was there. My twin facilitator has also reported seeing 11:11 everywhere. He is highly receptive, and his signs were showing up everywhere. Just yesterday, my mother accidently sent me a text that read – "*1111*" and she later texted, "*What? Accident.*" She didn't know how or why the message was sent. However, she sent it at the exact time I was working on these principles. So I knew that the Divine was working through her, sending me signs that she is also experiencing a connection with her guidance. It confirms that as she reads my book, she will be open to the idea of my presentation of these concepts and ideas. It was code 11:11 that also pointed me in the direction of writing this book and another part of my Divine mission. I will share more about this in *Key Code 11:11.*

When I was in the middle of my darkest hour, preparing to end my relationship and searching for a place to live, I was studying for my *Archangel Life Coaching Certification* with Charles Virtue, Doreen Virtue's son. I had narrowed my extensive search down to two condos. I said a prayer and asked to be shown which condo I should choose. Immediately following my prayer, I picked up the book I was studying by Doreen, "*Archangels 101.*" The number 101 was one of the unit numbers of condos I was considering. There was my answer.

In *Angel Numbers 101*, Doreen gives meaning to the number 101, defining it as learning to understand the fundamental principles of spiritual teachings and learning to *"let go and let God."* This increases your vibration, allowing you to attract all good things in your life. This was a powerful message to me. At that time, my mind was so boggled I could not make decisions on my own. In addition, I was having some health issues; I was so exhausted that the idea of hanging a picture on a wall, let alone moving, was something I had no energy for. However, this condo was completely furnished, including towels, dishes etc. It allowed me the opportunity to move in, ready to live. The slight increase in cost that I was concerned about was provided for. *I just had to "let go and let God" and show up; everything I needed was available.* It was as though the angels were taking care of me, knowing how ill, tired and exhausted I was. I had to allow by being open to receive and get out of my own way. Now I tell people I'm on a staycation.

I would highly recommend that you read the book, *Angels of Abundance – Heaven's 11 Messages to Help You Manifest Support, Supply and Every Form of Abundance*, by Doreen Virtue and her son Grant Virtue. Doreen and both her sons offer great resources that will assist you in connecting with your guides.

My twin and I got together for a spiritual field trip one day. Upon his arrival he was telling me about a movie that was coming out called *"The Gift."* Just before he arrived, his twin-flame facilitator had sent him a text message with a link premiering *"The Gift."* The timing of her message caught his attention; it was the second time he had seen *"The Gift"* presented. Later that day, we were driving and he pointed out to me a vehicle that had the license plate THE-GFT. I made the connection that these messages were due to his becoming open to receiving his spiritual gifts, activating his intuition and taking his understanding of his abilities to a deeper level. Since that time, I have had my own understanding and connection to that message *"The Gift."* I now realize it was also for me. My twin has given me *"The Gift"* of unconditional love by taking on the heavier karmic load, so that I could connect to my Divine purpose in life. That allowed me to find personal freedom – inner peace and happiness. With the assistance of my twin, I have found my way home.

During the time that my twin and I were working together with plans to open the spiritual community center, I was experiencing some fear and I received another mystical message. My concerns were that I had two prior failed business partnerships. I worried that something would go wrong again, and I was not willing to walk that path again. However, rather than running away from my fear, I asked for signs to show me if this was meant to be. While driving, I looked up and saw a license plate that read, THS-WRX. I shared my fears and this message with my twin and he suggested using *"It Works"* as the name of the company we were creating together. Later, after deciding not to follow through with our plans, I was driving and a car flew up, then swerved in front of me and slammed on the brakes. As it did so, I read the license plate – IT-WRKS.

I recently received another "mysterious message" while writing the Ascension Acceleration Process in *Key Code 4:4* which really signifies, *"The Pathway to Heaven or Enlightenment."* I was pumping gas in my SUV, and as I turned around, there was a pamphlet sitting on the pump where that handle had been. I didn't notice this paper when taking the handle off the pump, but as I went to reach for it, a breeze came along. It flew off the pump and I began chasing it across the parking lot. Something inside of me said that there was a message in it for me. I picked it up, and it read, *"What is Your Destination?"* As soon as I opened it, I read the bolded words inside, *"Romans' Map to Heaven."* Under that same section was a series of bible verses, which all followed the same process I had been shown to be the stages of Ascension. By taking on the burdens of the world, that being karma, we then realize that we must make the same self-sacrifice as Jesus by letting the karma go and creating an experience of our own death. By doing so, we can find eternal life in heaven on earth.

The following verse really captured my attention: *Romans 6:23 (NIV) – For the wages of sin is death, but "The Gift" of God is eternal life in[a] Christ Jesus our Lord.* This is what I had experienced by letting go:

feeling the death of myself and knowing that I had laid my burdens to rest. I too had resurrected by connecting to my higher self and was now living *"The Gift"* of unconditional love and sharing Christ consciousness for the remainder of eternity. This is when I realized the magnitude of *"The Gift"* that my twin had given me.

THE 11:11 *"WAKE UP CALL"*

11:11 is most commonly thought of as the angel number indicating that the angels are trying to communicate with you. Seeing this sequence of numbers is most often associated with your *"spiritual awakening"* which takes place at the beginning of the Ascension process. Twins from all over the world report seeing the 11:11 *"wake-up code"* just before or around the time of coming into physical connection with their twin flame. The following is a great definition of the full meaning of 11:11 and how it links to the connection of twin flames:

The 11 on the left side of 11:11 is the expression of the Divine feminine representing vibrational harmony when combining the masculine and the feminine energies that are found in the feminine twin flame. Likewise, the 11 on the right side of the 11:11 represents the masculine twin and is the harmonic balance of the masculine and feminine energies of the Divine masculine. Both twins must come into a harmonic balance of masculine-feminine energies individually before they can be in vibrational harmony together. *Therefore, 11:11 represents the merger of two harmonically-balanced Divine masculine and Divine feminine energies.* Once both reach this level of development, the two twin souls come together in physical union, becoming twin flames. This is required for them to complete the harmonic balance of both their masculine and feminine energies within each of themselves. I would like to point out here that my twin flame and I were in physical contact long before we were ready to balance our masculine-feminine energies. We also went into separation upon entering our *"dark night of the soul"* and this separation lasted for approximately a year and a half. As we each emerged out of the darkness and after we both were ready to work on balancing our masculine and feminine energies, we were then brought back together by the Divine — this time in a deeper way. We connected on a soul level, something that we had never done before. When it is time to fully unite, the goal is that two complete and whole individual souls merge, creating harmonic balance together.

11:11 and the Pyramidal Energies

The concept of 11:11 also links to the pyramid energy. If you multiply 1111 X 1111, it equals 1234321, which creates a pyramid structure. If you stack the numbers the energy associated with this sequence of numbers relate to the pyramid energies, which connects to the pyramids of Giza, in Egypt. I find this interesting being that twins are connected to Atlantis, which was located in the same region as Egypt. These same energies are found in the concept of sacred geometry, in which geometric shapes produce a defined energetic force depending on the shape of the sacred image and its configuration.

I work with many twins who feel a connection to Egypt and the pyramids. Generally, they all experienced some form of abandonment issues that need healing and forgiveness in order to move forward with their connection to their twin flame in this lifetime. Most have experienced soul trauma which has never been healed, caused from the energetic separation that ripped souls apart during the *Fall of Atlantis*. History has documented that to be an era where all twin flames originated and were together in union.

The energy found to be produced within the shape of the pyramid is the same as the Ankh sexual energy that is produced between twin flames once they have fully awakened by having let go and surrendered. Only then can they fully access their ability to tap into the higher-self galactic sacred sexual energies. This powerful orgasmic energy was thought to have been the force that was used to help build the pyramids in Egypt. I will discuss more about the idea of sacred sexuality and how it links to Divine creativity in *Key Code 10:10.*

It is these same pyramid energies and the *"wake-up call"* sign 11:11 that are also connected to the Alchemy of St. Germain. Alchemy transforms something or someone into something else by transforming lower states of energy into a higher state of energy. It is always associated with something positive or productive in nature. If you were to study some of the most successful companies in the world, such as McDonald's and Starbucks, they all have been infused with the Alchemy of St. Germain. St. Germain has indicated to me that the *"Twin-Flame Code Breaker"* is encoded with the same Alchemy principles as these highly successful worldwide companies. Receiving this information gave me confirmation that the information provided in *"Twin-Flame Code Breaker"* is a valuable message to the world.

I have been instructed to deliver this message as part of the new world order, which simply means we are moving from a lower vibrational planet returning to a state of Christ consciousness; the planet is shifting into a new way of life. In a nutshell, it is restoring heaven on earth, so everyone can find their way home. Being that I have a very deep connection with my spiritual guides, they have assured me that this is a very important and urgent message that is to be presented and launched on 11-11-2016. I am honored to have been *"The Chosen One"* and I accept this calling by sharing everything within this message the same way it has been shown to me. I am not surprised by the power that lies between these pages, my guidance want this information immediately available. Therefore, it must be something that the world is ready for and is part of Divine order. I can clearly see that this message is coming through me and not from me.

You can find countless theories and documented information circling the internet about the power of the numbers 11:11. But for a better visual demonstration, I will show you here how this pyramidal energy connects to the pyramids and how the sequences are constructed around the power of the number 1:

1 X 1 = 1
11 X 11 = 121
111 X111 = 12321
1111 X 1111 = 1234321
11111 X 11111 = 123454321

The sequence continues, but I think you get the idea. If you stacked any one of the product numbers in the sequences above, you can visually see the structure of a pyramid. For example, here I will use the product number: 1234321. This also demonstrates a visual presentation of its association with the A in Alchemy. The A creates the shape of a pyramid.

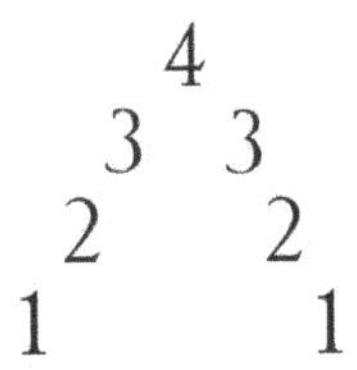

I think this would be a good time to remind you that the point of these examples is to help you understand the true nature of Divine order and to assure you that everything is in Divine order. *You can find freedom in letting go of control of your twin flame — practice patience and allow your twin-flame journey to set you free!* Once you arrive at this level of vibrational harmony, you begin to see that the outcome of your twin-flame journey is directed by the Universe. It makes it easier to let go and start working on yourself. As you continue to achieve this higher self-awareness, you will begin to know you are moving in the right direction and realize that everything is in Divine order!

Now is a perfect time to flip to *Key Code 8:8* as we continue to create a deeper understanding of the importance of becoming one with yourself by balancing your masculine-feminine energies. You are learning to connect to your higher self, so that you can become the Kings and Queens you were meant to be!

KEY CODE 8:8

Unify Your Twin Soul

"The primary quest of Divine Beings is to unify the harmonic balance of their respective masculine-feminine energies, creating oneness with self, creating oneness in a twin-flame union and creating oneness with the Creator." – Dr. Harmony

WHEN IT COMES TO CONNECTING with the Divine energetic forces, it takes the precise harmonic balance of the masculine and feminine energies. That is why each twin soul must balance their individual masculine and feminine energies before they can fully merge energetically. The Universal goal is to create oneness with self, the Creator, the twin-flame union and then the world. Oneness with self occurs once the masculine-feminine energies come into harmonic 50/50 balance. Typically, twin souls carry a 60/40 masculine-feminine energetic ratio or visa versa, creating an imbalance in the harmonic energetic laws of the Universe. *Source energy consist of equal parts masculine-feminine and twin souls must be in energetic harmony with the Creator and then their twin flame.* Most often, the feminine twin has paved the energetic pathway up to this point in the journey. Then a separation occurs that creates the shift in the balance of the Divine Masculine and Divine Feminine of each twin soul. Now the Divine Masculine twin flame becomes the primary generator of the energy necessary to carry out the mission. The masculine twin anchors and keeps the united energy grounded while generating energy for their feminine counterpart to magnetically expand outward. Conversely, it is the feminine twin soul that creates by adding fuel to the generated spark and together producing the flame, which is then magnified and multiplied into multi-dimensional energetic planes. This means that both twin flames must become one with self before putting their Divine mission into motion. Therefore, it is important that you first learn how to unify your individual twin soul before you can fully unite with your twin flame.

I have experienced this from both sides, performing roles as the generator and the electric. My true twin flame is the generator; during our interactions, it was his energy that I use to actively create. I experienced this after many energy sessions with him, where I would create programs for my clients. He "unconsciously" taught me many things I needed to learn for my Divine mission. Once, I completed a project I had been trying to accomplish for two years in half a day after one of our sessions. My twin flame could not visually see or understand the creativity being produced because he was behind the scenes. However, I could clearly see that his energy was providing a crystal-clear vision that enhanced and accelerated multiple projects I had worked on. Twin flames connect at the higher self, so he is still "unconsciously" contributing his energy that I am using to create *"Twin-Flame Code Breaker."* I had not made any conscious effort for his assistance.

Later, I became the generator for my twin-flame facilitator and he became the electric. This amongst many other things is the reason it took me longer than him to identify that we were experiencing a "true" twin-flame connection. "True" being that we were both indeed 'true" twin flames — just not each other's. *We were both operating from our higher selves, which is the difference between a twin-flame facilitator and a false twin flame. The false twin flame operates on the lower self planes because their energy vibration is not high enough to reach these higher self energetic planes; yet they are still needed for assistance to clear deep lower vibrational karma.* My twin facilitator always noticed the energy that I provided, which produced crystal-clear clarity. As I mentioned, it has been quite interesting experiencing a twin-flame triangle which has given me the rare opportunity to see the view from both sides of the fence. And it's quite intense, I might add! It did not take me long to realize that I was learning from both views in order to understand things that I would not have known otherwise.

Twin Flames Become Kings and Queens

After my twin and I made the decision to shift our attention back to working on our individual selves, I had a bizarre encounter with a man from London. And if you are a twin flame, you will understand this particular meaning of "bizarre." It helped me release the final karmic debris associated with my past life in England. He was a catalyst that opened my heart chakra to a new level, helping me to realize I had never had a "*man*" (masculine) to assist me in my life before because I didn't want assistance. For the first time, I was opening up in a new way and I realized that I wanted to be the Queen by being open to receiving and being taken care of. However, that meant I had to learn how to let go and ask for help and allow a King (masculine) to come and sweep me off my feet.

While working with twin flames, I see this to be a very common occurrence. It is generally the feminine twin who carries the heavier masculine energy and operates in a dominance masculine role and therefore is the driver of their own life — creating an imbalance within their energetic makeup. They intently seek to remain in control, so the number one lesson that their twin flame is teaching them is to let go, followed by practicing patience. Generally, how fast a union transpires typically is dependent on how fast the feminine twin is willing to let go of her masculine ways. Once the feminine twin learns how to let go, raise her energetic vibration and shift into unification, a harmonic balance of the masculine-feminine energies occurs; only then can the masculine twin shift into his masculine role. *So, rather than blaming your twin for what they are or are not doing, shift the focus towards unifying your own masculine-feminine energies.* Now you both can become the Kings and Queens that you desire to be.

What Does It Mean To Be A King Or Queen?

We are all Divine Beings! Therefore, it is our individual responsibility to open ourselves up to receive and allow ourselves to be treated like royalty rather than making someone else responsible for our own happiness. Because of soul trauma that has produced past pain, hurt, negative experiences and karmic patterns, we shut down our receptivity and block our blessings. Doing this energetically throws our Yin-Yang out of balance, which shifts us out of balance with Source. Since we are energetically made in the image of the Creator, we are considered royal Beings. It should be the mission of every soul to strive for oneness by being receptive to being Kings and Queens. In this instance, the Kings and Queens are representations of the Divine Masculine and Divine Feminine energies. Being a King or Queen has nothing to do with gender, nor does it play any specific role in the balance in our Being. *The primary quest of Divine Beings is to unify the harmonic balance of their respective masculine-feminine energies, creating oneness with self, creating oneness in a twin-flame union and creating oneness with the Creator.*

The King seeks outside the self with attempts to produce action, (i.e., the doer or the fixer). The Queen is receptive and nurtures the self by going inward, focusing on feelings and emotions. So, whether man or woman, the goal is to create unification balancing one's masculine and feminine energies in order to restore stability, inner peace and happiness. Having been an energy healer for nearly 20 years, I have tuned into the concept of energetic balance and helped many twins to do this with the use of not only energy healing sessions, but also balancing cognitive thinking with emotional stability. When thoughts, feelings, emotions and physical actions are imbalanced, it can create energetic blockages and an imbalance in the synchronicity of the Divine masculine-feminine energies.

When a Divine Being carries a heavier masculine energetic role, they intently focus on producing and pushing forward, losing site of their receptivity. In spite of their physical well-being, their logical thinking overrides the heart. They lose touch with their inner Being or inner child and separate themselves from their feelings and emotions.

This creates separation from the Creator. *Being that we are experiencing a global energetic shift from the 3D (dimensional) into the higher 5D (dimensional) energies, the increased energetic frequencies are also shifting into stabilized masculine-feminine energies collectively in order to restore oneness within the Universe.* This planetary shift aligns with the feminine energetic society of the *"Age of Aquarius"* bringing more love to the planet and preventing self-destruction.

When a Divine Being carries the heavier feminine energetic role, they typically become emotionally sensitive and can have their feelings hurt easily. They tend to be codependent by seeking outside themselves to fill the internal void. This sometimes can come across as clingy and energetically repels what they are seeking, causing it to shift further away from them. That includes your twin flame.

Unification of the Generator and the Electric Creates the Divine Mission

Shortly after accepting the assignment of being the vessel for *"Twin-Flame Code Breaker,"* I spent a couple of weeks processing and integrating information by taking notes, compiling thoughts and allowing Divine intelligence to flow through me. This intense process allowed me to compile many of the ideas and concepts that are presented throughout these *11:11 Key Codes.* In doing so, I revisited many experiences that helped me to integrate knowledge creating higher conscious awareness's. It helped me identify with my own words of wisdom and release my past to a greater level, while realizing that my twin was still teaching me in the process. To demonstrate the idea and that we need to learn to let go of perfectionism, I'll tell you that my kitchen and dining area looked and still looks as if a mad scientist had a chemical explosion. I tell friends who stop by not to mind the mess — my brain has exploded all over the kitchen! Viewing the mess, often makes me think that my twin flame has put me in time-out again, because I know he would really enjoy seeing it! Once, while fixing a leak under the kitchen sink, he put me in time-out, leaving stuff on the counter until we made sure the leak was fixed. After three weeks, I texted him and asked him if my time-out was finished and his reply was, "*If you have to ask, NO!*" This is a good example of how our twins can quickly pick up on what it is we need to work on within ourselves and create an experience that reflects back to us what we need to work on within ourselves.

During one of my many Einstein moments, I began making some interesting discoveries, which gave me a better understanding of how the harmonic balance or unification of the energetic conductors of the masculine and feminine energies when they scientifically merge. While processing this concept, I started relating masculine and feminine energies to the energy produced within a vortex, which is a pull of energy spiraling inward or outward depending on whether it was negative (masculine) or positive (feminine). I began to comprehend that the masculine energy or vortex is indeed the generator or magnetic, and the feminine energetic vortex energy is the creator or electric. So, I started to draw images that patterned these vortexes of the masculine and feminine energies. I realized I had previously drawn these same spiraling patterns a few times before in energy sessions with my twin flame. But at that time, I did not understand the significance of the symbols. This time I quickly saw that I was basically drawing the numbers **6** and **9**. Next, I consciously began to relate the number **6** vortex as the generating masculine energy and the number **9** vortex as feminine energy.

When I said I stepped inside of Einstein's head for a few days, I was not kidding! The vortex of the number **6** spins inward creating compression, which is grounding and restrictive energy; it is produced in the same Einstein formula: M = E/C (2), which contracts inward. The **9** produces positive energy as seen in the formula: E = MC (2) and it spins outward, creating expansive feminine energy. My conclusion was that when combining or merging these masculine-feminine energies, it creates neutrality (oneness) being that the negative and positive energy cancels each other out. *That in turn creates harmonic balance; there is no* *longer a positive or negative pull within the merger of the masculine-feminine energies, thus creating a completely balanced twin soul.* Then once each twin soul has unified by harmonizing their own perceptive energies, they now can unify into complete merger. I also compared the relation to the exact same energetic force that is producing the Christ consciousness energetic vibration in the unified field as seen in the image of the Sri Yantra (I will explain more about the unified field and Sri Yantra in *Key Code 10:10*).

I continued by drawing images combining the **6** and **9**, stacking the **9** over the **6** (**9/6** – I placed one on top of the other, allowing them to slightly overlap)

I could clearly see that merging these two numbers together created harmonic balance. I also saw that once the two energies united fully by linking together the **6** and the **9**, it creates an **8** — the infinity symbol and also a twin-flame code. The images I had in front of me resembled a custom ring and pair of earrings that I had made several years ago. Once, that ring had gotten caught in a bag of trash as I was throwing it in the dumpster. Being that my twin was coming for a session the next morning, I was forced to ask my twin to get it out for me. When I say forced, I mean it! I had always had trouble asking for help and now I was being forced to ask him to go dumpster diving. I also lost one of those earrings while visiting Egypt.

I spent several days processing and integrating these discoveries. Then I had another crystal-clear awakening: I was being asked to take on the assignment of writing this book. I understood that it was shifting me in alignment with my "Ultimate Calling" but I wondered how that was possible without the assistance of my twin. Divine mission is always a joint agreement, which would also require my twin flame to energetically be in harmonic balance. I knew that my twin had been working to stabilize his masculine energy. However, I was unaware of what stage of the process he was in. So I asked my Divine guidance the question, "*By agreeing to this Divine assignment, don't I need my twin's*

energy to assist with this mission? And if so, does that mean my twin has balanced his masculine and feminine energies, becoming the generator for the creation of this joint Divine mission?"

It was not long before I had my answer. While retrieving a voice mail one morning, there was a reference number that I had to write down. So, I began writing down BB11**6**88. Just as I started writing the number **6** it became a *"Key Code"* and immediately caught my attention — I had been processing and integrating the number **6** and understood it to represent masculine energy. Otherwise, I most likely would have never understood the significance of the reference code.

Before sharing its meaning, I would also like to point out that I have changed the letters BB out of respect for my twin flame's privacy. However, the BB represented initials of his first and last name. The **11** is unification of the masculine-feminine energies within the self (previously, in *Key Code* 7:7 I provided a complete explanation of the energetic relationship the number 11:11 has and how it links to the merger of unified twin souls). The **6** indicated that my twin had shifted into the masculine role, and the **88** was the infinity code representing the merger of twin souls creating harmonic balance — not only with oneself and their union, but also with the Creator of their combined energies. It was at that moment I realized that my twin had shifted into his masculine role and was energetically generating the energy for the Divine mission I was being asked to create. I recognized that since I'd been the one who had carried the heavier masculine role, I had to be the one who fully let go and shift into my feminine energy before my twin could shift into his masculine role. I had been working on shifting into the Divine feminine for at least a year and a half. This was by far the hardest lesson to accomplish and it took clearing all my negative karmic attachments to my past life in England. The man from London taught me to open my receptivity.

MAKE NOTE OF THIS SECTION: Unlocking these **very** important *"Key Codes"* and understanding the energies of the numbers

6 and **9** played a **very** significant role for another *"Code Breaker"* that I unlocked and will share with you in *Key Code 11:11.*

Characteristic of a King or Divine Masculine Energy

The Divine Masculine energy possesses logical and analytical thinking with a left-brain function. Those with it tend to rationalize and process in a linear fashion. They are very determined with a competitive spirit. They become the drivers of their own lives.

- Goal-oriented
- Expressing Self from the Head
- Black-and-White Thinking
- Being Assertive
- Constrictive Energy
- Singular Processing and Integration of Thought
- Won't Ask For Help
- Anger Outburst
- Need for Control
- Need for Power

Characteristics of a Queen – Divine Feminine Energy

The Divine Feminine energy intuitively connects by demonstrating compassion and empathy with the use of the right brain. Those with it tend to go with the flow while demonstrating ease and grace. They are flexible by nature.

- Open to Receive
- Nurture Inner Child
- Expressing Self from the Heart
- Creative – Energy Expansion
- Passionate

- Honor Oneness
- Suppresses Emotions – Passive
- Anger Turned Inward – Depression
- No Need for Control
- Self-Empowerment

Unifying The King and Queen or the Divine Masculine and Divine Feminine

In a world of chaos and energetic disorder, it can be challenging to create unity within our Divine Masculine and Divine Feminine energies. But 75% of the battle is accomplished by understanding the concept and identifying with the nature of oneness in self and then with others. Once you become consciously aware and understand the importance of these ideas, it is easier to learn ways to stay energetically in harmonic balance. Ultimately, oneness has two major components. The first is to keep a balance in right- and left- brain thinking. The second is to keep harmonic balance between head and heart in decision making.

Kings and Queens Don't Take Life on By Themselves!

The more I talk to people, and especially twin flames, about the topic of asking for help, the more I realize that the majority process their emotions by suppressing their feelings rather than expressing them. It seems as though it's easier to deal with what one might be facing alone (masculine-dominant) rather than allow others to help you. Asking and then allowing the support from others is a very humbling experience; it gives most people a false sense of weakness. And I will be the first to admit, this was one of the hardest lessons for me to learn. In all reality, it is what we perceive to be the weakness that creates our greatest inner strength (feminine empowerment). Asking for help from another person can be more challenging for most people than dealing with the life circumstance that they might be faced with. *"Why do we feel as though we have to take life on by ourselves?"* Think about this idea. If someone were to ask us for help, we are eager and ready to assist. Therefore, *"Why do we have so much trouble asking for assistance and try taking life on by ourselves?"*

Here are 5 suggestions to help you see the importance of stepping outside of one's own pride and stubbornness and becoming humble enough to allow others to support you during times of need. There is no need to take life on by yourself!

Suggestion 1: **Don't Be Afraid to Ask**. *"What are we afraid of, when asking for assistance?" That someone might say no? Of course not! We are afraid they might say yes!* Ultimately, we don't want their help. Usually it's because we feel like we are imposing and not wanting to put someone else out. But more often than not, it relates to the fact that we do not want to express our own emotions by demonstrating what it is like to be humble. Being humble represents our feminine side. Society views this as a weakness, but in all reality we need the balance of our whole spiritual Being. Life does not have to be so hard. It does not have to be push – push – push, drive – drive – drive. It's time to allow ourselves to come into harmonic balance by becoming one with ourselves and letting our softer side shine!

Suggestion 2: **Don't Block the Blessing**. When we let go and surrender to our softer side, we open our energetic receptivity as we progress along our journeys. By only giving away ourselves to others, we exercise the masculine energy which only allows us to give – give – give – blocking us from receiving. This creates a dysfunction in the laws of the Universe. *As Kings and Queens, we were designed to not only give but to allow and receive our blessings as well.* When we give, it multiplies a minimum of ten-fold; through the laws of the Universe, what you give away is programmed to return to you. So, when we block the receiving we are blocking *"The Gift"* of Spirit that tries to reward and honor our contributions to the Universe. It's time to open up and receive. This too allows our feminine side to shine.

Suggestion 3: **Don't Rob Others of Their Joy**. Most of the time, people feel good about being able to help. It allows others to feel like they are making a contribution as a whole. When they offer and you deny them that ability to let their light shine, it robs that person of their joy in being able to assist you. View receiving and accepting as allowing that other person to gain a sense of joy. This creates harmonic balance and oneness in the giving and receiving, and everyone feels a sense of joy. That is the "*The Gift*" that we are all to feel and experience. *Supreme joy then becomes the highest expression of unconditional love that any human can experience.* So next time someone offers; let go, relax and allow!

Suggestion 4: **Do Set Loving Boundaries**. The real "*Key*" to understanding how to demonstrate the principles of giving and receiving is this: it is important to set loving boundaries by not allowing people to take advantage of you. This is another reason why people have a hard time asking for or receiving help. It can open a doorway to being taken advantage of. That also creates an imbalance of the oneness of giving and receiving within the laws of the Universe. The flip side of the coin is that being the majority of people won't allow help from others, they also do not know how to say "No" when asked for help. In that case it is important to learn to say, "No." When out of balance your energy feels drained and puts you in the lower vibrational mindset, becoming afraid to speak up for yourself for fear of conflict and confrontation with the other person. So, if you feel like someone is taking too much from you energetically or otherwise, your harmonic energy is out of balance. This is where setting loving boundaries are important. *By setting these boundaries, you are restoring balance in giving and receiving. By saying "No," you are not only creating self-respect and self-worth for yourself, but you are* *also teaching the other person that it's not ok to take advantage of other people.* A simple response is all it takes. There is no need for explanation of why we are not able to assist. Either way, it's ok to set that boundary and do it in a loving way with no anticipation of conflict. Now we have exercised our feminine side.

Suggestion 5: **Know the Difference Between Walls vs. Boundaries.** It is important to assess an energetic exchange with others by asking, *"Are the laws of the Universe in oneness?"* This also helps us identify the difference between walls versus boundaries. When we learn to express ourselves without guilt by saying, "No," we are setting loving boundaries. This allows the other person to learn their lesson within the harmonic laws of giving and receiving — especially if they are trying to take advantage of you. *However, when we do not express ourselves in a loving way and we continue to give away our energy without receiving, we tend to build walls that block any energetic exchange and prevents us from having the best relationship we could have with that person.* So, it's time to drop the walls and set some loving boundaries. You are demonstrating self-respect and that other person will also learn to respect you as well. People only treat you the way you have allowed them too.

I will be the first to tell you that these are all tough lessons I have personally had to learn. I have made the statement more than once, *I feel as though I am a wild mustang horse about to be saddled for the first time, and it's going to be an exciting ride.* Of course, it's easier said than done, but when given the opportunity, use your challenges as learning experiences. Extract the lesson in such a way that it develops who you are — that becomes *"The Gift!"* I can tell you from experience that I will no longer be taking life on by myself. I have excitedly moved forward with ease and grace, allowing loving friends, family and relationships with people to assist me along the way. It is very rewarding!

How I Became a Queen

Ever since I was a child, I did not like being confined, constricted, hugged or embraced. I pushed anyone away who tried to cuddle or hug me. I basically skipped childhood because I was so headstrong that I started working at age 11 and kept that same job for 9 years. I might add this was by choice. It was the inner driving force within my soul that fed my perfectionism and ego-driven desires for accomplishment. I had very loving and supportive parents, but it was my desire to be independent and require no assistance from anyone. As a child, I not only cleaned my room, but organized the entire house without being asked. My father, being very strong in his faith and opinions, is also a very affectionate man who knows quite well how to express himself; he is in touch with his inner emotions. He has yet to meet a stranger and he is loved by all.

However, for whatever reason I have remained closed off to him my entire life. He has never been allowed to see the expression of my soul. I know that it partially pertains to his strong belief systems that do not align with mine. Even though I have never judged him, that has not stopped me from energetically pushing him away. Granted, his opinionated tactics can be quite overbearing at times. The differences we have were never verbalized because I have had no desire to attempt to prove my beliefs to be right. I have always passively refrained from the need to have to prove anything to anyone. I prefer to live a sermon than preach one — unlike my father.

By not being able to express myself, I learned how to build brick walls rather than learning to set loving boundaries, especially when it comes to crossing my energetic barriers. I always noticed that because of my spiritual gifts, I am highly energetically sensitive. Therefore, external chaos and disorder easily disrupts the homeostasis of my internal energetic environment. Not understanding this at a young age is one reason why I subconsciously protected my internal energetic space, and learned to build walls for energetic protection.

I would like to point out that it was I who did not know how to be open and expressive. It was I who chose to tune out rather than tune in. So, to be very clear, I am not placing any blame on my father. I love my father dearly, but I have never known how to show him that. My need for the strong masculine role created an energetic repelling between our energies, creating silent distance. This set the precedence for my romantic relationships — I remained in the dominating masculine role, while my feminine side lay dormant. Because of this, I have attracted feminine-dominant males and ones who did not know how to speak their truth or express themselves. I silently or "unconsciously" repeated a pattern of tuning out rather than in. So, to maintain harmonic balance, we have to equally align in our respective energetic roles.

If we seek something different, we have to be the ones to change in order to attract what will match our energetic vibration. This is one reason why relationships shift. As one partner shifts their energy, it creates an imbalance in their energetic union. If two masculine-dominating individuals are in a relationship it does not create balance, so the individuals repel. When working with twins, I have found masculine dominance by the feminine counterpart to be very common.

Prior to assisting my twin, while he was shifting into his masculine role, I had already become aware that I was shifting into my feminine role. I had been working on letting go and letting down my walls. I even thought that I had released my need for protection, until several encounters I had with my twin. I realized that I still had barriers remaining. His reflection mirrored back to me what I needed to work on within myself. My twin had issues expressing himself or speaking his truth, and I realized that attracting someone with those challenges was a repeated pattern for me. In trying to break that cycle, I had to create oneness within myself. I began to see that the only man who had ever fully expressed himself was my father — and I had shut him out my whole life. Then it hit me that I had never had a "man" (masculine) in my life because I never wanted one. I wanted to remain in the driver's seat and I was not willing to give up such a comfortable chair.

I was well aware of the core skeletons in my closet, but I still didn't know how to "fix" the deepest core of my Being. Mastering this lesson became the final *"Key Code"* I needed to release my driver role in order to harmonize so that I could fully express who I am. I realized this must be done before shifting into full radiance and allowing my flame to shine at its greatest potential. I always believed that everything in our lives happens to teach us lessons. Every encounter between two individuals becomes an opportunity to exchange by giving and receiving. Both parties always have something to teach and learn; this concept follows the magnetic laws of the Universe. So, the need to blame others or your twin flame for something that they are merely teaching you is something that must be let go of as you shift into oneness with yourself.

As I mentioned, it took the interaction I had with a man from London to open me up to the idea of accepting a "masculine" man into my life. And the Universe knew exactly what it was doing by sending me someone so far away to be my teacher. Even thousands of miles away, I wanted to run multiple times. The only reason I didn't was because I could see that it was what I needed to learn to open my feminine side and find a desire to want a "man" (masculine) in my life. That awareness helped me open enough to accept the experiences that I have received with my twin-flame facilitator. He is also miles away and our interactions have also caused me to want to run on multiple occasions. However, I am fully awakened to the areas I have needed to work on within myself. He has gotten to the core of my need for expression and opened up doors just outside of my soul. It is his ability to fully express himself that has been my greatest teacher. He is expressive in a similar way as my father — strong in his beliefs but he also knows how to be sensitive and he can connect to his inner emotions. This is what I had run from my whole life. I could see the connection, but it was not until a specific interaction that we had that brought the picture full circle.

Pre-proofing this book for content created a mirror that forced him to look at some of his core karma. My twin facilitator made multiple connections to some of his deep skeletons that he needed to clear, and it created some emotions that he needed to express. So, he sent me a series of texts in the middle of the night, which was his need to release. But it felt like he was dumping them on me. When I read them upon awakening, at first it felt like I was starting my day with "his issues." I had a full day of writing scheduled and my first thoughts were, "*I don't have time for this.*" But I tried to practice patience, empathy and compassion. I attempted to view the comments he had made from his viewpoint. However, I did text him letting him know I didn't appreciate his not waiting until we had time to verbally talk; we would have a discussion when the timing was right.

As the morning went on, the more I thought about his messages, the more emotions I started feeling. It started to make me angry. I noticed that the emotions were fueling my writing; I wrote an entire chapter that day — *Key Code 7:7.* The interesting thing was that he and I were both experiencing several things I had written about that day. *It's amazing how the Universe has a way of making every experience show up at just the right moment, giving us an opportunity to learn — should we choose to see it that way.* Also, I would have missed lessons or information that were shared in that "*Key Code*" had we not had that encounter that day!

Later that evening we had a talked and during our conversation, He asked the question, "*Why haven't you told your twin flame about writing this book yet?*" He had asked that question on multiple occasions and each time I answered: "*I plan to tell my twin when I am finished with the book. However, I cannot risk outside influence on this assignment. As intense as the process is, I am handling all that I can personally right now. I want to stay focused and by doing so would be self-serving of me to tell him at this moment just because I want to get it off my chest.*" I also realize it is important for you, the reader, not to interfere with what is to come through these "*Key Codes*" and I was not willing to interfere with Divine order.

Regardless, before answering him this time, I tried to take a step back and process how to explain it differently this time. I am a very effective communicator so I was trying to assemble words that would make sense to him. But he would interrupt me every time I attempted to respond, so I kept repeating myself. By the fourth time, I found myself "feeling" all the anger from the day resurfacing, and I was getting verbally expressive. He was perceiving my repetition as being degrading, which was not my intention. The conversation escalated and it even crossed both our minds to hang up on the other. I felt like a volcano that was ready to erupt. Now, you must know, this is not my normal nature. I stay composed, patient and I never find myself angry. But if we want to feel the good, we have to feel the bad. That is what helps us open up and expand our emotions.

In spite of it all, we continued to talk. By the time we got off the phone we were laughing. I even told him that if that is what it took to help me write an entire chapter in a day, then it was ok to "piss" me off again! And the running joke is: "*Don't make me tell you again!*" I continued to process and integrate what just happened, knowing it was out of character for me. I realized I was operating from my Divine feminine role and that I was actually learning to feel and express rather than suppress. Moreover, another conversation with him later that night opened me up to a deeper level of expression by sharing some really deep things from my past. The conversation also helped me bring full circle the idea that I had shut out my father from expressing himself and that I had never allowed a "man" (masculine) to play the Divine masculine role in my life. So, my anger was also part of my learning to let go of control in exchange for self-expression. We have had a few more encounters, not quite as intense as this one. On more than one occasion, we visited the idea of discounting our connection. But we both could see that there were lessons to be learned, so we allowed that to unfold. Since we are both highly in tune and operating from the higher self, everything is handled in a more respectful way than if responding from the lower self.

This example demonstrates the law of attraction by focusing on the importance of harmonic balance in the giving and receiving. For instance, my twin facilitator needed to immediately express himself to make himself feel better by sending a text in the middle of the night. I on the other hand, am not use to expressing myself, so I didn't understand his need to do so. Also, I am choosing to wait until after the book is completed to express myself and share this mission with my twin. My twin facilitator didn't understand my need to wait; he knows how to express himself and doesn't wait. So it wasn't that he didn't hear what I was saying for the 4th time, it was that he didn't understand why. In the bigger picture, this is teaching me the need for empathy, acceptance and expression and teaching him to practice patience. We are creating oneness within each of our respective selves. *Creating oneness and practicing the harmonic laws of the Universe are what all relationships are about, twin flame or not!* I challenge you to view your next dispute as a teacher and realize that the other person is just the vessel teaching you. Approach the situation with a thankful heart.

My twin facilitator has taught me to open my soul to a deeper level. I am able to express who I am, my feelings and my emotions, while remaining in harmonic balance of my masculine-feminine oneness. I will forever be grateful to him for teaching me! We often joke about meeting each other for the first time on the Ellen DeGeneres show after this book comes out – LOL! For the first time in my life, I accept royalty by sitting in the Queen's chair!

In closing of *Key Code 8:8*, I would like to challenge you to take a deeper look within your soul and see what you have yet to express to someone – good or bad. *Learn to let go of the need to be the Driver of your own life. Make a "conscious" decision to create unity within your soul!* I am enjoying the view while riding in the passenger's seat! Just yesterday, taking a break from writing, I was running. I stopped to notice a flock of birds congregating over me up in the air. As I looked up, I saw something falling from the sky but I could not tell what it was. I continued to watch. Then it became clear I was being rained on by bird feathers.

Angel wings were falling down on me. My masculine self would never have taken the time to notice the birds flying to begin with, much less find the beauty in being showered with God's perfection. This moment taught me that when we take time to get in touch with our Divine feminine self, we embrace the beauty of life!

Becoming Kings and Queens are a prerequisite to being able to harmonize your soul. Self-expression is mandatory in all dimensions of our lives. In *Key Code 9:9* we review in depth what the view looks like from the top of the Christmas tree, and the importance of harmonizing our souls so that we can radiate. I will use some of my own personal examples demonstrating how I have expressed and shared my inner light of oneness.

KEY CODE 9:9

Harmonize Your Twin Soul

"We become radiant once we are in perfect alignment with the Divine, which generates personal empowerment that produces supreme joy and spiritual enlightenment, as we live moment to moment in the – all that I AM presence!" – Dr. Harmony

ONCE YOU RELEASE YOUR PAST and transcend to your higher self by transitioning through the Ascension process, you'll find unification in your masculine-feminine energies. Then you begin to harmonize your soul and radiate like the North Star for others to follow. You will no longer have the desire to fill the void inside of you with your twin flame or anyone else because you have become filled with unconditional self-love. As your love vibration continues to rise, and your heart, soul and life aligns with your "*Ultimate Calling*," personal freedom resonates throughout because you have found your way home to inner peace and happiness. Now you are the High priest or High priestess of your own life. You are now experiencing personal empowerment (masculine) and expanded consciousness (feminine).

When your heart and your mind are in harmonic alignment, you are no longer robbed of your energy or spend time worrying. You trust the process as you gain inner empowerment that continues heightening your awareness. You begin to see clearly now what you could not see before. Your choices between ease and grace become second nature and you can quickly determine what is enhancing or robbing you of your life force. When you are loving what you do it gives you energy, rather than causing you to be exhausted. For example, I used to work 70-90 hours a week for many years — and YES it was exhausting! After a while, I was depleted in every area of my life. However, when you get in alignment, no matter how busy you might appear on the outside, it actually raises your energetic vibration on the inside; this ultimately attracts more abundance.

For instance, right now I am taking on the biggest challenge of my life by not only writing this book, but at the same time creating a twin-flame oracle card deck. I am rebranding, creating a website and marketing strategy, all to launch "*Twin-Flame Code Breaker*," and my guides allotted me a three-month window to accomplish this entire Divine mission. I'm pretty sure my guides are up there laughing at me, because they know that if they gave me more time than that, I would have gotten my head involved and this project would not have turned out the same as it is by coming from my heart. My old self would have been stressed by now. However, I am managing to stay in harmonic balance by still taking care of myself on every level — mind, body and soul — and at the same time seeing chiropractic patients and working with twins all over the world. The process of just showing up and doing what it is that is asked of me is fueling me. I don't have to be in control anymore and the load is much lighter. Everything I need for this journey has appeared. *When hitting what used to feel like a wall, now I stop resisting the process. If it's not moving forward with ease and grace, then it's time to stop and reroute.* If I don't know which direction to go next, I stop and ask my guides to direct me towards the path of least resistance and then I sit back and watch for my signs. They always point me in the right direction.

I will be the first to agree that this does take practicing patience and a lot of letting go. But my biggest reward has been finding inner peace in the still of the moment. So rather than exhausting my energy by pushing forward, I use that moment of silence to recharge. The only reason we become exhausted is because we don't see returns for our efforts. *As long as our efforts create a greater return than not, we are in alignment with our highest good.* In the vortex of all possibilities, the

Universe provides everything you need for your journey. All you have to do is show up and get out of your own way!

How Do We Get Out of Our Own Way?

Getting out of our own way is a major block to entering the vortex of all possibilities, letting our light shine and receiving our rewards. Shifting into radiance releases all mental chaos that has robbed us of our "*conscious clarity.*" I have experienced expanded consciousness over the last couple of days, which is the Universe's way of teaching me the examples I am to share with you. I did not consciously intend for *Key Code 8:8* and *Key Code 9:9* to be the last two chapters to complete, but once I began working on them, I realized exactly why they were saved for last. Writing this book helped me master these two "*Key Codes.*" My higher self knew exactly what final lessons these two "*Key Codes*" were to unlock inside of me, while bringing to my "*conscious awareness*" exactly what you, the reader, is to experience. With my newfound personal empowerment and expanded consciousness, it has not taken me long to make that final circle around the top of the Christmas tree. As I complete these final two "*Key Codes,*" you are witnessing my shifting into complete radiance, while I view everything from the top of the tree. Completion of this book officially adorns my soul with the North Star that shines brightly for others to find their way home.

The following are five suggestions to help you practice getting out of your own way.

Suggestion 1: **Be Who You Are.** Make no apologies for who you are. When we shift into radiance, we learn how to express ourselves and speak our truth. We no longer worry about what other people think because we become confident in ourselves and our abilities. One no longer listens to the mind-chatter telling them that they are not good enough, because now their mind has been purified. Now we can hear the song of our hearts.

Suggestion 2: **Let Go of Perfectionism.** Stop overthinking the process; learn to allow things to unfold and evolve. *When we stop trying to make things turn out the way our minds think it should be, rather than how our heart knows it is, we begin to view everything as perfect the way it is.* When something doesn't feel like it's aligning within the mind's eye, it is human nature to resist the process. Perfectionism is ego's way of having to get the last word in. But when we experience harmony of the soul and view every situation with our hearts, it creates expansion of our Being and we begin to show up as love.

Suggestion 3: **Stop Second-Guessing Yourself.** Once we raise our energetic vibration we begin to honor our own thoughts, feelings and emotions – and our receptivity heightens. We gain clarity in all situations and so we trust the flow of life. This allows us to become the leader of our lives; we no longer need approval from others. We can make decisions with confidence!

Suggestion 4: **Embrace Life with Your Heart.** By letting go of the need to question or analyze our experiences and seeing only love, we can now embrace life with the heart and not with the head. Life then becomes a more beautiful experience. This harmonizes our love channels and now our light becomes a reflection of the color of God shining with purpose rather than intention.

Suggestion 5: **Focus on What is in Front of You.** When we live a life of harmony, it does not mean that everything is perfect. It means you have learned to go with the flow by practicing patience and living moment to moment. Remind yourself that it is progress, not perfection. Let go of the need to push through life; resistance creates resistance. It only creates more struggle through our journey. Keep your mind focused on what is in front of you and watch how much further and faster you fly.

How I was Forced to Get Out of My Own Way

As I previously mentioned, I was literally shoved into alignment; connecting to my "*Ultimate Calling*" and becoming a twin-flame expert was not consciously planned. I am performing the same services I have performed for years — it was just a matter of expanding my wisdom and rerouting my direction by filling a purpose and serving other twin flames in need of my spiritual gifts. Now, most days I have to pinch myself just to make sure I'm not dreaming. It is as though I have been in training for this mission my entire life. My own twin-flame experience was a prerequisite in order to gain the wisdom I needed to help other twin flames on all planes and in every dimensions of life.

A few months ago, my twin flame and I were going to start a center for spiritual transformation in our community. We agreed that it was a way to give back to our community for what we had gained within our own spiritual development, and we each had our own reasons for wanting to help the other while doing so. One morning after we had painted the space the night before, I woke up and immediately knew something was not right —I was not able to breathe. Upon arising, I found a text message from my twin asking me to contact him when I woke up. I could feel that he felt the same way. We spent several days revisiting our plans. We both even reviewed the possibility of ego surfacing and the need to let go of control. We both had "*conscious awareness*" sending a mirrored reflection back to ourselves, pointing out what we each needed to work on personally. Although not being able to identify any specific conscious reasoning for either of our uneasy feelings, we decided it was not in our best interest to proceed.

Personally, I didn't have a clue what was wrong. But I knew that whatever it was, it was hitting the nail on the head. I wanted to run from everything and everyone and I didn't understand why. I spent several days in virtually nonstop meditation. I knew that we were both hitting some of our core karma. We stayed in close communication for several days trying to get to the heart of the matter, discussing options. He even offered use of the space to me and back out of the deal, so that I could move forward — but something didn't feel right. So, I told him that I thought it was best we both not move forward and that we each continue to work on ourselves.

The only thing I regret now was feeling I needed to get it off my chest by emailing him first thing in morning after making my decision, rather than having the patience to verbalize it later. I had done something that I taught him not to do. Later that day, I went to pick up a few things and return the keys, and I could tell he felt really bad. It hurt him because he had a desire to help me move forward as I was recreating myself. Even understanding that I should be in receptive mode, for whatever reason I couldn't move forward with his assistance. Looking back, I can see clearly that the block we experienced was necessary for our Divine mission to be carried out. Even though we could not consciously understand why our souls could not rest by moving forward with that center, our higher selves knew exactly what the plan was.

Trying to move forward without my twin's assistance didn't turn out so well either. I continued to hit my head against brick walls, trying to reinvent myself and attempting to shift into full alignment with my "*Ultimate Calling.*" The process had consumed all my funds. No matter how hard I worked to get things in forward motion, everything – and I mean everything – was being shut down! I went through three computers in one week trying to record a training video series that were to be a part of a new coaching program I was preparing to launch. I had hired three different website developers and was not able to get one website produced – not even after spending over six thousand dollars. I hired a branding coach and marketing strategist and everything she was attempting to help me with got completely shut down. The harder I tried, the louder the doors slammed in my face.

My twin and I had joked that if something didn't open up, I'd be living in a tent. I rarely joke about things like this, but I have to tell you – reality was setting in. I had friends who were opening their homes to me because that was the severity of my circumstances at the time. I had a six-week window and if something didn't shift, I would have potentially been homeless. I was in total dismay! I could not believe it. I had been faithful and made every step in the right direction to align with my purpose. I followed my intuition, instincts and Divine guidance. I was at the end of the rope — for the first time in my life, I had no idea what to do or which way to turn.

So what did I do? I let go of the rope and jumped. I decided that I was going to hang it all up. Being the "fixer" I had always been, I decided it was time to be realistic and get a job. I had not worked for anyone since I was 22 years old. Somewhere inside of me, I knew that I had not come this far to be left in the cold. Some of my friends said to me, *"You're a chiropractor and you have a part-time practice. Just start getting new patients and generating more revenue and do what you went to school for."* They did not understand! If I were going to continue practicing chiropractic full time, then why the hell did I give up a twelve-year practice several years ago and go into deep financial debt by taking on a business partner that failed (not my x-life partner)? Because I was trying to find what my soul was searching for. Besides, starting over required energy — energy that I did not have. I was officially bankrupt in all areas of my life, I was done, ready to let go – I surrender!

What did I do next? I submitted the first resume I ever wrote in my life to at least 20 companies. I could not believe that I had to resort to things like insurance audits, or processing and denying medical claims for chiropractic services that were most likely warranted. Talk about officially selling my soul to the devil — for money that I needed to survive! I found some humor in a serious situation — the first time I decided to see what positions were available, I ran across an online ad for an office assistant my twin had posted 4 hours prior. I almost applied as a joke (or not) – LOL.

One afternoon, after spending 4 hours filling out applications online, I decided to reconnect with a company in Great Britain that I had stumbled across a year prior. It was an independent contractor opportunity offering spiritual advice, remote energy healing and coaching. I liked the idea of assisting people online around the world and using my gifts, but I had been resistant because I didn't think it lined up with what "*I*" was supposed to do. However, I had always felt drawn to this particular company. When the opportunity first "*showed up in my life,*" I even purchased all the necessary equipment and had everything set up and ready to start. But at the last minute my x-life partner and I sold our business and my attention was redirected, so I never followed through. This time — and I must add, only since everything was already set up and ready to go — I decided to contact the company to see where it might lead me. By that afternoon, I was online making money!

I did it. I got out of my own way, and all I had to do was just show up. I had heard Dr. Dyer say this many times, and I can now say I attest to this truth. I knew I was in alignment because within hours I was working making meaningful money; within days, I had built a significant clientele. I was loving what I was doing and this was when the magic started! Twin flames started showing up immediately out of nowhere. I continued to hear the phrases: "*I was guided to you*" and "*I am so grateful I found you.*" I heard story after story of how they accidentally stumbled onto finding me. I frequently have people waiting in line to connect with me, all in need of my assistance. They were all just "*showing up.*"

In all my years of practice, I have never received such genuine appreciation for my gifts of service. I began to identify twin flames in a flash. I helped them to identify the importance of continuing their personal paths, to release their negative pasts and break the energetic barriers to their past lives. Story after story presented themselves, solidifying everything my twin and I had experienced, processed and integrated. Indeed, several women had uterine cancer. It did not take long until I was getting referrals from all over the world. I even began working with other twin-flame experts, helping them too break their energetic attachments and understand the nature of their journey, then implanting seeds of light so that they too could teach the same message I was sharing with them.

Recently, I discovered a phrase that I have started sharing with others, *"All heaven has broken loose."* Translation: let it rain – the floodgates of heaven have opened up. This is not a metaphor, it is real. I was directed by my Divine counsel to write this book, and for once in my life I didn't try to figure out how. I said, if this is my Divine mission, then send me what I need to make it happen. I just showed up to start writing. I have had money falling out of the sky – enough to cover the expense of editing and publishing this book. Over the last three weeks, money has been showing up everywhere: an unexpected tax refund, a significant settlement from my credit card processing company, an electric company refund and even a bank deposit error – a credit adjustment from 2014.

To enter this kind of vortex, much letting go has to occur. Getting in alignment begins by releasing the negative energies of your past karma, increasing your energetic vibration, and opening up to receive. Tapping into the higher energetic frequencies allows us to make a direct connection to our guides, angels and the Divine intelligence through the higher self. You can only reach these levels of manifestation after the soul has been purified and you move into unification and harmonization – only then can you tap into your highest potential and become a radiant light shining as an expression of the Creator.

Words of Wayne

When I began the Divine mission of writing this book, it was not my "*conscious*" intention to share as many stories or make mention of Dr. Wayne Dyer to the extent that I have. However, his presence miraculously showed up throughout this Divine assignment, which is my "*Ultimate Calling.*" As I previously mentioned, this book evolved with no conscious effort on my part — I AM just the vessel. As it continued to unfold, I began seeing *Words of Wayne* flow through me and I could feel his presence getting stronger as I learned the art of *"writing from my soul."* He was one of the most radiant Beings I have ever met; as you practice shifting into radiance, I cannot think of a better role model for you to follow. As you read this section, you will understand why I have placed the *Words of Wayne* in *Key Code 9:9 — Harmonize Your Twin Soul.* It perfectly demonstrates the example of getting out of our way and allowing things to show up!

During a session with my spiritual advisor yesterday, I was telling her about the *Words of Wayne* appearing within this book. I also shared with her what I had previously written in the front section of this book: "In Memory of Dr. Wayne Dyer." The memoir mentions a conversation I had with Dr. Wayne back in 2003, when I told him: *"As long as I'm living, your work will never die."* My advisor and I discussed the impact Wayne has made on the world and how the ripple effect of his teachings continues. This conversation reminded me of another significant impact Wayne made on me during the time before I was shoved into alignment with my Divine calling to become a twin-flame expert and write this book. I was fully surrendering to another battle between my head and heart, trying to come to terms with the reality of getting a job, which wasn't resonating with me. I was astonished that I had spent my whole life getting into, what I thought at that time was alignment. I kept reflecting on my obedience over the last couple of years. I had changed everything about my life to *"show up"* and do what I came here to do on this planet. So when the possibility of becoming homeless was nearing, I began to hear loud and clear the *Words of Wayne* as he responded to my comment back in 2003: *"I'm glad you won't be dying with your music still in you."* It was the *Words of Wayne* that encouraged me to let go of that rope that day and fully surrender. However, his words encouraged me not to give up on my *"Ultimate Calling."*

During that time, I had dreamt that I was in front of an audience and the lights were shining so brightly that I couldn't see anything but silhouettes. The experience was so real, including paralyzing fear. And at that moment, Wayne appeared out of nowhere and *he raised me up* and put me on his shoulders. As he did so, my fear disappeared and *"I could see clearly now."* He carried me off to a place where we sat down and spent the entire day together as he shared many *Words of Wayne* with me.

The next morning upon arising, I found a note pad laying on my night stand, which I had used while in Hawaii taking notes from Wayne as he taught what it meant to *"write from the soul."* How that note pad got there still amazes me to this day. I opened it up and the words I read constituted the answer I had been seeking. I will share those *Words of Wayne* with you later in this section. Shortly after reading those *Words of Wayne*, I heard the song, *"You Raise Me Up"* by Josh Groban. At that moment, I began to cry as I fully surrendered. I knew I did not come all this way in search of my Divine mission to give up before I found it. This was a defining moment – *I found my greatest breakthrough on the other side of my greatest resistance.* Once again the *Words of Wayne* were right on time. This made such a huge impact on me that I messaged Wayne's daughter, Serena Dyer, and thanked her for sharing her dad with the world; I also shared that story with her.

Fast forwarding to this morning, I woke up still thinking about how the *Words of Wayne* has made such an imprint on my life and how his essence remains within me. Then I heard him say that I was to put that story in this book — and I was to share those words that I read on that note pad that morning with you, the reader. I was clearly told this was to be placed in a section all its own called: *Words of Wayne. "I can see clearly now"* what those few words we exchanged back in 2003 really meant. I could feel my heart running over with gratitude while reflecting on his stories of gifting 19 homes to family and friends; paying his weekly visit to the bank just so he could tip the teller; and taking his daily morning walks with the intent to bless any homeless person that he might run across. Love does not get anymore unconditional than that. Then a *"crystal-clear awareness"* came to me. I want to pay forward and bless others to the same magnitude he has. I want to leave imprints on as many people as Wayne has, paying forward in honor of him for all he has done for me.

Then it gets even better – if that is possible! I was at my office just after those morning reflections. While waiting on a patient, I prepared an envelope to send my spiritual advisor a check for our session. I found myself writing a message to her that read: "Here is the answer that you have been searching for: *I can see clearly now.*" I have no idea why that came through, I just did what I was urged to do. My patient arrived just shortly after and asked me if she could pay me on Friday after she got paid and I agreed. She had had a head cold, so I performed a technique to open up her sinuses. As she came up and was getting off the table, she began singing, *"I can breathe clearly now."* In disbelieve, I intently asked, *"What did you say?"* She continued to sing, *"You know, the song – I can see clearly now."*

It did not take me long to decide that my patient will not be paying me for that visit on Friday. I will be paying it forward to her in memory of the *Words of Wayne.*

Before I share with you the *Words of Wayne* that were on my note pad that morning, I would like to mention that the "In Memory of Dr. Wayne Dyer" section and *Key Code 11:11* had already been written just a few days before being paid a visit by today's "mystical messengers." I think that it also demonstrates to you, the reader, the importance of watching for those "mysterious messages" and signifies just how important it is to ask for signs and then be open, willing and ready to receive.

The Words of Wayne Directed Me Towards My "Ultimate Calling"

The following *Words of Wayne* miraculously *"showed up"* on my night stand:

Ascension – I AM light – Jesus said, I AM the Ascension.

That which is real never changes. We are like a rose – the risk of remaining a bud is more painful than the risk of blossoming. The risk of not changing is greater than the risk of changing. If the door of perception were clearer, you would see everything as it actually is and that is infinite. Take a risk and go through that door. Have a mind that is open to everything and attached to nothing. *Find your Dharma – Your Ultimate Calling.* Don't look back and wish you would have had the courage to do what it is you came here to do. Live your life with no regrets and become the light that you were intended to be. Your soul doesn't want to be boxed in because it can't expand. The soul will resist anything that tells it that it can't be. *Your soul has a theme song: Don't fence me in and don't put me in a box.*

So what do you do when faced with making the decision to do what it is you came here to do? You Listen, You Let Go, You Let God!

When it comes to making decisions in life, there are only three choices you have to make:

1) **Willingness**
   Am I willing to listen and do what I AM being guided to do?
   80% of people focus on why they can't do something, rather than why they can.
2) **Determination**
   Am I determined to follow through with what it is I AM being guided to do?
   It is ALL laid out for us
   I can see clearly now
   I am going to get it done
   Figure it out – There is ALWAYS a way!
3) **Fearlessness**
   Am I fearless enough to listen to my heart and not my head, so I can do what I AM being guided to do?
   Fear comes from the mind
   Love comes from the heart
   ALWAYS choose to do what you LOVE!

Sharing The Radiant Words of Wayne

The next day, after writing *Words of Wayne*, I had a session scheduled with a client from Wales, UK. Out of all the many twin-flame stories I could share, with her permission this one warrants attention. This client stumbled onto me online and briefly experienced a sample of my gifts, but she had no idea how to contact me. She did not even know my name. All she knew is that she needed what I had to offer and she made it her mission to find me. After much searching, she contacted me on social media. We exchanged a few messages and she was ready to sign up for my *"Reboot Your Soul"* program. This is virtually the same program as my "Reboot Your Twin Soul." However, it was presented slightly different as she did not seek me out in need of twin-flame assistance. Therefore, I tailored the program to match her needs. She contacted me because she had been experiencing extreme fatigue and assumed it was related to health issues.

From her first session, I identified that her fatigue and exhaustion was coming from not being in alignment with her *"Ultimate Calling."* But we assessed all the possibilities of other health-related factors. Today was our fourth weekly session. Before every session with my clients, I always ask guidance to direct me to get to the heart of their issues and the root of what needs to be cleared faster. I felt guided to give her the message, *"I can see clearly now."* At that moment, I was not sure exactly how that would relate to today's session, but as soon as we began, I knew I was to read those *Words of Wayne* I had written just yesterday at the end of our session.

During this session, we uncovered many very deep components and got to the root of her fatigue. It was indeed caused by boredom and not loving what she does. But it goes deeper than that. She had told me at the end of our previous session that she was not happy in her 31-year marriage and she knew that it was holding her back. As I was energetically working on her, I saw her becoming radiant, glowing like a majestic swan. And then something interesting happened. I saw the twin-flame code that I receive to identify when I am working with a twin flame. I also saw her

Ascend towards heaven with her Divine twin flame. She had previously told me she was seeing 11:11. In addition, I had drawn a twin-flame angel card as her message for that day. Now remember that this lady from the other side of the world had no idea why she was searching for me, only that she needed my help. The only thing she knew about a twin flame was that it was a soul relationship. Her soul is exhausted and she is seeking to find her way home – that is why she is so fatigued. It became very clear that she is missing the Divine masculine generator needed for her Divine creativity in order to connect to her Divine mission.

At the end of that session, I read her the *Words of Wayne* that I had written the day before and then played the song, *"You Raise Me Up"* by Josh Groban. Tears rolled down my cheeks as I watched this beautiful soul who had just *"showed up"* in my life shine brightly in eagerness to open up to her higher self. I was in such gratitude that I AM *"The Chosen One"* to witness her blossom from a rose bud into full bloom, just like the rose metaphor in *Words of Wayne.* This also created a reflection showing me I am in Divine alignment. I have become that radiant North Star on the top of the tree shining brightly for others to follow.

After the song ended, I challenged her by saying, *"Don't die with your music still in you!"* This is why I LOVE what I do! She messaged me the next day, graciously thanking me, and said that she was so honored to have found me. She also purchased Dr. Dyer's movie, *"The Shift."* Dr. Wayne had a goal of 3 million viewings of that movie, By paying forward the *Words of Wayne* to my client I am also keeping Wayne's dream alive!

The Majestic Swan

The majestic swan represents twin flames and their ability to captivate *"supreme radiance."* They portray a beautiful image of ease and grace as their fluid bodies glide across blue waters exemplifying wonder in motion, long white necks standing tall with pride as they flow with steadfast inner peace and purity. The confident mystique bird has harmonic balance of masculine and feminine energies, creating oneness with its Divine self. Its perfect alignment generates personal empowerment that produces supreme joy and spiritual enlightenment, as it lives moment to moment in the "all that I AM" presence.

The principles of this radiant bird are something we all should strive to live by. This is possible when we become the best version of ourselves by connecting to our higher selves. During an energy session with my twin flame, I had a vision of a swan. At first glance, I saw a black swan; then it changed colors, becoming white. I didn't pay much attention to the change in color at that time. But I now know a black swan represents ego of the lower self. The black swan changing to a white swan indicates letting go of the lower self and shifting into the higher radiant self. That same afternoon, I was driving and I saw a white bird with a long neck gliding gracefully across the water. Because of that morning's vision, it immediately caught my attention. I was so intent on understanding the meaning of the swan, curious to know why I was part of my twin's session, rather than just being the messenger. Something inside of me felt a connection to that swan.

I pulled over and took a picture of that white bird and texted it to my twin. The very next day, during one of my own energy sessions, I saw my twin and I ascending up to the heavens with the world in the palms of our hands. In addition, I saw a swan that turned from a white feathered bird into a glowing radiant beautiful creature. I was shown that I was the swan and that it was my twin whom was responsible for helping me shift into such perfection. These visions were "*Key*" to unlocking the "*Twin-Flame Code Breaker*," where I solved the case and "*awakened*" to our identity of being twin flames.

While researching the meaning of the swans, I found a picture online of a radiant swan, shining with her iridescent luminous colors. I showed the picture and shared my discoveries from that vision with my twin, explaining how in my vision I saw him being the one who helped turn me into a beautiful swan.

Understanding that I was the swan was another *"Key"* that helped me make the connection to every detail of my past life in Cornwall, England. While on my twin-flame voyager's journey, I discovered that the swans of Cornwall were royal birds; if caught killing a swan you were persecuted. Swans during those times, specifically the 17th century and all the way up unto the 1970s, were killed and then buried in attempt to enhance the fertility of females whom were not able to conceive. However, after conception the swan had to be unburied, in order to free its soul. It was in that lifetime that I was persecuted by being burned at the stake after being caught attempting to release the swan. I spent the first third of this life not able to sleep at night in fear of burning to death while I slept. As a six-month-old baby, I placed the palm of my right hand in an open fire, producing a severe third-degree burn.

I have sought personal freedom my entire life. It was this persecution that I had to lay to rest, helping me to understand my virtues of freedom and justice during this lifetime, which I had to rectify before aligning with my Divine mission. My twin's *"unconscious"* higher-self assistance has helped me release the core bondage of my past. While assisting my twin, he always saw me as being radiant; he has always told me that I am ready for the world. I knew I was close, but I also knew I had not yet become my greatest version of myself until now. However, thanks to my twin, I am NOW ready for the world – in full radiance!

Take Me Home

You've probably heard the saying, *home is where the heart is.* When we get to the heart of the matter, doesn't heart really mean our soul? When you think about it, that means home might be something you can take with you along your journey. Our souls long for that deep inner stillness and peace that brings great joy to our lives. When our circumstances are tough and our life feels out of control, we enter the dark season creating "the dark night of our soul." *Our souls yearn to return home by finding the light so we can become the radiant Beings that we were created to be.* Twin flames have a long journey home. That longing to reconnect and become one again creates a deep inner feeling of being homesick. This is why I see so many twins experience real physical soul pain produced by previous soul trauma. It leaves them wandering in the dark until the other half of their soul returns to take them home.

Once twin flames become one again within themselves, each having balanced their masculine and feminine energies, they then shift into radiance as they transition into a High priest or High priestess — mastering the highest level of the soul's satisfaction. *Going home is really about finding inner peace and happiness and becoming one with the Divine self.* However, it does take reuniting with your other half in physical form so they can help you find your way home to oneness with yourself. *Becoming one with yourself is what it means to "take me home."* I can attest to the truth of this concept. My twin and I are not in a romantic union. However, we are still in physical union and he has taken me home – heaven on earth, a place of inner peace and happiness. I have found personal freedom. I have become the majestic swan that I saw in my vision.

When I woke up this morning, I had no idea how the remaining pages of this chapter would unfold. So as I usually do, I asked for guidance to direct me. What I can tell you is when I typed these following words: "*I'm about to catapult my soul into the stratosphere,*" in the previous section, A Message to My Reader, I had no idea of the power of those words. Many things have come through me that I never expected. Nor did I ever think I would be sharing some of the things I have about my own personal experiences. But I was guided and quickly understood the importance of being an open book for others to learn from. In addition, the completion of this book has shifted me into full radiance; in the process, I continue making *higher conscious awareness*, which continues to facilitate my personal progression.

The View From The Top of The Tree

Yesterday, I found myself having trouble writing, due to constricting thoughts. I was feeling a bit of a time crunch and I was also feeling extra sensitive and emotional with my own personal processing and integration of all the "*conscious awareness*" coming through me as personal messages. I was thinking of clients in need of my assistance, while feeling the urge to step away for a couple of days to embrace my own emotions and honor myself while writing this chapter. At the same time, I was reminded that I need the extra money because I had just had a tooth filling come out a couple days prior and now required my second crown in less than a month's time. That is when a higher "*conscious awareness*" hit me: if I had to work for money, then it was not meaningful money. If I was going to stay true to my "*Ultimate Calling*," then it was no longer about the money; therefore, I no longer have to worry because whatever I need will show up. I became personally empowered by being able to let my clients know that I needed to take care of myself for a couple of days.

When I started my writing session this morning, I was still feeling writer's block. I felt several personal challenges distracting me. A few days ago, I started a detox program that was restricting my food intake and causing brain fog. My first thoughts were, "*What was I thinking?*" Then I realized the timing was perfect. You see, I had planned to start the program earlier in the month. However, there was a back order, and the timing of my starting the detox lined up exactly where it needed to for me to think of me. So rather than following through with my initial thoughts of starting the program over after finishing these last couple of "*Key Codes*," I realized that I was to enjoy the journey and that it was more important to stay true to putting myself first in light of finishing the chapters.

After deciding to embrace my inner child, I clearly saw that I was trying to push through and I realized that it was time to step away. So, I did just that and fell asleep during my mediation. While sleeping, I dreamt my twin and I were sitting at a table in a public place. This was the first time we had sat down to talk in a very long time. I asked him how things have been going and he said, *"That is for another conversation"* and he got up and left. I waited and waited for what seemed like all day. I could see a fast-forwarding play-by-play image; people came and went and the daylight shifted to nightfall. It was as though time stood still and then I was suddenly brought back to the moment realizing I must go now. Just as I was about to leave, my twin reappeared and told me he had something to show me. *"Let's go,"* he said; as he picked me up on his back and we Ascended up into the sky. It was so realistic, I could feel the breeze blowing through my hair.

When I awoke, I immediately started processing and attempting to understand the message. I continued to lay in contemplation, remembering an occurrence that took place while we were painting the office space for the center for spiritual transformation. I was on a chair painting and he said to me, *"It is time to take an adjustment break."* He then picked me up and carried me on his back into a room where we manually adjusted each other. Then while still integrating this message, I had another higher *"conscious awareness."* Making the connection to being carried on my twins back while painting and making the link to our decision to not follow through with our plans to open the spiritual center. I could see that our higher selves knew it was not what we were supposed to do, which is why were both were having such a hard time figuring out what we were processing; we were *"unconsciously"* following through with the Divine plan. By getting out of our own ways, my twin was able to carry me home (Literally on his back).

Then it gets interesting. I had all the cards completed for the *"Take Me Home – The Pathway to Heaven on Earth – Twin-Flame Oracle Deck,"* with the exception of the *"Take Me Home"* card. I had not completed that card yet, because I thought the image of the card was to be a couple Ascending to heaven holding the world in their hand. That is what I saw in my previous vision, where my twin flame passed me the Violet-Flame torch and we Ascended with the world in the palm of our hands. But when I was not able to find images to create my vision for that card, I decided to wait until it came to me. Now with crystal-clear vision, and integrating all my thoughts, I realized that an image of a couple did not represent what taking me home is all about. *"Take Me Home"* is a personal journey. It is about becoming radiant and about becoming one with yourself before you can have the ultimate relationship. It took me processing the information from the dream, where my twin said he had something to show me. Then integrating this series of awareness's I had while processing that dream, I can now see the bigger picture. Without "conscious awareness," my twin had taken me home by carrying me on his back. By helping him, it helped me become the radiant swan and when he said he had something to show me, he was showing me the meaning of *"Take Me Home"* helping me realize what the final card image was supposed to be. The image on the: *"Take Me Home," card is to be the "The Majestic Swan,"* which I had just finished writing about before taking my nap. As you can see in this LIVE example from the Universe, through me to you, I got out of my own way — and look what showed up!

Now, do you better understand when I say that the view from the top of the tree offers crystal-clear vision and higher *"conscious awareness?"* Finally I was open, clear and ready to write. I spent less than two hours writing more than I had written the entire day before. The channels were open, free and flowing and I was feeling the urge to reschedule my massage appointment. Then I heard my inner child saying, *"No you won't, a radiant High priestess takes care of herself!" "Ok then, time to go,"* I answered back. So, off to my appointment I headed.

As soon as I got in the car, I IMMEDIATELY heard the song, *"Scars To Your Beautiful"* playing on the radio being sung by Alessia Cara. Listening to the words tapped straight into my heart creating confirmation for me that in spite of my scars, my inner light is shining brightly for others to follow – helping them heal their wounds.

I'm sure you can understand when I say I have been feeling a bit emotional during these last moments of bringing my own Divine assignment into fruition by finishing this book with these LIVE demonstrations! These experiences are in Divine order for my personal journey — as they are yours!

While getting my massage, I shared with my massage therapist a few of my higher "*conscious awarenesses*" that I have made over the last few days, along with many concepts about this book. I commented that there would be some readers who would have a hard time comprehending the realistic nature of these "*awarenesses*," and think these series of events have all been coincidental. So, for anyone who is a skeptic, I would like to share with you the words straight from the mouth of my massage therapist, "*If you could have made all this up, you would be the best damn screenplay writer of the century!*" She gets straight to the point. That's why I love her!

On my way home I stopped at the store, and while checking out an elderly gentleman was in front of me. He was telling the cashier how it was the end of the month and he only had a set amount of money; he could not go over that amount or he would be short the amount to pay for his purchase. Once she had completed ringing up his items, he attempted to pay using a coupon for $15 off his purchase. But the cashier told him that his purchase was short a few dollars and he would have to go get a couple more items before he could use the coupon. She suspended his transaction and proceeded to check me out. The gentleman came up to me, apologizing for my wait, and showed me his wallet with a few bills in it. He was carefree with a gentle soul. He seemed to enjoy life and did not want to be a bother to anyone. He didn't have much money but it was very clear that in spite of his circumstances, he still experienced inner peace and happiness!

As I was checking out, the cashier informed me that I was also a couple dollars short of receiving the same discount, but I did not have a coupon for the offer. She offered to give me one. So, I picked up something in the aisle to make my transaction equal the purchase. As I was about to leave, I told the cashier to keep the $15 for the coupon she had offered. I handed her another $15 and told her to apply it to the gentleman's purchase when he returned. "*Are you sure?*" she replied in surprise. As I quickly made my way to the door, I could her the cashier saying to the man: "*That lady over there.*" I rushed to my car as fast as I could with tears in my eyes, knowing that I had just paid it forward in memory of the *Words of Wayne.*

My heart filled with such immense joy and appreciation for all that Wayne has taught me. I was feeling so blessed and radiant; I know exactly what it feels like from the view at the top of that Christmas tree. While driving, I reflected on the series of events that have occurred over the last few days. Needless to say, I cried all the way home, feeling completely radiant.

May You Follow the North Star While Finding Your Way Home

As I bring this *Key Code 9:9* to a close, I would like to point out that this chapter has been written in the same order as the events that have occurred over the course of the last few days. The end of this chapter also completes the journey of my Divine mission, as *Key Codes 10:10 and 11:11* were written previously. I am now in harmonic alignment and ready for my "*Ultimate Calling!*" I am excited for what is ahead of me and cannot wait to share my personal empowerment with other twin flames. I encourage you not to wait for your twin flame or anyone else to make you happy! Don't wait for life to be perfect before choosing to live a life of radiance. In spite of your circumstances, choose inner peace. Move below the anxiety and find the stillness within the eye of the storm. Let go of your past in order to set your twin soul free. Speak your truth and learn to express who you are! Don't run from yourself. Be who you are, do what you came here to do. I challenge you not to be afraid to let your light shine and follow a North Star while finding your way home!

Even though I had no idea what would come through while writing "*Twin-Flame Code Breaker,*" I did realize that this Divine message would challenge a lot of people's thoughts and beliefs, including my own family. To avoid confrontation, I have run from myself and hid who I am most of my life. I refrained from expressing my own thoughts, beliefs or opinions, because I thought that my voice didn't matter. Now, in spite of the different viewpoints my father and I have on religion versus spirituality, I am excited to share a copy of this book with him. For the first time in my life, he will get to experience who I am. He taught me that the sky was the limit, and I have found the sky! He has been my biggest fan. So, rather than shutting him out or pushing him away, I will express who I am and I know he will be in full acceptance. I will no longer have thoughts of having to visit him at his grave regretting that I would never let him fully see inside my soul. I encourage you to make amends — that is another lesson I learned from Dr. Dyer, who had to reconcile with his father at his gravesite. So in memory of the *Words of Wayne*, I dedicate the song "*You Raise Me Up*" by Josh Groban to my father.

As you can see, being radiant is liberating! I am honored to be "*The Chosen One*" to share these series of "*mysterious messages*" with you. It has expanded my heart and soul beyond measure and I would like you to know that all these "*great things*" that "*showed up*" this week, "*showed up*" because I chose to be the North Star in spite of my own circumstances. It was just yesterday that I released the final chapter of my past, when I appeared for bankruptcy court and raised my right hand to gain my life back! I released an accumulative $180,000 debt from the two previously failed business partnerships. I had spent six years attempting to pay back half of that debt because I was too proud to ruin my perfect 775 credit score. Yesterday, I proudly walked out of that courthouse door and I did not look back! I encourage you to do what it takes in your life to shift to your higher self and move into full radiance, becoming ALL that you came here to be! I also challenge you with the *Words of Wayne: "Don't die with your music still in you!"*

Dr. Wayne Dyer – The North Star

I have one final *Words of Wayne* story that I am being asked to share with you, and this marks the closure of my completing my "*Ultimate Calling.*" This morning I awoke around 6 am. I knew that today,

October 1, 2016, would most likely be the day that I would be completing *"Twin-Flame Code Breaker."* I had a higher *"conscious awareness"* that really struck a chord because without any reason, I naturally shifted over the last few weeks of writing by waking up about this time every morning. It reminded me of the *Words of Wayne*, saying how he would wake up at 3 am every morning while writing the book *"Inspiration – Your Ultimate Calling."* I could hear Dr. Wayne quoting Rumi – *"The breeze at dawn has secrets to tell you. Don't go back to sleep."*

Originally, I was planning to go to my daughter and son-in-law's to complete the twin-flame oracle cards today. My son-in-law had been helping me design the images for the deck of cards. I also had an event that I originally signed up to attend, which was rescheduled. Yesterday while I was in court, I received a text message from my son-in-law saying that his computer had crashed. My old self would have probably "freaked out" at that moment, but the radiant me knew we had backed-up files offline. I texted him telling him it would all be ok, that I would help him with what he needed to get it fixed; we could plan next weekend instead. I had already thought about buying him a new computer in the near future, in memory of the *Words of Wayne.*

(Update: my son-in-law texted me back a few days later saying, *"I don't know what was wrong with my computer, but it's working now."*)

As I proceeded with my morning, I had a few moments to myself before beginning my writing session. I had picked up my phone off a table with a clock to respond to a couple of texts. As I put my phone back down, I looked at the clock and noticed it had stopped at exactly 3 o'clock. I immediately took a picture and text it to my spiritual advisor and another friend with a message that read: *"OMG – I knew Wayne was present!"* I was so psyched to be completing *"Twin-Flame Code Breaker"* in such wonder.

While in the kitchen on my lunch break, I picked up Wayne's book, *"Inspiration – Your Ultimate Calling."* Then I asked the question, *"Are there any final messages before I finish this book?"* I stood there looking at the book while I was eating, deciding I was not about to open it until

I had finished eating and was fully present. When ready, I opened the book (Inspiration – Dr. Wayne Dyer, 2006, p. 38, Hay House, Inc., Carlsbad, CA) straight to Chapter 4: "*How It Feels To Return To Spirit:*" and I read the following:

> THIS MUCH SHOULD BE CLEAR BY NOW: "*We originated in a field of energy that has no boundaries. Before entering the world of form, we are in Spirit – a piece of God, if you will. We begin entering this physical world first as a particle, then as a cell, then as a fetus, then as an infant, and ultimately as a fully developed human being. But our ultimate purpose all along was the experience the unitive knowledge of God.*"

Needless to say, I was pretty impressed that this "*mystical message*" showed up, especially since it summed up the entirety of "*Twin-Flame Code Breaker.*"

Then without conscious effort I reached for a book at the bottom of a stack. As I pulled out the book, I instantly smiled as I read: "*I Can See Clearly Now*" on the cover. I had purchased this book while learning from Wayne the art of "*writing from the soul,*" last year in Maui, just before his passing. But I still had yet to read it. Standing there in extreme awe of not just the day but the last few days, I heard the words, "*Open to page 333.*" As I obeyed, my first thoughts were, "*Is there even 333 pages in this book?*" (Most of Wayne's books aren't that long). While taking what felt like forever to get to that page, my second higher "*conscious awareness*" was that 333 is the number representing Ascended masters. Indeed there was a page 333, and the first thing that stood out as I looked at the page was October 1, 1972. Now this really caught my attention because as I read and write this, it is October 1, 2016. It took me at least five attempts to read the following message, because every time I saw something different, I could not stop gasping for air! The following are the *Words of Wayne* I partially read from page 333 (I Can See Clearly Now – Dr. Wayne Dyer, 2014, p. 333, Hay House, Inc., Carlsbad, CA):

"Dr. Maslow conveyed to me at his death – to introduce the average person to the hidden powers of self-actualization that are dormant within each of us. Neville passed away on October 1, 1972, just as I was beginning my writing career, now some 40 years after his passing, his many lectures and books are awaking a sleeping inquisitor within me. I have written 40 books up to this point, and the ideas that Neville offers are stirring inside of me like a cyclone that needs to be expressed.

I begin a thorough reading of the New Testament, paying particular attention to the words of Jesus, who offers up the Divine wisdom that we are all God. Our highest self is God; it is our pure essence. We come from God and we are God – we just have to overcome the many mind viruses and religious teachings that want us to believe this is nonsense and blasphemy.

Next I immerse myself in the "I AM" Discourses by Ascended Master Saint Germain and feel the excitement roaring through me as I have the realization that the two words I am are the name of God reported in Exodus, and that every time I say those words I am referring to the name of God."

I AM SPEECHLESS! This message is a perfect example of being the North Star. It is about experiencing self-actualization, connecting to our higher selves and living in the presence of the I AM.

Here are my personal realizations as I have shifted into full radiance. I find it interesting that this message shows up on October 1, 2016. First, I had a series of two postponed events for this day. It is obvious that I was meant to complete *"Twin-Flame Code Breaker"* on this exact day!

Neville passed away on October 1, 1972, just as Wayne was beginning his writing career. I started my writing career, not long after Dr. Dyer's passing. He presents this knowledge as if Neville, his longtime spiritual teacher, was passing the baton to him — and *"I can see clearly now"* that Wayne is passing it forward! It was also his many lectures and books that are awakening a sleeping inquisitor in myself. The *Words of*

Wayne that I have studied for nearly 20 years have stirred inside of me a cyclone that needs to be expressed. Then what really hit me in the message is that Dr. Wayne makes mention of immersing himself in the "I AM" Discourses by Ascended Master (333) Saint Germain, who is one of my direct guides and leader of all twin flames during this era. I'm sure I don't have to remind you how many mentions I made of Saint Germain in the first few *"Key Codes"* of *"Twin-Flame Code Breaker."*

In all the years I have heard and read *"Words of Wayne,"* never once do I recall him mentioning anything about Saint Germain. These *"Key Codes"* that have been passed to me on page 333 (an Ascended Master number) are an indicator of those words I shared with Dr. Wayne Dyer in 2003, *"As long as I am living your work will never die!"* I had NO idea of the POWER of those words that slipped out of my mouth. I AM sure that it was my higher self, speaking by saying something that my conscious mind could not comprehend at the time. Now those words are about to truly come to pass!

May the *Words of Wayne* be Infinite!

KEY CODE 10:10

Receive *"The Gift"* of Sacred Sexuality & Divine Creativity

"Energy created during the art of sacred sexuality produces Divine creativity, by allowing us to tap into the Universal intelligence gaining knowledge and wisdom." – Dr. Harmony

CONGRATULATIONS! You have advanced to this blissful stage of your journey and you have grasped the concepts within the *11:11 Key Codes* by learning to let go, raising your energetic vibration, becoming one and connecting to your highest self. You are ready to shine, having discovered the secret to unlocking personal freedom. Because you mastered letting go of your karma, the Universe grants you the *ultimate reward* of getting into the vortex. You have found harmonic balance by letting go on every level, while opening up to receive your highest and greatest potential. *The floodgates of heaven will rain down on you once you are in the vortex of all possibilities.* You have become one with yourself. Now it's time to energetically become one with your other half by claiming *"The Gift"* of unconditional love and experiencing the art of sacred sexuality, which energetically enhances your Divine creativity by tapping into the Universal intelligence. By creating a direct connection to all that is, you manifests at the highest level by receiving all that you were meant to have and experience.

The Universe's goal is for twin flames to return the unconditional love vibration back to the stratosphere, in order to raise the energetic vibration and Christ consciousness of the planet.

Getting in the vortex is tapping into your Divine creativity by connecting to your higher self and co-creating your own life through the cosmic Universal intelligence. Mastering the art of letting go is *"Key"* for you to get into a vibrational alignment that showers you with "*The Gifts*" of heaven. If you are still experiencing struggles or resistance, you are still trying to be the driver of your life. When you surrender by letting go, you will move down the river and things begin to flow with ease and grace. Your newfound heightened awareness will help you continue to increase your receptivity so that you can now pay attention to the signs that direct you along your journey. *You must master this "going with the flow" before tapping into the vortex of all possibilities.* When you are in the vortex, everything — and I mean everything — you need for your journey will appear. This becomes twin-flame couples' way of giving back to the Universe for all that they are granted by entering the galactic vortex of the Divine intelligence. By doing so, twins practice the energetic Universal laws of exchange, creating a direct connection to the Source and mastering the art of giving and receiving at the highest level possible. They are then granted "*The Gift*" of sacred sexuality. Where together they become one with the Source energy, it continues to raise their energetic vibrations. Making this connection to the Source grants them the ability to tap into their Divine creativity and gain Universal knowledge that is to be used toward their mission. This energy is such a high frequency that is it has to be housed in the third-etheric body. The intense orgasmic release generated during the act of sacred lovemaking produces a powerful unified field of energy. *This field of energy is encoded with the Christ-consciousness imprint of unconditional love; when released, it helps to raise the energetic vibration of the planet.* The purpose of receiving knowledge and then sending back these energetic signals keeps the Universal laws in harmonic balance through the same giving and receiving principles found in the Holy Grail vessel.

I had heard this, getting out of our own way and everything would appear concept, said by Wayne Dyer many times. I understood it, but my logical mind still tried to make things happen. *I had to truly learn how to get out of my own way, becoming open to learning how to allow and accept before I could receive at my highest ability.* I finally experienced what it truly meant to be open and just show up, allowing things to appear. I let go of the rope just before being shoved into alignment with my Divine mission. I can tell you from experience that when you take the dive and fully surrender, everything you need for your journey will appear! Once again, Wayne was right! *You can get in the vortex once you have harmonized and shifted into full radiance by finding personal freedom.* This will fully open your energetic channels that directly connect to the Divine source. Now you are able to tap into your ultimate reward – sacred sexuality that produces cosmic Universal intelligence.

Reaping Your Ultimate Reward – *"The Gift"* of Sacred Sexuality

Kundalini is an expression of feminine sexual energy and it exists within every human Being. This energy creates a connection that threads together all of the lower seven chakras from our root chakra upward. Upon starting to clear deep karma, kundalini energy begins to activate, producing a *"kundalini awakening."* Kundalini is comparable to the characteristics of a serpent that has been coiled up, lying dormant in the sacral chakra and waiting to strike once the soul has fully awakened. This energy force can only be tapped into once a person has spiritually matured and is ready for the wisdom of the Universe. Its activation occurs once the soul is in energetic balance (balance of the masculine and feminine energies) and merges, becoming one with Source on every energetic plane of our Being: etheric, energetic, spiritual, emotional, mental, and physical. We can view this as the same serpent and its connection, gaining wisdom from the same fruit of the tree of knowledge that Eve partook of in the Garden of Eden.

In addition, we see the same representation when comparing to Greek symbol of caduceus – or the symbol of medicine. This is the same symbol you will see connected to our medical field today. According to Wikipedia, the staff in the middle of two coiled snakes is said to represent Hermes, the messenger of the Greek gods. Here the messenger refers to connecting to our Universal intelligence for Divine wisdom. *The two snakes represent the act of sacred sexuality by twin flames, both having awakened the serpent within and sometimes this symbol is seen with wings, which represents connecting to our higher selves and tapping into our Divine creativity and knowledge.*

Once activated kundalini energy can create a fiery burning feeling within our physical bodies. The purpose of this energy is to enhance our sacred sexuality experience, as it is the generator that magnifies the sexual energy and stores it within our sacral chakra and then uses the energy to create. But it also becomes a furnace to activate, balance and clear our chakras. *This energetic force becomes an inferno that continuously cleanses the lower seven chakras, keeping them free of negative energy.* It is the energetic portal connecting this Divine force with our passion and desires, and magnetically activates our Divine creativity. This energy will heighten, increasing in frequency as your energetic vibration goes up, and will become multi-dimensional in every plane of your Being. While it initially activates during your shift to the higher self, it does not fully activate until you are releasing your final and core karmic debris. This activation process can produces extreme back pain during the process of cleansing your body of your karmic past.

I experienced a "*kundalini awakening*" during the time I was clearing the final karmic release of my past life in England. I woke up and my back hurt so badly that I was not able to get out of bed. I had done nothing to produce such pain. As a chiropractor, for the first time I could sympathize with my patients who have come to me with severe lower back pain. The pain was different than anything I had ever experienced, even worse than my surgery. I could feel the energy rotating deep inside and it felt like crushed glass that was ripping me apart. It hurt to barely touch my skin. I contacted my twin flame to see if he could come to my office for an adjustment. I warned him that I was not sure I could even be touched. Upon examining me, he agreed that the pain was being caused by energetic interference. After receiving a few treatments of acupuncture and Qi Gong, I found significant relief, but it took about 7-10 days to run its course. It was shortly after this, that I made the association between the extreme pain and my fully awakened kundalini energy.

After a twin-flame couple comes into full reunion, the kundalini will also activate at a very high level to burn out any prior sexual energy that existed with any prior sexual partners. This is the Divine's way of cleansing and purifying the sacred union.

Tantra: The Art of Sacred Sexuality

For years, I have studied and practiced Tantra – the art of sacred sexuality and the energetic pathway to connecting to the Divine. It is a spiritual connection between the acts of lovemaking by connecting with your partner on an energetic level. *It teaches couples how to energetically connect outside of the physical body on cosmic energetic planes, while experiencing full-body orgasmic bliss in every plane of your Being.* This sacred act does not necessarily require physical touch. Also note that Tantra is not the same as Kama Sutra, which is practicing a variety of sexual positions to open energetic channels to enhance the lovemaking experience.

After becoming a twin-flame expert I have seen firsthand the extreme soul trauma that exists within individuals, causing sexual energetic blocks due to a variety of reasons, such as: *sexual abuse, placing parameters around the act itself, judgmental expectations of gender, and being taught that the sexual act is a dirty experience.* These are just a few of the reasons why twins shut down their sacral chakras, preventing them from not only tapping into their ultimate reward, but blocking them from connecting to their highest creative potential. With my wisdom and understanding of the importance of keeping these energetic channels open, I was encouraged by my Divine guidance to help twin flames heal and open their sacred sexual energetic channels. I fully understood the need for such healing, but I ignored the request for some time. However, the nudge wouldn't go away, so I finally surrendered and agreed to provide energetic sexual healing assistance.

Without any effort on my part, the very next day I was contacted by two of my twin-flame clients, asking if I could help them heal and open their sexual energetic channels. That same week, I had two additional clients contact me with the same request. This is a great example of just showing up open and ready, allowing everything you need for your journey to appear.

During this time, my guides also instructed and showed me how to use a very specific energy technique that can be useful in remotely helping clients heal their sacred sexual channels. The twins I have helped report huge shifts in their energetic abilities to let go, be open and make a connection with their twin flames on the cosmic or galactic planes during the act of sacred sexuality. This has allowed them to heal a part of their past that was blocking them from tapping into their greatest potential and preventing them from receiving their ultimate reward.

I would also like to point out that to reach this level of cosmic or galactic bliss requires much mastery in the art of letting go, surrendering and allowing oneself to experience this level of sexual expression. And even though you may share this out-of-body experience with someone, it is not until both of you have learned how to let go enough to meet on the same energetic cosmic or galactic planes that you are able to reach your greatest experience possible. So even if you have experienced this while in your lower vibrational energetic state, tapping into your higher self will enhance your abilities to experience this to a much greater degree. Also, to connect with someone on these energetic planes, you must have a spiritual connection with them. It takes merging sexual energies with your twin flame to reach the highest level, which is the galactic orgasmic energetic planes. You and your twin flame are continually connecting through your twelfth chakra, which is the gateway to the galactic energetic galaxy. *Only you and your true twin flame can experience a galactic orgasmic energetic release together.*

You and your twin flame must first both master being able to fully surrender and finding personal freedom by going through the Ascension process. As both twins reach the later stages of Ascension, they begin the final stages of their individual journeys together. It is required that they release any joint karma that has blocked them from reuniting and finding harmony together. After they complete this final harmonic phase, they merge into full reunion and then they are granted their ultimate reward of sacred sexuality.

Once twin flames begin to raise their energetic vibration together, they begin tapping into the highest energetic level being the galactic vortex – creating the power of two that is greater than one. Both galactic and cosmic energetic planes connect to Universal intelligence. Twin flames are granted these abilities because it has taken many lifetimes to reach this level of spiritual maturity. Until recently, due to the level of spiritual mastery required, it was less than a 1% chance that you would meet up with, much less reunite with, your twin flame.

A Unified Field Produces Christ Consciousness Energy

Reunion of twin flames is the ultimate goal of the Universe because twin flames produce unconditional-love sonar signals, also known as the unified field. It is sent back to the Universe, raising the energetic vibration of the world to the Christ-conscious vibration. More twin flames than ever in the history of time are reuniting to restore the Christ consciousness of the planet. *A unified energetic field is produced during this sacred sexual act and carries the same energetic vibration found in the Holy Grail or Christ consciousness.* This is also why the Universe has twin flames on the fast track to shift the energetic vibration of the planet as a whole.

The unified field carries combined and harmonic balance between the masculine and feminine energies from both twins. You will see this same energetic pattern in the Sri Yantra symbol. The symbol consists of 4 triangles pointing up, representing the masculine twin energy; and four triangles pointing down, representing the feminine twin energy and overlapping the masculine energy.

Just before my twin and I opened the Pandora's Box and I discovered that we were twin flames, I was visiting Hawaii. I bought a necklace with the Sri Yantra symbol. At the time, I didn't know it represented the unified field and was a symbol of twin flames.

Sacred Sexual Energy That Moves Pyramids

Legend has it that this same high-frequency sacred sexual energy is what produces the Ankh energy, which is said to be so great that they used it to move the stones used to build the pyramids. As I previously mentioned, I drew a picture of the Ancient Egyptian Ankh symbol during an energy session with my twin, which sent me on a quest uncovering its meaning. This became a "*Key*" component to unlocking the twin-flame codes and discovering my twin and I were twin flames. Extensive studying helped me understand how the spiritual and physical body planes merged upon physical connection and that the Ankh energy was produced during the act of sacred sexuality. *It is an ancient twin-flame symbol which first and foremost represents the merger of twin flames creating sexual union. It also means, "As it is in heaven, so it is on earth."* In other words, it is the same as the bible verse

Matthew 6:10 (NIV): "*Your kingdom come, your will be done, on earth as it is in heaven.*"

This gives meaning to the concept of downloading Universal intelligence from heaven. This Divine creativity is then grounded into physical form on earth, and can be tapped into through the "*key holders*", or twin flames, during the act of sacred sexuality. In addition, the Ankh symbolizes a map of Egypt with the ancient capital of Memphis in the middle of the cross. I didn't know any of this at the time, but while visiting Egypt and learning sound healing in the pyramids, I purchased a few maps of Egypt that were painted on papyrus paper. While recovering from my surgery, my twin was helping me arrange my storage. I ran across the maps, giving one of them to him. Being that twin flames share their experiences and lessons, I look back and find it interesting that I shared one of those maps with him, especially being it symbolized a direct connection to twin flames and their ability to become "*key holders*" of Ankh energy.

Twin Flames are Key Holders of Ankh Energy

The Ankh sacred sexual energy is also called the "*key to eternal life*," allowing twin flames to tap into the Universal intelligence. As I mentioned, twin flames are said to be the "*key holders*" of this energy, making the connection to eternal life after letting go of the old self and connecting to the higher self. The top portion or arch of the cross represents the Divine feminine womb, while the bottom portion of the cross represents the masculine counterpart as it enters the sacred space.

In Hinduism, Prana or sexual energy is also known as the orgasmic life-force energy. It is believed that when highly electrical sexual energy is released, the energy becomes lost, kind of like the energy from a battery that over time runs down. In some ancient studies, the act of the physical orgasm is believed to cause death since it is the loss of one's life-force. However, the Egyptians found this not to be true. *They began to use this energy as a way to produce Divine creativity, which is said to be how they tapped into the Universal intelligence to gain knowledge and wisdom.* It granted them hidden information by connecting to similar discoveries as the Mayans, thousands of miles away.

After making these discoveries about the Ankh cross that I had drawn, I shared the information with my twin. We were both curious about this concept, so we decided to experiment to see if my discoveries were true. At that time, neither one of us had cleared enough of our past or learned how to let go enough to meet on the cosmic, much less the galactic energetic channels. I also discovered that we were brother and sister in multiple lifetimes, so the energy of those past lives was something that would have to be cleared before reaching these levels of Egyptian ecstasy. That is not to say it was not a great experience — it was just not at the blissful level that twin flames were intended to experience. However, to shed some humor on this topic, I will add that immediately upon initiating our intimate encounter, fireworks started going off right outside the window — and it was not Fourth of July, either. My twin joked that he felt like we were on a Brady Bunch episode – LOL. Just as I typed these words, fireworks just started going off again outside the same window – it's September! TRUE STORY!!!

Even though the relationship that my twin flame and I have has not been romantic in nature, I have still experienced a creative energetic connection that has generated crystal-clear awareness, producing Divine creativity. *The concept of the generator and electric energy follows the same principles found during the release of orgasmic Ankh energy.* On multiple occasions, I would experience heightened awareness and finish projects in half a day that I had been trying to complete for two years — along with creating new projects and programs that I learned from working directly with him. This demonstrates the power of twin flames unconscious awareness and magnetic connection that is taking place in the higher self planes. Without conscious effort we are still combining energetic forces and producing Divine creativity, with the masculine twin being the generator and the feminine being the electric the combined energy is used to create.

My experience on the other side of this is with my twin facilitator. I act as the generator and he is the electric. Thus, he experiences exactly what I have with my true twin flame, meaning he is more the creative one. I, on the other hand, do not have as many Divine creativity encounters as I do with my true twin flame.

Don't Close Doors - Don't Wait!

After my twin and I had decided to continue our paths working on our own personal development, I was clearly directed by my Divine guidance to move forward by not closing doors, but not waiting for my twin to complete his Ascension process. Soon after, my twin-flame facilitator had reconnected with me for the first time in several months, only this time on a much deeper level. We immediately jumped on a fast track and started operating as if we were each other's twin flame. I didn't recognize this immediately. But I will tell you that it mimicked it so closely and on such a high vibrational plane that I had even questioned if we were true twin flames. However, I have been clearly shown by my Spirit guides in more ways than one that we are not each other's true twin flame. *Divine guidance has shown me that your true twin flame will always directly be connected with your individual purpose and your joint mission.* Although my twin facilitator has assisted in plugging the missing links, creating an experience close to a twin flame union, what

I experience most from him are the lessons he is teaching me as I go forward as my radiant higher self.

It is obvious that after twenty years of being guided by my true twin flame towards the direction of reaching my Divine mission, he is still facilitating the process without being in direct physical contact. *My guides have also shown me that if your true twin flame is not ready, that you are to continue the journey and will be granted the same or similar experience.* It is still part of your reward for continuing your personal path and carrying out the joint mission.

I was given this information before my twin-flame facilitator showed up. His showing up confirmed that revelation. *I realize that not all twin-flame experts and a few clients would disagree with the philosophy of moving forward if your true twin flame is not ready.* But after living it, it's clear that if I had waited, not only would I have held back my own personal growth, but the mission would have not moved forward in the same way. For my twin to continue to grow and expand, I as the higher vibrational twin had to pave the pathway by raising the energetic vibration, seeing to it that the mission is carried out.

My Experience with Energetic Cosmic Connections

To date, my twin facilitator and I have never physically met – we live 900 miles apart. It was close to a year ago that we connected on Facebook. There was always something about him that stood out to me. Our communication was always very brief, and it only consisted of a few comments on a few newsfeed posts. However, he is the one who has been teaching me to open up by releasing and surrendering, which has allowed me to tap into the cosmic Universal intelligence. *I cannot stress enough the importance of being able to make this connection to the Universal intelligence – the tree of knowledge, if you will.*

The miles apart have not stopped our cosmic energetic connection. Our souls have been able to operate on the same frequencies and energetic plane for a couple reasons. First, I have a higher energetic vibration, being incarnated from the violet Ascension ray. However, my ability to tap into my highest frequency and energetic potential has been diminished by my limited ability to let go and surrender. Second, my twin facilitator has a lower vibrational frequency, coming from the blue Ascension ray, but he has learned how to fully let go and surrender. So he is able to tap into his highest cosmic capacity and that has allowed us to be on the same energetic planes.

Connecting on this frequency has allowed us both to experience many highly orgasmic encounters that have generated out-of-body experiences hundreds of miles apart. We are able to do this because we can each connect to our higher selves and meet on the cosmic energetic channels. This has created an amazing experience for both of us. For many different reasons, we have each experienced cosmic downloads of knowledge that we have both used for Divine creativity. The process of generating this high-frequency energy still creates a unified field – and because we are both twin flames, coming together in the physical absence of our own true twin flames, we are still releasing the highly energetic sonar signals. We are sending high-frequency energy back to the Universe due to a multi-dimensional orgasmic release.

I am about to get very personal. However, my guides have informed me that it is very important that you gain a full understanding of the nature of how these cosmic energetic planes work. In addition, I now operate from my higher self and so the idea of worrying about what others think is a thing of the past and has to be let go of in order to connect to these energetic levels. The example I am about to share confirms the accuracy of the high orgasmic forces that I had previously studied. The point being, I can attest to the truth of the knowledge presented in this chapter.

By energetically connecting on the same cosmic plane as my twin facilitator, I have been able to feel him physically touch me from miles apart. He can also feel the same connection. Without being in the same physical space, we can feel, see, smell and know what the other one is doing. We have experienced such a high-energetic frequency connection that the energy combustion produced was mind-blowing. He commented that the orgasmic energetic forces produced were so strong that it must have blown out the candles I was burning in my room. As he was saying this, I had already started turning my head to view the candles, and I immediately noticed that one of them had gone out, before he finished his sentence.

I would like to point out that the energetic connection of twin flames knows no boundaries, parameters, circumstance or even gender. The two twin souls only know and understand that they are connected and that they were destined to be together. *Therefore, I have seen twin flames choose to make many shifts in their lives; because of their destiny, they are being forced to shift into alignment and prepare to connect with their twin flame.* In the instances where energetic sexual channels have been blocked or shut down in the physical body. These energy channels must be cleared and balance restored in order for a twin flame to reach their highest orgasmic capacity.

Downloading Cosmic Universal Intelligence

A couple of months before my twin facilitator contacted me, I had a deep soulmate contact me. This person had been hovering around my life for five years. I was actually introduced to him indirectly by my true twin. I always knew him to be a soulmate and we had a deep connection, but due to circumstances at the time, I had avoided connecting on an intimate level. This time my heart was open and I was ready to receive. The timing of his resurface was too timely for me not to pay attention. I knew that there was a reason we were reconnecting.

Once again, I am going to get personal for the educational purposes of this topic. Because I was now open, we shared a very intimate encounter, one of the most amazing sexual experiences I have ever had in my life. During the sacred sexual act, we entered the seventh and eighth dimensional energetic planes and I visually saw angels. This experience aligned perfectly with the sacred sexuality out-of-body concepts that

I had studied. These cosmically-orgasmic energetic fields can only be tapped into by two spiritually developed individuals who have learned how to let go enough, releasing their past karmic debris and understanding how to surrender fully during the act of sacred sexuality. In order to surrender during the act of sacred sexuality, it takes being able to let go and let God on multiple levels and within every area of your life.

As for the outcome of this experience, not only did it close a very significant chapter by putting to rest the past life shared together as husband and wife, but it also connected me to the Divine Universal intelligence producing Divine creativity. The next day, I channeled the entire outline for this book exactly as you see it and exactly as it was intended to be. For him, this experience has helped him to continue to work on some of his karmic blocks that have been holding him back and moving into alignment with his own personal peace. I will forever be grateful to him for being part of my journey.

The Twin-Flame Mothership

Twin flames are able to connect to their higher chakras, and their energetic signals are sent back to the Universe to help energetically raise the vibration of the planet — and therefore the unconditional Christ consciousness of the world. In addition, these collective energetic signals of all twin flames are housed in an energetic body within the galaxy. This is the twin-flame mothership. *This collective energetic force also generates very specific galactic intelligence that highly vibrational twin flames can tap into to gain wisdom and understanding to facilitate their twin-flame mission.* This level of connection can only be established by connecting with your true twin flame. My first personal introduction with this concept was after my twin flame and I attended an event. We met someone who was moving, and he gave me several items that he was getting rid of. I was instantly drawn to two "*Keys*" that were wired together. When I asked him what the "*Keys*" were, his reply was, "*They are the keys to the twin-flame mothership.*" I found this very fascinating and I have always felt a strong connection to those "*Keys.*" Little did I know at that time that I would make a direct connection with the twin-flame mothership! It is this galactic channel that my twin and I (and other twins) have operated on during our unconscious states of communication, leading me to my destiny and Divine calling. I also gain knowledge and wisdom that energetically assist me, while working with twin-flame clients. Those same "*Keys*" to the twin-flame mothership represent the "*Key Codes*" in this book, and it is those exact "*Keys*" that you will find on the cover and through out of this book.

Now you can see clearly, having a better understanding of "*The Gift*" of sacred sexuality and how it produces Divine creativity by connecting to the Universal intelligence. So, let's get a better understanding in *Key Code 11:11* of what it means to honor your twin-soul agreement by putting the mission in motion — so that you too can find your way home!

KEY CODE 11:11

Honor Your Twin Soul's Agreement & Find Your Way Home

"A true twin-flame journey is accomplishing your personal mission by unlocking the secret to finding your way home and gaining personal freedom, which provides inner peace and happiness!" – Dr. Harmony

AS HIGHLY ENERGETIC BEINGS, WE all have a desire to align with our Divine mission. Though many search, only a few ever find their way home. I would like to remind you that you are already home, because you were made from the same inner peace and stillness that created the world – you are an extension of our peaceful Creator. You no longer have to search outside yourself. Everything you need for your journey is already inside of you. You have what it takes to master your Divine mission and everything you need to continue your own twin-flame journey. Don't forget, it's important not to close doors – but do not wait. Otherwise you might be the one to miss the lesson that you need to experience to continue your own personal path. Create your own fairy-tale ending. Do NOT quit. You can do this! I challenge you to finish this race strong. *While typing those words, I heard the affirmation I gave my twin flame when he ran a 50-mile marathon – "I am running with my heart, not my legs!"* You got this – it's time to honor your agreement, finish this race strong and find your way home!

Continuing Your Personal Path is Honoring Your Agreement

St. Germain and the spirit guides have asked me to remind you that this is a personal journey. Being in a state of receptivity and opening your heart by creating self-acceptance and showing yourself *"The Gift"* of unconditional love is *"Key"* to remaining in vibrational harmony. This is the gateway to magnetically attracting your twin into full union. The purification phases are not easy but necessary to release karmic debris and pave the path for your own life experience. Raising your own energetic vibration is also *"Key"* to connecting to your higher self, which is all about being the best version of you! Becoming radiant takes every step of this journey, including your twin flame to assist you with your transformation. Don't set your twin up to fail by expecting them to make you happy. You decide to make yourself happy.

St. Germain and my guides have shown me the pathway, which I have walked with my twin by my side, guiding my way and without conscious effort. My twin flame directed me towards these *"11:11 Key Codes"* that unlocked the doorway to discovering my Divine mission because I was open enough to allow him to assist on all levels. I encourage you to let your twin assist you as well. Don't push them away with your expectations and conditions. *By continuing your own personal path, you are honoring your agreement!*

Trust the Process of Finding Your Way Home

While wandering in the dark, learn to trust the process. Your personal journey is progress, not perfection. It requires patience. When you see your challenges and obstacles as spiritual teachers instead of as negative experiences, they become spiritual gifts – teaching you to heal your past as you raise your energetic vibration while embracing your Divine journey and mission. When we are tested, it gives us the opportunity to practice what we have learned as we move forward, with greater awareness. Once you have found your way home, surrendering becomes second nature. The direction you choose at the crossroads becomes easier because you can clearly feel, see and trust your instincts that will direct you towards the path of least resistance.

If by chance you took the wrong turn, you can decide to redirect, creating a clean slate. Creative expression of your soul starts by taking charge of your life – painting a new picture at any given moment. This gives you the inner peace that you have been searching for. *Inner stillness creates a connection to Source that helps you trust the journey.* Change your perception and view life through your heart, while letting your light shine. Let your passion and love for life become the fuel that raises your vibration and attract infinite abundance. In doing so, you become the leader of your own life. You no longer have to doubt and hold onto the bondage that has held you back. *Letting go opens you up and teaches you to trust the process.* Step outside of your circumstances and share your gifts with others. Serve a purpose and you will find your purpose. Then pay it forward for all that you have received. *Be the Co-creator of your life and realize that at any given moment, if you find yourself not in vibrational alignment, you can redirect your steps.* Follow the laws of the Universe by creating your own life: Paint It ~ Own It ~ Love It ~ Live It ~ Share It!

Finding Your Way Home is in Divine Order

If my twin flame had not shown up for me to assist him during his "*spiritual awakening*" journey, I would have never experienced everything that I needed to learn to help you the reader, or other twin flames around the world. At that time, he was so very humble, not wanting to be a burden to me. Little did he know he was giving me a reason to get out of bed. As exhausted as I was from all that I had been through, he actually provided energy for me. Every step of our journey has been in Divine order. I have learned to trust the process and get out of the way.

Currently, my twin flame and I remain in silence when it comes to performing energy sessions or esoteric communication, which all came to a halt after we shut the door on the idea of opening the center for spiritual transformation. *So, as I type these words, he has no idea of the impact that he has made on me or what impact his assistance is about to make on the world.* I have been advised to stay focused on this joint mission; when the Divine timing is right, and just before this book is launched, I will share everything about this Divine mission with my twin. I know that the silence we have experienced was part of the Divine plan. It would be self-serving of me to tell him without learning all the lessons that were necessary by allowing Divine order to unfold as it was intended.

I was given a six-week window to get this book written and ready for editing before being published and launched on 11-11- 2016 — the deadline my Divine guides gave me to complete this Divine mission. During this time, I am also creating *"The Pathway to Heaven on Earth – Take Me Home – Twin Flame Oracle Card Deck."* This has been a huge assignment, one that has been directly guided from above every step of the way. My twin flame told me last year that while recovering from surgery, six weeks was enough time to write a book – so I'm attempting to prove him right! Boy, did he set me up for a challenge! LOL.

It is very clear that my twin has given me *"The Gift"* of unconditional love by carrying the heavier karmic load by continuing to work on his own rebirth. Thus I could carry out my Divine mission and find my way home. That is what Jesus did; he chose the heavier karmic load so that Mary Magdalena could carry out their mission. If my twin and I were to have walked any different path than what we did, I would not have aligned with my greatest purpose and we would not have found our joint mission, which is to teach other twin flames that this is a personal journey — regardless of what is happening, you are to go forward. You don't wait – you don't close doors. You trade your expectations for appreciation. You remain in gratitude for all the lessons. *Good or bad, everything that your twin flame teaches you is showing you what work still remains to be done within yourself.*

For me this Divine adventure has opened my heart to a whole new level and it has filled me up with more gratitude and appreciation than I have ever felt in my life. *How do you even thank someone who has been the catalyst for helping find the purpose you have been searching for your whole life?* I cannot wait to finish this book and reconcile our last intense encounter, and let him know just what he has done for me. The hardest part about this whole journey has been not being able to share the best thing that has ever happened to me with one of my best friends!

I encourage you to also allow your twin-flame journey to unfold as you continue your path home. Let go of self-desires and the need for control. Let go of your twin. You have heard the saying, *"If you love someone, set them free; if they come back to you it was meant to be, if they don't it never was."* When you get out of your own way, everything will align in perfect order.

Honoring My Twin-Flame Agreement

After I created the outline of this book, it sat for about a month. Since I work with twins daily, I understood the importance of the message in this book and knew that the *"11:11 Key Code"* principles were something that the world needed. But for many reasons, I wasn't sure if I was ready to complete this Divine mission. I kept feeling a nudge that would not go away. It was around this same time that my twin-flame facilitator and I were jumping on the intense twin-flame fast track. So, I sought a session with my own spiritual advisor. Before even getting started with that session, she said to me, *"You are supposed to write a book about your twin-flame journey and the outline is to follow a specific sequence."* Then she gave me the details and the outline. It had already been created following that exact format. She also said, *"You are to create a twin-flame oracle deck of cards."* I had already tried purchasing one but could not find one deck available online. So, I had it on my to-do-list to create, for my own purposes. When she told me this, *"bells and whistles"* started going off in my head! *I heard it loud and clear: "It is time to move full speed ahead."* I immediately went to work to honor my twin-flame agreement and complete my Divine mission.

She proceeded to tell me that I needed to use a deck of playing cards as the inspiration to create the twin-flame oracle deck of cards. After our session, *I remembered seeing a deck of playing cards already in a drawer in my completely furnished condo (Remember 101- It was in Divine order that I show up at this condo).* When I pulled out the deck of cards and opened them, I discovered that they were a legitimate poker deck of cards that had officially been used in Las Vegas. As I opened the lid on the box, I noticed on the seal that the date the cards were used was 2-11-11. Remember the sequence example producing the pyramid structure producing the number 1234321 (1111 X1111 = 1234321)? In addition, the table number where this deck of cards were used was the same day as my twin flame's birthday. Despite all that I have studied, experienced and understood as I channel and receive guidance from my counsel on a daily basis – I was still blown away.

Talk about a *"higher conscious awakening."* I immediately understood that part of my twin-flame Divine mission was to launch a twin-flame deck of cards with this book. I feel that it is part of my own prophecy to share and help guide and direct other twin flames towards harmonization. Finding this deck of cards was no accident – it was confirmation from my own guides that I was in full alignment. I was to complete this request that has been directly guided by the instruction of St. Germain.

It should be the Divine mission of every twin flame to clear their own karma and honor their agreement to continue their own path and complete the Divine mission of their twin-flame union. I can tell you from my personal experiences, along with my Divine guidance, you will know you are honoring your own contract when you take the focus off of what your twin flame is doing. See your twin with only unconditional love. Do not have expectations and do not focus on what your twin is doing. Having compassion for your twin is the purest and highest form of unconditional love which only the truest of twin flames can ever experience. It allows them to fulfill and honor their agreements and complete their mission. My twin-flame journey is an excellent example of the purest form of spiritual love that twin flames can experience. It is a Divine connection that supersedes the ego and self-desires on the earthly plane. We have not had a relationship romantic in nature, yet we have remained closely connected. Without our *conscious awareness*, we shifted into full alignment while on our individual paths, and still completed our Divine mission.

My twin has been the generator of my career the majority of our journey. Although knowing this, I never realized until recently that it took his energy to generate the evolution of my Divine mission. I never imagined in a million years that all the work that my twin and I did while experimenting on energetic planes and while I was assisting him along the path of his *"spiritual awakening"* that I was training for my Divine mission. This still amazes me every day. I show up and love what I do. I make meaningful money, while enjoying my livelihood.

A Message to My Twin Flame – Thank You for Honoring Your Agreement

Not in a gazillion years could I repay you for *"The Gift"* you have given me! But I know I don't even have to try, because I know that everything you have done for me, you have done unconditionally with no expectations of anything in return. I know that somewhere deep within the connection of our souls, you chose the heavier karmic path so that I could carry out this Divine mission. I also know that somewhere up in our higher selves, this is exactly how we planned it. Whether your conscious mind can comprehend this or not, you have honored your agreement and therefore, the mission has been accomplished. *If anything had happened differently, I would have not found my way home and I would not have aligned with the mission that has been accomplished.* Now this mission is about to change the world by helping other twin flames learn to follow our footsteps. *Together, we have created a blueprint, paving the way for others to find their way home – helping restore heaven on earth as has been intended since the beginning of time.* Doing something of this magnitude does not surprise me since we are two of the strongest humans alive, with endurance beyond measure. A mission of this significance proves that the power of two is greater than one!

"I can see clearly now" that unconditional love has been the premises of our twenty-year friendship. Neither one of us have ever placed conditions or expectations on the other. Everything we have experienced together has been unconditional. I also know it has taken the silence that we have experienced over the last few months to accomplish this mission. *There have been things I would have never learned about the twin-flame process had we chosen a different path.* I would not have shifted into alignment with this Divine mission. So, I know that we chose the right path by not opening the center for spiritual transformation. I also believe that going forward, we will continue in the right direction — not only in this lifetime, but for the remainder of eternity.

I want you to know that I don't need romance from you because I have been able to touch, feel, see and know the deepest and best parts of your Being. I am honored to be *"The Chosen One"* who experienced the deepest and the best side of who you are. And as I have told you more than once, what we share has always been enough for me. As far as I'm concerned, we have and will always be in a full-union relationship. You have been there for me during some of the darkest seasons of my life – as I have been for you. I know that will never change. Thank you for a friendship that runs deeper than romance! I appreciate you more than words can say!

I contemplated whether to listen to my head or my heart as to whether to add this personal message to you in this book. I knew I should be listening to my gut, but I fought the thoughts of how long it has been since we talked about the topic of twin flames. I had been reflecting on how much has changed since we had our last conversation and knew that I would have tell you all about this journey when I see you again. The song, "See You Again" by Wiz Khalifa came on the radio then. As always, I follow the signs, so this message for you has been added to this section. I have heard this song at least a 1000 times – but it was as though I heard this song for the first time. I will tell you all about it when I see you again — and may you find your way home! I dedicate this song to you.

I Can See Clearly Now

Reflecting back on this twenty-plus-year journey, paralleling paths with my twin flame, *"I Can See Clearly Now!"* My awareness has heightened and I can see that every piece of my entire life has come full circle. Accepting the assignment of writing this book and helping other twin flames has become my own *"Code Breaker"* — the missing *"Key Code"* that I needed to open the doorway that led me to the *"lost puzzle piece,"* which I needed to gain a clear image of my Divine mission. I never gave up searching for what I needed to complete my soul, and now I have arrived – I have found my way home!

While driving to my office a few days ago, I had a crystal-clear revelation by making the connection to the title, *"Twin-Flame Code Breaker,"* which had come through me at the same time of the outline, at least a month prior to writing this book. I find it interesting how I have lived out the *"11:11 Key Codes," while at the same time harmonizing my own unconditional love and finding my way home.* As this light bulb went off, once again I could hear the *Words of Wayne* saying, *"I Can See Clearly Now,"* which is the title of one of his more recent books. At that exact moment the song *"I Can See Clearly Now"* came on the radio.

Not long before his passing, I had heard Wayne say that he was trying to come up with the title of that book and he had been asking for soul guidance. While waiting for his answer, one day he heard the song, *"I Can See Clearly Now."* I could feel massive goose bumps all over my body and tears swell in my eyes. I did it —mission accomplished! I no longer question my mystical messages. They have become a way of life for me because *"I Can See Clearly Now!"*

That was only half the story. I had asked my guides to show me when the content of this book was to be completed. A few days prior to receiving this bone-chilling message from Wayne, I received another clear message. I was also driving and I looked up and saw a license plate that read: HOM-RUN. I was so happy that I had received my answer that I almost failed to notice that the car was the exact same car my twin drives, aside from color.

With only days away from completing my Divine mission and accomplishing the challenge of writing this book in just six weeks — just like my twin had said I could do — I can hear my own affirmation coming through: *"I am writing with my heart and not my head!"*

2B or Not 2B

I am always being asked by my clients, *"Why are you not in physical union with your own twin flame?"* I feel that the answer to this question is very complex, but I will summarize the answer by saying, *"We are in full union. We have been by each other's side every step of the way."* We have honored our agreements and we have accomplished the Divine mission. That is what a twin-flame journey is all about. We don't need romance or words to express our unconditional love for each other or the world. This book is living proof of that! *A true twin-flame journey is accomplishing YOUR personal mission by unlocking "The Secret" to finding your way home and gaining personal freedom, which provides inner peace and happiness.*

Once you are in alignment and you have reached a heightened state of awareness, the mystical messages you receive come through with even greater clarity. With that said, I had my most prominent revelation to date after being Divinely guided. I made a connection between a series of events that took place over the last several months. At the time my twin and I were going to open the center for spiritual transformation, I had the awareness that we were not only anchoring our spiritual energy in the heart chakra of the United States, but his office space that we were going to use was the heart of the heart chakra. When I shared this with my twin, I know he didn't fully understand that. At the time, I didn't even realize the power and accuracy of my words either.

A couple weeks ago, I was driving into the complex where my twin and I both practice; we are only three buildings apart. Upon pulling in, for the first time creating a *"conscious awareness,"* I realized that there is a pyramid structure right in the front of my building that partially reads Triad. Moreover, part of our street name is Triad. Then it hit me — the Center we were considering really was in the heart of the heart chakra, anchoring the pyramid energies in the center of the United States. I was so shocked, I took pictures of the pyramid and sent them to my twin-flame facilitator. I knew that this was a *"higher conscious awakening."* I had driven by this sign for years and never made this connection.

A few weeks prior I had been writing about the pyramid energies and their association with the numbers 11:11 and twin flames. *Now here was a pyramid and Triad, included in the sign and street name where we both practice, in the heart of the heart of the nation!* Now it really gets interesting, I mentioned prior about making the discovery linking the masculine and female energies to the numbers **6** and **9**. The number **6** is linked to the masculine or the generator energy by creating contraction and grounding the energy, while **9** is the feminine electric energy, creating expansion by producing creativity. That same night just before drifting off to sleep, I suddenly had a vision. It was both my twin's and my street numbers, sitting side by side. It was lit up, but two of the numbers lit so brightly, it made me open my eyes. They were the numbers **6** and **9**. You see, our street numbers are exactly the same, with the exception of his containing a **6** and mine containing a **9**. For the purposes of privacy, I will change the actual street numbers, but this is an example of what I saw – 14**6**2 and 14**9**2.

I had made the connection — linking our location as the heart and anchoring the harmonic balance of energy for the nation. *As if that was not enough, now I was shown how we are doing it by merging the combination of our masculine and feminine energies.* He was the generator and I was the electric, together creating harmonic balance needed to complete our Divine mission! Talk about a *"Twin-Flame Code Breaker!"* The next day, as I was sharing this revelation with my massage therapist, out of nowhere, I had another *"highly conscious awareness"* and made another connection – my unit is **#2** and his is **B**. That equals **2B**.

Dr. Wayne had appeared again — he always chose seat number **2B** on all his flights!

In closing, I would like to give a more complex answer to the question, *"Will I ever be with my twin flame?"* Is it **2B** or not **2B**? Only our higher selves know. Did we both agree that our destiny would be to not only honor our agreement by clearing our own karmic pasts but also to honor our karmic vows to help change the world with this Divine mission, which would make us worthy of the ultimate reward of a full sacred union? Or, did we agree to pay our reward forward, in order to help clear the karmic patterns for the Universe by letting go of self-desires and making the choice to sacrifice a romantic relationship? – By making that sacrifice, we chose to change the world instead – allowing others to view our physical union through the Christ-conscious heart of God so that we could help save this world from self-destruction.

Either way, I know that my twin flame is my King, my generator, because I know from the bottom of my heart that he chose the heavier karmic load, so I would not have to. *In doing so, he has been my greatest teacher – giving me "The Gift" of the greatest amount of unconditional love known to man.* I know him and I know that he would have done this so I could complete our Divine mission. He has taken me home. As I shifted through the Ascension process transcending to heaven on earth, I found inner peace and eternal joy. I have found unconditional love and personal freedom during this lifetime! *Now, I offer him in return that same unconditional love by placing no expectation or conditions on him!* Why? Because I trust that whatever is meant to happen that it was our agreement. Everything up until this point has been in Divine alignment and so I know that I don't have to place attention on outcomes or figure out anything in the process.

Therefore, this makes our physical union one of the most selfless, Christ-conscious demonstration of unconditional love to all mankind. Together, we have created a new blueprint for a true twin-flame experience so that others can follow the *"Twin-Flame Code Breaker" – 11:11 Key Codes* The Secret *to Unlocking Unconditional Love & Finding Your Way Home — "The Gift" to the new world so you too can find your way home!*

Our separation has created the necessary silence so that you, the reader, could hear the music of two unconditional twin hearts beating as one. The symphony took place while you were reading this book! The reality is, I get to live happily ever after! I got my fairy-tale ending!

And So It Is!

2B Continued…

A P P E N D I X

The Freedom Celebration

The following is a passage I wrote while performing a *"Freedom Celebration"* after identifying and breaking my karmic pattern. It was in an open field where I released a butterfly balloon. On that balloon I wrote everything on one side that I was letting go of. On the other side, I wrote everything that I wanted to come to pass in my new life going forward. I shared this *"Freedom Celebration"* with my twin when he released his karmic pattern, and I gave him a dragon fly balloon to release during his celebration. I encourage you to perform the same *"Freedom Celebration."* There is power in action. May YOU experience personal freedom and find your way home!

Freedom Celebration

I _______________________, am now FREE to release ALL my (burdens) past pain, suffering and old patterns of action. I now DECLARE the purest form of love and light into my life. I place all my heart's desires into the breath of God. I vow to live a life of Peace, Purpose and Passion. I have learned to trust my instincts and my inner guidance. From this day forward I will speak my truth with clarity. I trust that God will supply ALL my needs and I no longer have to worry about my finances or personal relationships. I agree to live out my life in the Divine order that it was intended to be: I will paint it – I will own it – I will love it – I will live it – I will SHARE IT!

Now, with the release of this butterfly/dragonfly, I unleash all my inner potential and I will be taught how to fly into new dimensions in every area of my life: body, mind and soul. Let there be POWER in this expression of my trust in the higher good of the Universe. As I go forward into the world, I will let my light shine for others to see and become an extension of the Divine flame. Through this ripple effect, may I be an inspiration and touch the lives of others.

I am open for guidance and I am ready to receive blessings beyond belief!

And so it is, with ease and grace, I fly into the wind and I will FOREVER... See myself FREE!!!

Namaste

Drop the Rock, Lighten the Load

Here's a very simple, yet powerful tip that you can practice to help you lighten your load by physically letting go! You may have heard this story and I am not sure of its origin, but here is my version:

Once there was a little boy who went swimming with his friends. They were playing with rocks and tossing them into the water and were all having fun until the little boy realized that he had gone too far out into the deep water and so he began to panic, still holding onto his rock. He began to fight the process and he struggled and struggled to stay afloat. His friends noticed his despair and they hollered, *"Drop the rock, Drop the rock!"* The little boy was too busy fighting for his life to even hear what his friends were yelling at him. So, he continued to fight and he continued to hold onto the rock and before long he could no longer keep his head above water and unfortunately, he drowned. This is the same thing we do in life when we encounter stressful experiences. We find ourselves continuing to hold on and we forget to drop the rock or let go of our past. The moral of the story is to drop the rock, lighten your load, raise your vibration, and reclaim your life.

Drop the Rock, Lighten Your Load in Action:

- Place a small stone in your pocket and when you find that your load is heavy and you need to be reminded to drop the rock and let go, place your hand in your pocket and squeeze the stone, then drop it as a reminder that it's time to lighten your load.
- If you like to write, then take a few minutes to journal about the situation that the stone represents and what it feels like to symbolically let it completely go.
- Make this an easy experience – don't think about spelling or punctuation or whether or not you are a good writer. Just try to stay open emotionally and say every word that you need to say without judgment. When you have said it all, you will most likely know it because you will come to a comfortable stop on your own.
- Let Go and Let God – Now Go Forward with Peace!

PAYING FORWARD THE WORDS OF WAYNE

In Memory of Dr. Wayne Dyer

"You are a creature of Divine Love connected at all times to Source. Divine Love is when you see God in everything and everyone you encounter" – Dr. Wayne Dyer

If you found the words of *"Twin-Flame Code Breaker"* to be inspiring, I invite you to pay forward seeds of radiance to everyone you encounter by sharing Divine Love in memory of the *Words of Wayne.* Wayne exemplified radiance in everything he did and everywhere he went. I challenge you to follow the North Star as you find your way home. There is no better example than Wayne!

Here are a few examples of paying radiance forward in memory of the *Words of Wayne.*

- Share a smile
- Redirect a gift
- Practice being kind
- Pay the toll behind you
- Share a meal with the homeless
- Hold the door for the person behind you
- Practice patience by listening to someone
- Pay for the car behind you in the drive-through
- Watch and share "The Shift" movie – Dr. Dyer had a goal of 3 million viewers. It currently has just over 1 million.

4 Steps to Staying Energetically Grounded

If you often find yourself feeling out of synchronicity, your energy may not be grounded. This can cause an array of symptoms including fatigue, anxiety, dizziness, buzzing in your ears or increase in sensitivity. There are many circumstances and social environments that can generate distortion in your energetic circuit system. Therefore, it is important to stay grounded, shielded and protected. This also includes keeping your energetic field around you cleansed and cleared. Stagnant energy can create congestion in your aura. The following 4 steps will help you ground, shield and protect your energy.

Step 1: **Grounding**. Grounding yourself helps you stay centered and connected to the earth. Earth is the Divine masculine energy that keeps you energetically planted. The first step is to sit in a comfortable position, preferably with bare feet on the floor and palms facing upward. This helps to pull in the Divine feminine energy through the palms. So you are receiving through your hands, and releasing through your feet. This keeps balance in the flow of energy that moves throughout your physical body.

- Sit in an upright position and picture yourself planted in a tree trunk position with spine erect.
- Next, take a deep breath in through your nose and out through your mouth. With each inhale, imagine energy coming in through the palms of your hands; with each exhale, imagine it exiting the bottoms of your feet and energetically connecting to the core of the earth. Repeat the breath for 5 cycles.
- Then, visualize a beam of blue light entering the top of your head extending down through the middle of your spine, and exiting the bottoms of your feet and connecting to the core of planet earth.
- Walking barefoot in the grass is a great way to ground your energy.

Step 2: **Clear Toxic Energies.** Now that you are relaxed and grounded, remain in your upright position.

- First take 5 cleansing breaths.
- Then envision your body immersed in a non-permeable Violet Flame that will cleanse and purify toxic energy debris from every plane of your Being.
- It will also transmute the negative energies that you have and then absorbs them back into positive energies.

Step 3: **Shield**. Shielding is very effective to keep out any negative energy or energetic attachments. It is similar to protecting your space with a wall.

- Take 5 cleansing breaths.
- Then picture yourself encased inside a mirrored box with the mirror pointing outward.
- This will send any negative energies back where they came from.

Step 4: **Protect**. After you have grounded yourself and released all toxic energy debris from your body and your energy field (aura), you are ready apply a protective shield around the mirrored box.

- First take 5 cleansing breaths.
- Then imagine the mirrored box, enveloped by a rainbow-colored light.

Perform as needed, preferably morning and night. But you can also perform these grounding techniques, any time you are entering an environmental space that has negative energies or while in large crowds where there are a lot of chaotic energies.

You Must Lose Your Way Home to Find It

What a beautiful place in life it is when you shift out of the darkness and realize you have finally arrived – you found your way home after being lost in the dark! Reflecting back on your journey, you didn't know what you were searching for your entire life. Yet you remained in tune with your instincts, and in spite of your circumstance, you continued that search.

You never gave up. You listened to that inner wisdom, deep within your spirit, that evolved into a strong voice that never stopped speaking to your heart — a nudge that never ceased; it gave you the burning desire to continue searching deeper within your soul. As time passed and unforeseen circumstances persisted, you were forced to stop and listen to that inner voice.

Finally, you understand exactly what it's been saying. Then it hits you like a bolt of lightning creating a crystal-clear vision and lighting up your path. The fog lifts and you can see your way. You realize it took processing and integrating enough pieces of the obstacles before seeing the bigger picture. You know you have been Divinely guided every step of the way. Now there is no turning back. The light up ahead becomes brighter. Somehow you find the courage, the strength and the will power to continue your journey. Reaching the light at the end of the tunnel, you understand that this is the destination that you had been searching for all along. You made it – you aligned with destiny – you found your mission. It is one so large, there is no way you could have consciously mapped out this quest by yourself. You can rest now because you have found your way home – heaven on earth!

ACKNOWLEDGEMENTS

I would like to extend my heart and unconditional love by acknowledging all twin flames who signed up for this unconditional love journey during this lifetime and era. Every one of you have made many self-sacrifices to get to this point in your journey. You deserve to be applauded! Do not give up; continue the course. My wish for you is to experience all the possibilities that are available to you in "*Twin-Flame Code Breaker.*" May it become a light that helps you find your way home!

First and foremost, I would like to thank my father for teaching me that the sky is the limit and that possibilities are endless. You didn't just teach me to dream — you taught me to dream BIG. You have always given unconditionally and taught me what a Christ-conscious radiant heart is all about! Thank you mom for all that you are and for your unconditional gentle loving radiance. You are a giver of the Divine's Eternal love and I am honored that you are my mother. I am so blessed to have experienced you both!

Thank You! To both of my children, Heather (and family) and VJ who made many sacrifices growing up, while I was searching to find what my soul has been longing for my whole life! I am very proud of both of you. You have both become amazing young adults and I love you both to the moon and beyond!

To my brother Billy, I cannot thank you enough for being there for me during such a great time of need! In my "*darkest hour*" you were there, no questions asked – A true representation of unconditional love – Thank you from the bottom of my heart!

I would like to express my unconditional gratitude to two of my greatest friends, Debbie and Claudia. You both have been there for me through my "*pitfalls of hell!*" I immensely appreciate you both and I feel so blessed to experience such deep and unconditionally loving friendships!

A special thank you to my massage therapist, Rita for not only all your many massages and words of wisdom, but also proofing

"Twin-Flame Code Breaker." You have been a part of my journey while shifting from the *"dark night of my soul"* to becoming a radiant North Star for others to follow. I truly appreciate you!

Eric and Beverly, thank you for being a part of my journey and being there for me with complete unconditional love and support! There are not enough words to express my gratitude – Thank you!

In addition, I would like to express a very special thank you and unconditional love and light to you, my dearest Leo! I am not sure how to express something so big and so deep. However I think in this case, no words are needed. I unconditionally love you Leo!

My dearest Kathryn, it is no accident that our paths crossed! Wayne new what he was doing in advance when he brought us together! I will be eternally grateful to you for all your advice, healing sessions and rich unconditional love! You are a gift to the world by sharing the Eternal love of the Creator. I cannot thank you enough for creating my *"awakening"* and confirming for me the need to following through with my Divine mission! I appreciate you more than words can say!

Parthenia, the speed at which this Divine message flowed through me would not have been possible without your prior direction. Your guidance, along with teaching me developmental editing, structure and how to create an outline, all became a *"Key"* component for my being able to assemble the format of this book. I cannot thank you enough for believing in me, and seeing the music that resided deep within my soul.

I also would like to thank two very important catalysts who played major roles facilitating the direction of my journey! First, Dr. Dan Morter and the Morter Health family: It took our paths crossing to direct me towards the understanding of B.E.S.T – Bio-Energetic Synchronicity Technique. Experiencing it firsthand as your patient has changed my life for the better. Not only did it help with the physical pain that I had after multiple car accidents, but your guidance as my field doctor has taught me so much! I cannot thank you enough! And last but not least, I would like to thank not only a friend but fellow chiropractor, Dr. Kevin Winkle! Kevin, I was at a crossroads, not knowing which way to turn and searching for my mission when you shared with me that you were going to chiropractic college. You became my beacon that directed my path to my destiny! Thank You!

ABOUT THE AUTHOR

Dr. Harmony is a twin-flame expert and spiritual advisor with a background in holistic chiropractic, vibrational medicine and intuitive energy healing. For nearly 20 years, she has helped people remove energetic blocks that kept them stuck in life. She helps them make the connection between body, mind and soul and find their way home. She too has found her way home to heaven on earth – a place of inner peace and happiness. She has aligned with her Divine mission through her own twin-flame experience, extensive research, Divine guidance and expertise. Her *"Reboot Your Twin-Soul Blueprint"* facilitates soul transformation by building a bridge from the *"dark night of the soul"* through the Ascension process, and connecting to one's higher self.

Dr. Harmony is on a mission to teach over a million people how to find their way home by connecting to their higher selves and connecting to their souls' purpose. Her approach offers a bondage-free life, creating personal freedom by transforming mindsets and creating breakthroughs in all dimensions. Her approach helps others equip themselves with tools that empower and encourage them to take inward journeys, discovering transforming mindsets that help them create a life that will radiate outwardly as an expression of the inner dimensions of the soul. Dr. Harmony offers inspiration by living a sermon rather than preaching one.

Dr. Harmony is also the founder of Global Paws For Peace – A Global Canine Peace Movement that is Creating Unity Amongst All Breeds. Please visit: www.GlobalPawsForPeace.org

Lightning Source UK Ltd.
Milton Keynes UK
UKHW02f2214090418
320768UK00017B/1697/P

9 780692 794920